ACING DEPRESSION

A Tennis Champion's Toughest Match

ACING DEPRESSION

A Tennis Champion's Toughest Match

CLIFF RICHEY WITH HILAIRE RICHEY KALLENDORF, PhD

Foreword by Jimmy Connors

NEW CHAPTER PRESS

Acing Depression: A Tennis Champion's Toughest Match is published by
New Chapter Press (www.NewChapterMedia.com) and distributed by the
Independent Publisher's Group (www.IPGBook.com).

This book tells the life experience of Cliff Richey in dealing with certain
mental health issues. While it is hoped that this information might provide
insight, neither of the authors is trained or licensed in the mental health
field and nothing in this book should be taken as any type of recommenda-
tion or as any form of professional advice.

ISBN - 978-0942257663

Cover photo is courtesy of Brian Connelly. All other photos in the book
are courtesy of Cliff Richey, except for the photo on page 93 (U.S. Davis
Cup team) which is courtesy of Russ Adams, the photo on page 141
(Rosewall-Richey at Wimbledon) which is courtesy of Getty Images, and
the photo on page 257 (Cliff and Amy Richey) which is courtesy of Brian
Connelly.

New Chapter Press would also like to thank Bill Simons, Joel Drucker, Bill
Mountford, Ewing Walker, Kirsten Navin, Irene Tan and Manfred Wenas
for help with this project.

Cover & book design by Kirsten Navin.

Printed in Canada.

Contents

Foreword.. *i*

From the Authors: Set Up, Break Down ....*v*

1 *Sudden Death Victory*...1

2 *Night Terrors* 5

3 *West Texas Roots*.. 13

4 *Richey, Inc.*.. 24

5 *High School Drop-Out* 35

6 *The Old Shamateur Game*...................................... 51

7 *Boycotting Wimbledon* 61

8 *Uptown Girl* 70

9 *Pressure Flakes* 81

10 *It Ain't All Autographs & Sunglasses*......................... 97

11 *Playing at High Altitudes* 118

12 *Bull in a China Closet*...................................... 131

13 *Gut Strings* 151

14 *In the Zone*..165

15 *Starting to Choke*...177

16 *Black Bags*...188

17 *Change a Losing Game*...198

18 *Comeback Kid*..214

19 *Real Men Do Cry*..227

20 *Mulligans* 236

21 *"Never Give Up"* 248

    Epilogue..265

    Acknowledgements 266

"Keep Fighting, Cliff"

Not so long ago I received a call from my friend Cliff Richey. Over the years, we have stayed in touch, so I thought it was one of those "catch up" calls. You know the ones: "How's the family? Playing any golf? Everything OK?" But this one was different. It wasn't the same old Cliff . . . this one was more serious. Out came the question. "Jimmy, I have just written a book with my daughter and would like for you to write the foreword." Well—I must say, I was flattered. "Sure," I said, "What is the gist of the book?" When he told me it was about his battling depression, I suddenly remembered some of our past conversations from years ago and his admitting to me that he was having a tough time. He was depressed constantly and it was affecting his life and the lives of those around him.

Let me be clear, I am no doctor and don't pretend to be. But I know Cliff Richey. Our paths first crossed almost 40 years ago. I was a young upstart on the professional tennis circuit, and Cliff— well, he was the one to beat. He was what I wanted to watch and try to learn from. He had that "never-say-die" attitude and the will to win at all costs. Grind it out till the end and after the match was over, he would be satisfied that he had no regrets.

I learned a lot about Cliff just by watching him practice. He would put every ounce of energy he had into every shot. He had his own style and his own attitude and he really wasn't looking to please anyone but himself. He played boldly and was willing to take the good with the bad. He never made any excuses.

What made Cliff Richey what he was on the tennis court has certainly carried over into this book. His story has taken a subject, depression—which has affected him personally—and put it out there for everyone to see. Depression has been a subject that no one really talks about. Few people even admit to having such a condition. But Cliff is not afraid to be bold and reveal what he has gone through and what it takes to get a handle on this disease. He has the ability (as a well-known sports personality) to use his celebrity to bring attention to a condition that affects millions of people around the world. His courage to step forward and admit his problem is one thing, but to have a book written about it . . . well, I told you I admired his guts. This is just one more accomplishment for Cliff to add to his legacy. He goes beyond the idea that you have to "be a man and just deal with it." He opens up with vulnerability about a cause he now stands for.

As you read this book, understand that depression is starting to receive more attention every day. And Cliff Richey is part of that process. He has laid it all on the line and while he is winning his battle with depression, it is an everyday fight. Just as Cliff played tennis, he is studying how depression works; what its weaknesses are; and what strategies you can use against it. His hope is that people who read his story can learn—learn about the disease and learn that people who suffer can have a better quality of life. Things can get better. There is hope.

Cliff is my friend and his crusade to draw more attention to depression will not be easy. But he has never been afraid of a fight. With his energy and focus, it is a challenge that can be met.

Keep fighting, Cliff. Fighting for something worthwhile is never easy. But then again, hard work is something you have never been afraid of. You have a tough opponent but I know you will not let depression get the better of you. Stay with it.

Jimmy Connors
Five-time U.S. Open Champion

Set Up, Break Down

The interviews leading up to the process of writing this book were a new experience for me. They would have been for anyone, even a pro athlete or so-called celebrity with 40 years of experience in responding to the media. From decades of sports interviews, I was accustomed to always trying to paint myself in a good light and keeping my public persona or "image" intact.

My daughter is a successful professional in her own right. And yet she was willing to spend time with me on a project that concerned so many important issues: career, family, fatherhood. Instinctively, I knew I couldn't bullshit with my daughter.

Only my daughter could have gotten inside my soul the way she did. Only my daughter could have asked the questions she asked. I could not have been so totally open and honest with anyone else on such personal matters. It was—in hindsight—an enormous leap of faith. I trusted her to write candidly and beautifully about our shared tragedy.

The experience turned out to be deeply healing for me and, I hope, for Hilaire. A new form of family healing took on a life of its own as the book progressed. This could only have been possible with total honesty. Anything less would have created still more wounds, more dysfunction—set down on paper, never to be

---

reconciled for all time. In writing this book, I decided to start the rest of my life with a clean slate. I'm asking my family to give me a mulligan.

I believe that, by divulging "weakness," I'm really gaining strength. Honesty is the only way toward real help and hope.

Cliff Richey
Phoenix, Arizona
September 1, 2009

• • •

Growing up in the world of celebrity sports wasn't easy. As a toddler, I took my first steps in airports and on the stairwells of hotels. Yes, I got to hang out at some fancy resorts, but my dad wasn't there for me most of the time. My mother practically raised us on her own. My sisters and I agree that our father, famous celebrity or not, was among the top few flaming assholes of all time.

What we didn't know back then was that he suffered from clinical depression. Thank God he was diagnosed (by his dermatologist, no less!) and finally got help. I remember his drunken rages, inevitably followed by a depressive stupor. To this day, I wake up with a panicky feeling in my stomach, afraid at some subconscious level that he's going to yell at me for something I didn't do. The traumatic effects on family members of clinical depression are real and lasting. Nothing about depression is normal.

Having said that, I am tired of reading the pronouncement that depression cannot be described. As a "words" person, I believe in the power of language. Perhaps no one has tried hard enough to describe it yet. My goal in this project has been to apply a researcher's scientific precision to determine as closely as possible what happened to my father and why. With his honesty and my gift for words, coupled with a deep understanding of our (shared) personality, perhaps we can begin to conquer this thing by at least giving it more names. In exorcism—one of the topics of my academic research—an exorcist is believed to hold great power over the demon once he can finally figure out its name. Perhaps we as a society can begin to win the battle over this adversary by identifying it with greater accuracy.

Most of the events recounted in this book occurred before I was born, but I remember going with my father to San Francisco as a child to see the court where he won his "Sudden Death" match. Writing this book has been a journey back to that tennis court, as well as so many others.

When I was a little girl, I would often spend the night at my grandparents' home. Behind their house was our family's tennis court. Many times, I would wake up and find myself all alone, early in the morning. Still in my nightgown, I would scamper down to the tennis court. I knew where to find them.

I can still hear the sound of the tennis ball echoing back and forth, back and forth, as I approached. That, to me, was the most reassuring sound in the world. It meant stability, regularity—the comfort of knowing that ball was in the hands of a master. I used to believe, with the simple faith of a child, that that sound would go on echoing forever. Or at least until whoever was hitting it wanted to stop. One thing was for certain: as long as they kept hitting that tennis ball, the players in my family would almost never, ever miss.

If only the entirety of my childhood had been as happy as that. If only the predictable sound of that tennis ball could have sheltered me from all the heartache and the unpredictability of clinical depression. It could not do that; but even still, for as long as it lasted, that sound was a powerful amulet. Sometimes I can hear it still, in my dreams. Nobody uses that tennis court any more. Now even the echo of the echo has fallen silent.

This should have been just another great tennis tale, like the ones I remember hearing from my childhood. (How many times did I hear my father begin to tell a story about one of his matches: "Well, I was a set up and a break down, and then . . ." ?) By all rights, his life story should have sounded like a longer version of just another one of those.

In some ways, the first half of it pretty much does. The average age of onset for clinical depression is 27. Until he was roughly that age, my father had a remarkable career; however, up to that point—with regard to his psyche, at least—he had led a fairly unremarkable life.

But then something terrible happened to him. As we talked, I began to see how his loss of sanity actually formed a surprisingly close parallel to his loss of skill in tennis. I began to realize that his career had been the perfect setup for a breakdown. That was the point where, for a professional comparatist like myself, things really started to get interesting. . . .

In the course of writing this book, my father and I have spent over 200 hours together, reliving his past. When he first called and asked me to undertake this project, I knew it would be a labor of love. What I didn't bargain for was how much I would learn in the process. In a way, I discovered, this is what I've really been writing about all along, even in my academic books. I started writing about exorcism after hearing my father speak about "fighting his personal demons." I wrote about casuistry in response to our family's collective moral dilemmas. Finally, it was time to hit the subject matter head-on. I was tired of doing only academic projects. I was ready to write something with "heart."

What follows is the tangible result of that experiment. At my father's own request, I have boldly tried to get inside his head. Some of these pages are a direct transcription of his words, *verbatim*. More often I have written in his voice as if it were mine.

As a literary critic, I am all too familiar with the age-old debate over form vs. content and which of those is more important in fashioning an object of literary art. In crafting the form of this memoir, I have self-consciously tried to replicate both the experience of depression and the experience of certain types of cognitive therapy. The pages that follow, my father assures me, mirror the experience of depression in that they start out simply. Then they slowly add layer upon layer of greater complexity. What many people do not realize is that depression is a progressive disease. Simultaneously, these pages also mirror a type of cognitive therapy which, ironically enough, is most often used in jail. It is a technique whereby prison inmates learn to empathize with their victims by writing stories in the victim's own voice. As a child, I did feel imprisoned by my family of origin, although that part of the analogy would have to end here. However, it has been a tremendously liberating and healing experience for me to learn how to empathize with a person who—at least at one point—used to be capable of wounding me so deeply.

We're an unlikely combination, the jock and the scholar. But we've come to identify with each other so closely that at some points, it has been almost frightening. All in all, this has been a magnificent adventure. Besides, isn't that the true definition of empathy?

Hilaire Richey Kallendorf, PhD
College Station, Texas
September 1, 2009

• CHAPTER ONE •

Sudden Death Victory

Saturday, October 3, 1970. The famous "Sudden Death" match. Incredible as it may seem, the No. 1 tennis ranking in the United States rested on a single point. I was playing against Stan Smith at the Berkeley Tennis Club near San Francisco, California. The score was four points all, six games all in the fifth set.

It's the only match I ever played where there was a simultaneous match point for both players. It can't happen any more because they don't use that kind of tiebreaker now. The nine-point tiebreaker was called "sudden death." I always enjoyed playing "sudden death" tiebreakers, myself. I kind of liked them. I guess I've always liked to live on the edge.

We all knew the No. 1 ranking was up for grabs until the very end. Stan had beaten me two matches to one that year. But I had had a better year over all, and we were both ahead of all the other players. I felt like if I could beat him one more time, I would be ranked No. 1 in the country.

Stan and I had an emotional rivalry. We really didn't like each other that well. We had high respect for one another, but I just hated losing to that guy. And vice versa. It was probably as much that as worrying about the ranking.

My sister Nancy, who was the top-ranked American woman

herself in 1964, 1965, 1968 and 1969, helped me with my serve the day before. For most matches in general, I would not go out and practice my serve that way. But we both knew exactly what that match meant. She knew and I knew. I remember trying to wind myself up to go out there the next day. Stan had a serve-and-volley, attacking style of play. I was more defensive with my playing style.

The match was on hard court. Everyone knew that the surface favored Stan. But I was better on fast surfaces than people gave me credit for. Nonetheless, the perception was that I was invading his bailiwick, his backyard. I knew I had to get a high percentage of first serves in. I needed to feel comfortable with my serve.

So Nancy and I went out the afternoon before to work on it. I got a basket of 40-50 used balls. I practiced my serve for at least an hour and a half. I knew I was running the risk of ending up the next day with a dead arm. But in my mind, if I had a bad day serving the next day, I would not win. My serve had never been my biggest strength.

In my characteristically obsessive way, I hit at least 200 practice serves that afternoon before. Nancy acted as another pair of eyes. She knew my game. What I tended to work on. I'd ask her if the toss looked high enough or if my shoulders were rotating into the court. She was an enormous help to me that day.

Going into the match, my mental state was good. I was coming down off of an unbelievably good year. I had won eight of the 26 tournaments I entered and was in the finals of five more. I was in the semifinals of eight or nine more still, including the French and U.S. Opens. A fellow player came up to me at the end of that year and asked, "Cliff, do you know how good of a year you just had?"

But as good as the year was, it was tiring. I don't care if you're young, you can still get tired. If you take just the one month leading up to that match, it was exhausting. Nonetheless, I had a lot of confidence. Emotionally, I was up.

So now we had just one more point to play. I missed my first serve. I threw in a little chicken-shit second serve. It was just a hit and a hope. The first order of business was just somehow to get the ball in the court. I came to the net off of that serve. He hit the return of serve. And then he came to the net! So we were both at the net! I dived for a backhand volley. I did a 360-degree turn. I just instinctually went for where I thought the ball was going to be. Stan thought he had passed me on the last shot, but I reached out and hit a winner. I hit a winning forehand volley. He still thinks it bounced off the wood frame of my racquet. I disagree. It certainly doesn't matter now. . . . And then it was over. I was No. 1.

Stan recalls that right after that, I sort of went into a trance for about five minutes after shaking hands. I was in that "zone" people talk about. It was like I kind of flipped out or something. I was beside myself with excitement. I went back over to him and gave him a hug. After four hours, the winning score was 7-6, 6-7, 6-3, 4-6, 7-6 (5-4).

It was not my destiny for that to be my only "sudden death" experience. With emotional illness, a swift spiral downward can also seem like a "sudden death." I used to say to Dad, "I'm the most blessed person I know. I ought to be the happiest person in the world. What's wrong with me?" Dad would point to the wall and ask, "Don't those trophies mean anything to you?" I would say, "No, they mock me."

Perhaps I didn't adjust well mentally as I went along. Eddie Marinaro, the football player, once said to me, "You've got the successful man's disease." When you have trophies hanging on the wall and a nice bank account and a nice house and no debts, but you still aren't happy, you have to realize the problem might be with you.

I made it to the top in tennis in all age divisions—midgets to seniors. I had major breakdowns all in between. While playing 1,500 tennis matches in 500 tournaments, I was like a fair-haired person who gets skin cancer from staying out in the sun too long. Genetically, I was predisposed for what happened, but circumstances also combined to produce my condition.

When I won that "sudden death" victory, I was at the top of my game. I had no idea at that point that I was already emotionally sick. I would have scoffed at the idea if someone had told me then, when I was 23, that my next 40 years would bear the stamp of clinical depression.

CHAPTER TWO

Night Terrors

You get these reactions from people when you start talking about your depression. They don't want to hear about it. Don't want to know about it. I'm just wanting to say, "You don't know me." Depression has formed me in so many ways but nobody wants to acknowledge that part of who I am. They want to talk about my tennis career. But they don't want to talk about my depression. You want to be known for who you really are. I'm a depressed person. It's not a choice!

I was born on New Year's Eve, 1946, in San Angelo, Texas, in the middle of a blizzard. That was almost like an omen or something. It never snows in the desert of West Texas! But somehow, in my case, that almost seemed appropriate. As it turned out, my subsequent life and career would be about as unusual as—well, as a snow storm in the West Texas desert.

I had a happy childhood, albeit a short one. I did typical things up until the time I was 12. My career started early in life. So childhood for me was everything before that.

I don't remember sleeping in a cardboard box as a baby—but it happened. Our little house was nothing but a cardboard box itself. It didn't matter to me. I never felt deprived as a kid. I didn't perceive myself as living in poverty. I always had enough to eat. I had

I won my first tennis trophy in the "midget" division at age 8 in 1955 in Ft. Wayne, Indiana at the tennis club where Dad had a summer job.

two parents who loved me and an older sister. I also had plenty of neighborhood kids to play with. Life was good.

My sister Nancy has memories of growing up on a chicken farm. Six months after I was born, we moved to Houston. We lived there until I was 11. During the summers we would sometimes go to upstate New York, where my dad would take short-term jobs teaching tennis. Herbie Fitzgibbon, a fellow tour player, recalls seeing me chasing frogs by the side of the tennis court at the Gypsy Trail Country Club in Mahopac, New York. I remember hitting balls against a wire fence when I was five or six years old. I don't remember a time when I didn't have a racquet in my hand.

My earliest childhood memory dates back to that same summer, 1951. We lived in a rented farmhouse. There was a summer camp for kids in the woods nearby. I got to be friendly with some of them. We stumbled onto some cigarettes. Took a few puffs. I guess Mom smelled it on my breath. I couldn't believe she had such powers to know I had been smoking! Her uncanny ability to divine when I had gotten into trouble would only grow keener in later years.

I had a pretty normal childhood. I loved goofing around with my buddies. I'd sometimes ride my bike as far as three miles from home. No one thought anything of it back then. My parents gave me pretty free rein. I used to run around wearing a coon-skin cap because I wanted to look like Davy Crockett.

Mom was a real good cook—homestyle, Southern cooking. Like buttermilk biscuits, cornbread and fried okra. My two favorite things she made were tapioca and rice pudding.

When I was very small, I didn't want to let Mom out of my sight. That was probably a natural phase little boys have. Between the ages of five and nine, I can remember messing around, playing on our gravel road there in Houston. One day she was getting in the car to go to the grocery store. I was playing with some kids. I ran over to go with her because I didn't want her to leave without me.

Dad used to give tennis lessons on some courts at the Shamrock Hotel. Mom would be tending me while he gave the lessons. To keep me occupied, she would challenge me to walk all the way around this big circle driveway. She watched carefully the entire time. It made me feel like a big grownup that I could walk the whole thing. But I probably wouldn't have done it if she had been out of my sight.

It was during those years that my mother was diagnosed with a neurosis. I remember some of it. I remember Dad would leave to go to his job as tennis pro at the Houston Country Club. It was hard for my mother to be left alone with us. She was afraid something terrible might happen. I was like five or six years old at that time. Dad wrote down the pro shop number for me in case I needed to call him. I overheard her say she didn't want him to leave.

It was just horrible for Mom to live with so much fear. I didn't have the reaction to it that you'd think. It was never like I didn't want to be around her. I loved her so much. I was unaware at the time how much anguish and misery she was in. I was too young to comprehend that part of it. A kid can't understand that kind of emotional pain. I don't remember seeing her cry very much. She certainly was never a nonfunctioning mother because of it.

She went to a psychiatrist a couple of times to find out what was wrong with her. She definitely had a breakdown of sorts. She felt like there was a long period when she was in a black pit. Her Christian faith pulled her out. She just kept hanging on to Jesus.

Maybe she was like that from when I was born. If not, I still might never have noticed the difference. I don't remember if she suddenly became ill or if she was always that way. She has always been afraid she might slip back into that darkness. So she used to say she could relate to what I have been through.

I have good memories of Dad taking me over to Moody Park in Houston, six blocks from our house. We'd go shoot beebee guns. I enjoyed that. I was a pretty good shot. In that same park, he taught me peewee league baseball. He also used to drive over there and run laps around it to stay in shape. He had weak lungs. I remember sitting in the car, watching him run.

When I was 10 years old and Dad had a job at Golf Crest Country Club, Nancy and I used to play a game on a ping pong table where we'd let the ball bounce on the floor once before hitting it back. We called it "gnip gnop," for "ping pong" spelled backwards. We'd listen to Elvis Presley on the radio while we played.

I used to get in trouble, like most kids do. Mom was the disciplinarian. She's the one who spanked me. Dad didn't like it when she did that. We'd still be at the tennis club, and she would say I was going to get a spanking when we returned home. We lived 20 minutes away. That was far worse than the actual punishment—the anticipation. I was praying for every red light!

I picked up tennis balls to earn my first bicycle. Dad would pay me a little money for picking up the balls when he gave lessons. When I had earned enough to buy the bike, I promptly quit. He was so mad!

I had won my first trophy at age eight, but I wasn't serious about tennis yet. Mom really encouraged me to get out there at least once a week just to keep whatever skill I had going. She would ask me to fill the fourth slot with her friends to play doubles. I don't think she had it in her mind necessarily that I would be a professional player. She probably just wanted me to get some exercise.

In Houston, we lived in what I would have to call, kindly, a one-room shack. It really was the premier example of a shotgun house. You could open the front door and the back door and see right through it. There was a bathroom and a little kitchen. Fairly early on, Mom and Dad built a bedroom for themselves off to the side. They later built a front sitting room where I slept on a couch which converted into a pull-out bed. Nancy slept in the middle of the house. It was a fairly good-sized property. We had a lot more land than floor space.

You didn't have to worry about crime back then, like you do

these days. All the kids would just wander the neighborhood. The street wasn't even paved. Everybody had a ditch in the front yard. It was a drainage system for the rain. We used to hunt crawdads there after a storm.

The critter population wasn't limited to the outdoors, unfortunately. Inside the house we had two cockroaches we just never could seem to get rid of. Finally, Dad gave them names: Dixie and Sckockie. He said Nancy should keep them as pets, seeing as how she didn't have any friends.

We lived in a tough neighborhood. It was a typical below-middle-class area. My friend David's father was a repair man for Sears. Mr. Bowley. On one corner there was a Mexican family, the Quintanillas. A guy who lived next door to us, his name was Shorty. There was an empty lot across from us. Toward the end of when we lived there, someone built a brick house on that empty lot—1100-1400 square feet. It looked like a palace to us. The owners left their garage door open one day. Somehow we got ahold of these persimmons and splattered them all over the garage walls. They called the cops. That was the only time I got in trouble with the police.

The friends I was running around with used to go out, stealing hubcaps. I remember them getting arrested for that. There were also whispers of marijuana use. That was a huge big deal in those days. I lived in fear of someone stealing my bicycle. I would try to hide it in the carport so it wouldn't get stolen. I think there was some trauma growing up just because we lived in a pretty rough end of town.

At my elementary school, Looscan, a lot of kids would show up with white skull caps because they had lice. Mom wanted me to switch to a school with a little better clientele. When I started fifth grade, I did change schools. The new one was much nicer.

I didn't look to big sister to defend me. But Nancy, for her part, felt protective of me. During some of those years in Houston, one of the neighborhood kids used to pick on me. Nancy saw him as a bully. She went after him and beat him up! He left me alone after that.

One night, I was having this awful dream. The only thing I remember is that I woke up, and my dad and I were sitting in his car, in the carport, on the backseat. The reason for that, he said, was that I had gone to his room in the middle of the night. He thought I was awake. I was so frightened, I felt like I had to grab him and go to the car. It was a 1954 Ford, dark blue. He didn't realize I was asleep until I woke up, sitting there, and asked him what we were doing out in the car.

My childhood night terrors might have been an early form of panic attacks. I probably had quite a few of them, but some I don't remember. The part of your brain that's experiencing it goes underground later and gets lost. One can only imagine how much it affected me at the time.

It's hard to describe the sensations you experience during a night terror. It's a nightmare. It's a dream that's just so realistic. From what I remember, night terrors are kind of like scared sleepwalking, but with your eyes open.

Kids are more prone to night terrors than adults. I had quite a few of them over a period of about a year and a half when I was seven or eight years old when we were living in Houston. They would usually happen within an hour of when I went to sleep. Some were not as frightening as others. I don't remember the story content of the terror. I think I probably walked in my sleep quite a bit.

The Merck Manual of Diagnosis and Therapy says night terrors are an indication of extreme anxiety. Maybe the night terrors were a sign of sublimated fear. Was I afraid of getting beaten up by neighborhood bullies? I have no idea. And then, one day, they subsided just as quickly as they had come on.

Before we left Houston, my best childhood friend, David, came over and said goodbye to me. I remember watching him walk away. That was pretty hard.

Some 30 years later, I drove back to that same neighborhood in Houston. I saw that kid Nancy had beaten up, still sitting there on that same front porch. I used to walk into that house like it was my own. He got up and said, "You came back!" They used to see my picture in the paper. He remembered and was real glad to see me.

But by then he was schizophrenic. He had become a chain smoker. I think he had been in Vietnam. It really freaked him out. I asked his keeper if he was dangerous. He intimated that he could be. I stayed and talked a while. Maybe I should have been more worried for my safety, but I wasn't. That was my old neighborhood, after all.

I was never schizophrenic, nor did I fight in Vietnam. But in my own way, I realized, I was as messed up as that childhood friend of mine. When I saw him again, it was not a case of "there, but by the grace of God, go I." No, it was far, far worse than that. It was more like I could empathize with his pain. Like his condition was only an extreme manifestation of what I, too, was feeling.

We all have to fight our personal demons. His was schizophrenia; mine was clinical depression. Who's to say which one is worse? Post-Traumatic Stress Disorder can take many forms. The kind he had was only the most blatantly obvious. He thought I was the big hero, returning in triumph. How surprised he would have been to discover that I, too, get skittish.

There was something that drove me to go back there. The psychologists would call it a desire to return to the womb. It was more curiosity than anything else. Curiosity and a certain sentimentality. Nostalgia. The reality I found there was a shock to my system—and all the more so because, in a way, it was like looking in a mirror. And the image I saw there was none too pretty.

CHAPTER THREE

West Texas Roots

In the fall of 1958, Dad gave up three jobs: coaching the tennis team at Rice University, teaching tennis at Golf Crest Country Club in Houston, and a summer job at the Century Country Club on Long Island—all at once. He had a scare with skin cancer. Decided he could no longer spend all day out in the sun.

I remember seeing him out on the front porch of our house on Elser Street in Houston. He was telling Mom what he felt like he had to do. He was crying. I was 11 years old. I had never seen him cry very much. That affected me big time. It was unsettling. It didn't throw me into a tizzy, but I can remember it vividly. I could tell he was going through hell.

The next job Dad had was a temporary one in Albany, New York in the summer of 1960. He had to wear pants, a long-sleeved shirt, a floppy hat, and sunglasses. The sunscreen they made back then was lousy. It didn't work too well. So he had to cover every inch of his skin. He looked like a mummy! People did not even recognize him in the pro shop.

In the mean time, we moved to San Angelo to be near Dad's parents. I think he was trying to regroup. We moved into a little house on Harrison Street, out there in West Texas. It was a fifth the size of the one my kids would later grow up in. We ate red beans and rice and goat meat for three years until my dad got another good job.

All while I was growing up, we moved around a lot. That meant I went to a lot of different schools as a kid. By my count, I attended at least eight different schools in the ten years I went to school. That was a little unusual and probably also a little bit stressful.

The first day at Santa Rita Elementary School in San Angelo, in November of 1958, the principal took me down to my class. My teacher's name was Mr. Ritchie, like my name, only spelled differently. He was my favorite teacher—a neat guy. He made everything pretty fun. He's the teacher I remember most out of all the teachers I ever had.

That year, two friends (Henry Eckert and Jinx Riley) and I called ourselves the Scorpion Gang. At Halloween, we set fire to paper bags full of shit. The idea was to ring a doorbell and run away, leaving the bag burning on the front porch. The people were supposed to open the door and start stomping on it. But it didn't turn out like we thought. It wasn't a well-executed prank. We also used to raise Cain at different movie theaters in town. We would go in there and make noises during the show and bother everybody until finally we'd get kicked out. We were good for nothing! We were not a gang to be feared. We were The Three Stooges and didn't know it. Three punky little kids who would have run at the sound of a firecracker. The only thing scary about us was the name. We stole candy off of a candy truck one night. It was just the silly, goofy things that kids do.

I distinctly remember being subjected to corporal punishment in middle school. That was still Santa Rita when I was in the sixth grade. The principal's name was Bozarth. We grabbed this kid in the schoolyard. The gang and I poured Kool-aid mix on the kid's head. Bozarth brought us in, and we got paddled. I was the second in line, which means I had to listen to the first. I heard some popping going on. He had a spat board with holes in it. We didn't have to pull our pants down. He gave me a few good swats on my butt. I remember bending over. When Dad found out, he did not take kindly to hav-

Here I am with Dad at the Golf Crest Country Club in Houston.

ing anything like that happen outside of his control. He went over there and raised hell. He was mad about not being consulted.

No doubt about it: Dad liked to be in charge. His first pupil ever in terms of serious tennis coaching was Tut Bartzen. He was 19 years older than I. In 1959, Tut was traveling on the amateur tour. He called Dad and said he would be in Dallas the next week. He said he'd been having some trouble with his game. He asked Dad to join him in Dallas to help him prepare for the tournament. Nancy was 16 at the time and playing some real good tennis. She went with Dad to help Tut in Ft. Worth. I was left at home with Mom. I was 12 years old. I had asked if I could go too. They said, "No, this is business. You'd get in the way."

Well, that really hit me big-time hard. I didn't like that at all.

15

They were planning to be gone seven days. There was a tennis court at Santa Rita (it's still there). I grabbed Mom. We found a box of 20 balls. My goal was to get so good in a week that next time, they wouldn't be so dismissive. They wouldn't want to leave me at home. We went down to that court every day that week. She fed me drills out of that box. I was rejected, and I couldn't handle it. That was when I said, "OK, I'll show them." And I've been pounding some kind of a ball ever since!

The only things Dad really ever spanked me for were stealing and cheating. We were at a tennis tournament in Abilene, in the spring of 1959. I was in the sixth grade, but they let me play on the junior high tennis team. We used to travel to tournaments all over. Mike McCarty, another player on the team, said he was going in the shop to steal something. I went with him and stole a leather racquet grip. The pro knew we had done it. The high school coach told Dad. He took me out in the front yard and beat the crap out of me!

The next year, I went to Washington Junior High, which was just the seventh grade by itself. There were some bullies from Lee Junior High. These guys came up to the high school one day when I was playing tennis. They started to bully me. They thought tennis was for sissies. I went after them with my tennis racquet and pounded the shit out of them. They threatened me that they would "get" me when I went to Lee Junior High. I was 13. I remembered they had said that. The first week at Lee, I came out the back of the building. There were six or seven kids who formed a circle. They were shoving me back and forth. The next thing I knew, a fist came out of nowhere and knocked me down cold. I was late to my next class. I was lying unconscious there under the bushes. I remember the only punishment those boys got from the school was a couple days of not being allowed to participate in football! That hardly seemed fair.

I played a junior tournament or two in Albany, New York in the summer of 1960. We played on clay up there. I was almost good enough to beat Nancy. I was getting real close. She knew it and I knew it. I was calling some close lines on her. I wanted to beat her so badly that I started wishing some of her balls out. Dad was watching one of our matches. On clay courts, the ball leaves a mark. This time she contested a line call. She told Dad I had cheated her. He called me into the shop. He was spanking me, giving me a pretty good thrashing, even though he wasn't normally big on spanking. I went back onto the court. I knew where the mark was. She had taken her finger and increased what the ball mark looked like. I said "Dad, look what she's done." She sheepishly had to admit that this time, she was the one cheating. She was the one who got in trouble then!

Dad didn't like to spank us because his father had been very unpredictable with him. He'd never know as a child, coming home, if his father would be in a good mood or a bad one. Dad would come home and arbitrarily either get a whipping or high praise. He never knew which. His father was also an embarrassment to him with his friends.

My grandfather was an alcoholic. He was born in 1893. When we lived in San Angelo from 1958-61, my grandparents lived 20 miles away in Miles, Texas. I remember one time being out there visiting them in Miles. He was pretty snookered. For some reason he wanted to get back to San Angelo. I was only 12 years old, but I had to drive that whole way by myself. I could hardly see above the steering wheel! He used to let me drive his car on those country roads. Nobody was around, really. But that day, he wasn't doing it to give me a thrill. He was so drunk, he couldn't drive. It was definitely his idea. He knew he couldn't do it. I literally was barely able to get us there.

He was a binge drinker, so he would go on a one-, two-, or even three-week winder. He always drank and then would sober up for a few weeks. He would get off of it and be pretty grouchy. His nerves would be out on end. He would be in a bad area emotionally before

17

he kind of recuperated. Dadda used to go on these bouts of drinking and then go to church to cleanse it out of his system. I went with him once to the Miles Presbyterian Church. This preacher said, "All it takes is faith the size of a mustard seed to be saved." I'll never forget that sermon. It made a big impression on me.

Five or six years before my grandfather died, we drove out from Dallas to play a men's regional tournament in Midland. Dad and I drove to Midland, and either on the way out there or on the way back, we stopped in Miles. Dadda didn't think I heard him tell Dad what he did. He said to Dad, "I'm having trouble getting off of it this time." His heart used to palpitate. He put himself through hell with that alcohol.

When he was drinking, he loved to get on the phone to people. As soon as the phone would ring, Dad would get on the line and then tell us, "He's drinking again." Dadda loved to go to the Lowake Steak House. His was a wasted talent. His drinking really affected the quality of all the lives around him. But he was a character, very funny and made friends easily. He also played the piano with flair.

His nickname was Kewpie, like the Kewpie dolls, because he was bald. He was only 5'5" but weighed 200 pounds. He always wanted to be a big shot. He used to think it was the real deal to get to know the newspaper people. Newspaper people, to him, were big shots. He knew the editor of the sports section in the local paper all during the '40s and '50s. They would go out and get soused together with their drinking buddies.

My grandfather was an intelligent man. He was Goodyear tire salesman of the year. At one time, he was worth quite a bit of money. He was sharp. He taught my dad about stocks and investments. Even when Dadda was "lit" with alcohol, he was usually still rational enough to talk stocks and bonds. Just about the time he'd had one too many drinks, he'd look at me and say with a slur, "Hold your head up. You're a Richey." He could hardly hold his own head up! It was ridiculous. . . . Another time, coming back from winning the U.S. Junior Indoors in St. Louis, he was with us there in the car and suddenly he had to go to the bathroom. He grabbed some newspapers we had in the front seat and went behind a tree by the side of the road. It was only later that I realized he had used some of my very first press clippings for toilet paper!

My guess is that my grandfather, Dadda, had depression too. One time he said to Mom, "I have these fears." I think that was his way of describing depression, anxieties, and the whole syndrome I inherited. I really believe Dadda drank as self-medication for mental and emotional disorders they didn't know how to treat back then.

My grandmother, Garnie, was a neurotic. She was obsessive-compulsive. She checked the door a million times. They fit together. She was neurotic because of his drinking. He in turn drank because she was neurotic.

Garnie came from a Czech family. She was one of the kindest people you could ever meet—and she would give you anything. She loved animals and would feed any creature that came to her back door. She had nearly 50 cats and Dadda didn't like them. He would take her cats and twist their necks off and throw them in the garbage. His nerves were right out there on his skin as he was coming off a drinking bout. There was some high dysfunction. On a given day, Garnie would be acting fine, but then all of a sudden she would go off, and it was like a completely different person. She was also pretty unpredictable.

When we moved back to San Angelo in 1958, the next spring there was a tournament called the Thunderbird Invitational. Dadda, Mom, Dad, and Nancy drove out to Phoenix for Nancy to play in it. Garnie stayed behind to take care of me in the Harrison Street house. She always felt that she was left to do menial jobs. She called herself a kitchen mechanic, "KM" for short. She just always kind of felt picked on. They left for Phoenix. At first, everything was fine. Then all of a sudden, she went on a two-day jag. It almost scared me. She got into this neurotic binge and felt like everybody was picking on her. It was totally unlike her normal self.

She was kind-hearted, but she was just neurotic. That's where Dad got all his germ stuff. She was afraid of germs. I would come in from playing tennis, and she wanted me to take a shower immediately because she was afraid I would catch cold. She was the most negative person you could be around. She would go off into this rage. It was like, "Gosh, what sparked this?" It was like a four-days-delayed reaction. She would just go off into this tissy fit. Dad always said that I was like Dadda, while Nancy's personality was a lot more like Garnie's.

There is a history of mental illness in our family. Some of my ancestors were undoubtedly depressives who went undiagnosed. Alcoholism often skips a generation to be passed down from the child to the grandchild. That's what happened with me. My mother was also prone to some emotional and mental health issues. Genetically, that might be a factor with me, too. So when you look at my pedigree, there are warning signs all over the place. I've never had what you would consider normal emotional content.

My dad wanted to control his world. He craved stability. He didn't want his world to be unstable and fall apart again. He had as much of an addiction to trying to control his environment as his father did to alcohol. He was always addicted to control.

I'm trying to do mirror images here, between generations. Dadda spanked Dad even when he didn't deserve it. Total inconsistency. So Dad never wanted to spank me at all. That's the mirror image of Dad's control thing: chaos. You want to control everything. You don't want to feel that pain any more. I can see how Dad wanted to make his world right. His goal was to make his world forevermore secure and not to have that chaos once he got out on his own.

There's the inverse of a lot of that stuff you start feeling. Dad probably wanted a closer family than he had growing up. And for

20

the opposite reasons, I wanted a less close one.

As human beings, we all run from pain. We get painless and feel good in so many different ways. My drug of choice was success. Dadda's was alcohol. But both are very strong drugs.

When Dad was a kid, he got so good at marbles that no one would play against him. He played for keeps. He was also good at throwing knives, or anything else that required hand-eye coordination. He always had to be the top dog—the leader of the pack. Anyone who was going to be a friend of George Richey basically had to be a subordinate. He did give people quality time, but he had to be in the superior role. That's a pretty tough attitude to apply across the board to the society you're living in!

Dad's extreme competitiveness stemmed from both nature and nurture. Dadda was also a type A. He was not a reticent soul. He had a hot temper. That temper has been handed down through at least three generations. But Dad was pretty cool in a crunch. A pretty cool cookie. He had his wits about him and was a good competitor.

Early on, Dad perceived my maternal Grandmother as someone he would have to fight to control Mom. Dad always regarded Grandmother as a little bit of a threat. And Dad didn't take too kindly to threats. . . . Dad always loved to be in control.

Mom was caught between her mother and her husband. In their row, she was caught in the middle. The psychiatrist told Mom she needed to find a way to alleviate that tension. I think Dad created a difficult situation for Mom, for all of us. It shouldn't have been as strained a relationship as it was.

There were times my mother wanted to go visit her family. But family relations were tough and Mom had a hard time knowing how to handle that. I remember the first time I went with her to Electra, Texas. Grandaddy picked us up at the bus terminal. He was postmaster of the town. I was a little afraid of him. He was a total stranger to me. Later Grandaddy would come and visit us some in

Dallas. He would come alone. It wasn't a secret that Grandmother and my dad didn't get along very well.

I never felt that close to Grandmother and Grandaddy. That's a sad thing, in a way. I remember Grandaddy being a kind man, a good man—a real gentle soul. When I was older, I would write to them from trips I took abroad. They tried the best they could to be close to us. They had a subscription to *World Tennis* magazine. That is how they kept up with our career. Grandmother would highlight some of the stories about us. All the results were printed in the back pages. She would highlight the scores of our matches.

We got a phone call in Dallas in the fall of 1964, saying that Mom better come home, because her father wasn't doing well. He had skin cancer which had metastasized. Mom left Dallas and went home to Electra. That night in bed, somehow I knew that he had died. I had the distinct feeling that his spirit started at the back of the house where Nancy was, glided down the hall, and came into my bedroom. To this day I'm convinced that his spirit entered our house and took a walk around. We got another phone call the next day. My mother told me he had passed away. I said, "I know" and told her what time it was. I was not surprised to hear that the hour matched.

That paranormal experience was, in some ways, the opposite of the night terrors I used to have as a child. Grandaddy's ghost was a comforting presence, not to be feared. I already had enough fears to contend with. . . .

By that time, I was 18 years old and already prone to intense anxiety. I was rising fast in the tennis world, but it never seemed to be enough. My grandfather's passing signaled to me that my childhood was over. A calm, stabilizing influence would henceforth be missing from my life.

Having said that, if my father had had my mother's parents instead of his own, I might never have had a great tennis career. Dadda was the original firewood, the fuel, which fed the syndrome I now call Richey, Inc.

Out of dysfunction came excellence. I am convinced that that is a pattern which is repeated through the ages. At least, that was the case for my family and me. . . .

CHAPTER FOUR

Richey, Inc.

Richey, Inc., I call it, not in a derogatory way. We moved as a unit. People referred to us simply as "The Richeys." From the outside, it looked like the perfect little family. In some ways, it was. But it was too much of a good thing. Winning was the be-all and the end-all. It was our life, our business, our religion. We didn't grow into this syndrome of Richey, Inc. It was never any other way.

We thought we did not need anything or anyone else if we could throw "winning" at the situation. That handled everything. The strategy that evolved was not plotted or thought out. It worked most of the time; but it created mounting pressure also. We just operated in a certain manner: kept others at arm's length, let our racquets do the talking. We'd better win if we acted and talked like we did! We took a cue from the late, great Pancho Gonzalez. Whenever there was a problem, his solution was: "Just play better. That will shut them up."

The way we approached it, it was life or death. Winning or losing. You bet it was. You're often told that one of the good things about sports is that it teaches you so much about life. That always made me mad. How can you find out about something you don't have? There wasn't any other life for me to go back to—none apart from tennis. Tennis was my life.

Richey, Inc. is my retrospective name for a creed and an enterprise. It entailed inordinate success, a strong work ethic, fidelity in marriage, and a conservative approach to finances. Some of our slogans were: "If there's adversity, then flip it on its side" or "Don't stop with a brick wall" and "Change your attitude."

Richey, Inc. gave me my whole life: my profession, my bank account, world travel, an education I couldn't have gotten any other way. But it can be a little bit suffocating when you're spending more time together than most people would, under more stressful conditions than most families experience. I don't have a negative feeling toward all of it but you reach a point where you want your independence. To be your own person. I didn't do that until very late in life. . . .

Dad had a summer job teaching tennis in Fort Wayne, Indiana when I was eight years old. I won my first tournament up there— my first little trophy. I put some books under it to make it look as tall as Nancy's. There was another family who would come visit us up there. Dad didn't like that. It was a distraction. His goal was to have Nancy win those junior girls' tournaments. It was pretty darn serious from the beginning. Not just a fun, social thing to do.

Back in Houston, when I'd go to Golf Crest Country Club on the weekends, both of my parents would be out there. I had both of my parents tending to me all the time. I had a real sense of family closeness, which is important to a kid. There aren't a lot of kids who get to spend that much time at country clubs, whether the family works there or not. It was a nice atmosphere. I probably could have just as easily gone into golf as a profession. I caddied to earn a few bucks and shagged balls for the golf pro. Dad also used to take me with him to coach tennis at Rice University. I had some hero worship going for some of the guys on his team. They must have been only 18 years old, but they sure looked like men to me!

When Nancy got to be 13 or 14, I was about 10. It was an excit-

Richey, Inc.—Dad, Nancy, Mom and me—at Memorial Park Tennis Center in Houston in 1957.

ing thing to get in the car to go up East to see the national girls' tournaments she played in. I was one of the first people ever to see Billie Jean Moffitt (later Billie Jean King) play outside of California. We would drive from Texas to these different towns. There was like a little series of events surrounding the national 15-and-unders or 18-and-unders. From 1956 to 1958 or 1959, I got to tag along. It was fun. I was traveling to places like Philadelphia and made many different friends that I would see the following year.

In 1959, at age 12, I decided to become a "real" tennis player. We were both young enough at that point that Nancy still only played 15 tournaments a year, max. I played a few tournaments in the summer. During the rest of the year, Nancy and I would put together a fictional tournament against each other and tack it up on the bulletin board in Dad's pro shop. We had the cities written on a schedule and everything. The members would come in and get a kick out of it. We imagined when we went out to play a match that we were in, say, New Orleans that night. The goal was to make it seem real. You treated every point seriously and pretended it was a tournament match. That was one of Dad's methods. He just knew instinctively that if he could make his practice matches seem important enough, then in the tournament it wouldn't be so much of a shock to his system. The goal was to get "tournament tough." Who won our little play tournament? I'm not sure. I bet you she did, since I don't remember!

By the time I was a teenager, I had started to get good enough to clip her at times. She might have had a slight edge on me when I was 14. But by the time I was 15, I had gotten too strong and could beat her. The first time I ever beat her was in Albany, New York when she was getting ready for the summer tour that concluded with the U.S. Championships at Forest Hills.

In essence, I had a career already at ages 13, 14, 15, and 16. At age 14, I won the Texas 15-and-under championship in Houston. Even though it was kids' tennis, it was big-time kids' tennis and we approached it with a professional attitude. I had an agenda, a bottom line, starting very young. I wanted to become a very good tennis player. My whole life was dedicated to becoming somebody. I wanted to be a star.

Meanwhile, some of the socialites in Dallas were concerned for my well-being. They thought I could get into a private school on account of my tennis and maybe eventually even be offered a college scholarship. I went along with that idea far enough to take the entrance exam at St. Mark's, a ritzy prep school, when I was 14 years old. I still remember the essay question: "Write an essay on President Kennedy's trip to Europe." I hardly knew he was president! Somehow or other, I barely passed the exam, although I'm convinced to this day it was only because they wanted me to play on their tennis team. By that point, I had already decided that prep school was not for me. . . .

In high school, I played a tennis tournament called the Cotton Bowl Invitational. We played in the automobile exposition building at the Texas State Fair. Mine was the only entry from Highland Park High School. I won the two or three different divisions I was allowed to enter. I won the team trophy, even though I was only one person! There was no team, just little old me. The trophy is still there at Highland Park to this day. I went back years later and saw that trophy still sitting there in that trophy case.

As a sophomore, I won the Texas High School Championship. I was a teenage "phenom" in tennis and my name started to appear in the paper a lot. I found out that there was a National Interscholastic Championship and I wanted to play. I went to see the athletic director at Highland Park High School, a guy named Tugboat Jones, and asked him to send me to the tournament that was held at Williams College in Massachusetts. He said he'd send me if I promised I'd come out for football the next season. I said, "No, I'm afraid I'll get hurt." He grinned and said he'd send me anyway. He had just wanted to see what I would say. . . .

I lost in the final of the Interscholastic to Mike Belkin. He had won the National 15-and-unders in 1960, the year I couldn't play that tournament because I had mononucleosis. I was only 13 at the time.

Dad always said he thought that illness was the best thing that ever happened to me, because he knew I wasn't ready yet. He didn't want to put me in over my head too soon. You don't want to throw a kid into too tough a competition, early on. That can beat him down. My dad didn't want me to get in the habit of losing.

Another early tournament I remember from my high school days in Dallas was the Sugar Bowl Invitational, which was held in New Orleans. I played a guy in the final, Ham Richardson, who had been ranked the No. 1 player in the United States. I was way up in the match, but then I got a little choky. Suddenly, I found myself cramping in the fifth set. I was down 5-2 in the fifth, but miraculously, I ended up winning, 9-7. This was a real men's event, not just a junior tournament. So it was a big win for a kid. I was still clutching my trophy in the car. I said to Mom and Dad, "Those kids out partying in high school, they have no idea what kind of fun this is. They have no idea what this kind of high feels like." What they were involved in, the pep rallies and the football games, didn't even look like fun to me. I was not belittling them, but I didn't covet what they had. . . .

George Richey was chairman of the board of Richey, Inc. It was Richey, Inc. against the world. That's all I knew. We upset a lot of people in a lot of different areas. I would say now: rightfully so.

My dad was such a huge part of the reason I became a success. He maybe played through us in some ways. You bet there's dysfunction there. But it would be hard for a competitor not to play through you. That's almost the definition of a good coach.

Dad was absolutely dedicated to us. It was in large part because of him that we became what we were. He was financial advisor, confessor, coach, not just a father. It is NOT my father's fault that I have clinical depression. These are surrounding facts, not excuses.

So much of the dysfunction, on the flip side, is trying to attain excellence. It's all about drive. You can't polish a fantastic diamond without the dross that floats off in the refining process.

Dad played some professional tennis in his day. I know how good a player Dad was. He reached No. 8 in the world among the pros. I probably would have had respect for him anyway, but it helped that my dad knew what it was like to play competitively. I do remember that when he played and lost, Dad would rant and rave at his opponents all the way home. He just couldn't wait to get back at the same guy the next time. His reaction to losses was over the edge. . . .

He was not the strongest person physically. He didn't have as strong a constitution as I had. Dad was probably 5'8" but he had weak lungs. He had had bad bronchitis as a kid. He also topped out at 150 pounds. I'm 5'9"and played at 170 pounds. I had more innate strength. Dad always said I was a bigger and better version of himself. He felt like I had everything he would have liked to have had. He wasn't jealous. He was just proud of me. In his heart, he was really a player first and a coach second. But he was never resentful of the careers we had. And that's exceptionally admirable in a man. Dad's timing with his career was all wrong. Mine was all right; but instead of being resentful, he was happy for me. Dad was always pleased when I did well. That shows you what a wonderful man he really was.

At first, as a child, Dad had wanted to play baseball. But then, at age 16, he fell out of a moving car and injured his right arm. So he taught himself tennis, a "one-arm" sport, with his left hand. Dad never learned to play with his natural arm. What he did do was to practice eating left-handedly and doing other things left-handedly besides tennis to make it feel more natural. Serving, for him—because it's a throwing motion—was always more difficult than ground-strokes. Hitting overheads was also hard. From my dad's point of view, when he coached Nancy and me, whenever we would complain about anything having to do with playing conditions, opponents, or competition, he would say, "Well, try doing it with your unnatural arm!" That "no excuses, get the job done" mentality was always underscored by the fact that he did do it with his left hand.

He was a very good player. He was an excellent athlete and had fine physical coordination. His career was engendered by adversity and evolved from there. The amateur tour was only right for single guys, which he was not. Dad had to teach at club jobs to earn a living for his family. So by definition he was a professional, which meant he wasn't even eligible for amateur events. He had no venue to play (or hardly any—just a few isolated pro tournaments here and there). At that time, it was not really possible to earn a living with pro tennis.

Dad had a family to feed at a relatively young age. He had it about the toughest you could imagine. In contrast, I had it pretty easy. He was pleased for me, but he wasn't about to cut me any slack. He was living in a trailer by the side of the road with a squawking baby and didn't know where his next meal was going to come from. As a man, I can't imagine what it feels like not to know how I'm going to provide for my family. I guess the kid always has it easier than the parent. . . .

He liked to be called Pro. It happens in golf and tennis: the pro at a club is usually nicknamed "Pro." Even Nancy and I would call him that. Later on, our practice partners did the same. It was an endearing, nice term we could all use in a common way. When I got married later, my wife called him that too. It was less awkward than "dad" since he wasn't her father. When the grandkids came along, he didn't want to be called "Grandpa." That made him feel old. So eventually, they also called him "Pro."

Pro loved playing the game more than anything else. His second choice would have been just teaching us. His third choice would have been giving lessons at a club, which is what he had to do for much of his career. Personality-wise and from his upbringing, he

31

resisted being social. Being a club pro was hard for him—catering to rich people, being nice to them. Dad told the story of how at one of his club jobs, sensing that he wasn't the strongest person physically, he started trying to figure out how much money he needed to save so he could retire and not be tied to something that was hard for him. He also discovered he had skin cancer in the late 1950s. So when he quit those three jobs and we moved back to San Angelo, he jumped in and started coaching us right away. He enjoyed the fact that now he had free time to teach us.

When we won, he got an immense thrill out of it. Nancy and I did perceive that he had some unfulfilled dreams and desires that he satisfied through us. But nonetheless he gave us his undivided attention. He was 100 percent committed. "Don't give in to human weakness"—that was the attitude he brought to the table. The positives always outweighed the negatives. . . .

If there's one word that would describe my dad in every area, it is *extreme*. Whether it's tennis or saving money, he was damn sure gonna be the best at it. He wasn't gonna come in second if he could help it. His generation lived through the Depression and the World Wars. We had only one car, one TV set, one phone. Dad was what you might call a dry alcoholic. He was always trying to control his environment. He was damaged goods. He was an extremist. But I'd rather have had him that way than for him not to have cared.

My father was domineering. There's no doubt about that. That's an honest assessment. But that's an asset when you're going out on the battlefield to compete. You want to have a strong figure in your corner. While we were growing up, he used to say, "If you want me to help you with your tennis, you'd better give 110 percent or I'm not interested." You can stomach a lot of willful personality if you know deep down that he really wants to help.

Dad was a competitor, a driven person but he had a soft heart underneath his hard shell. It helped me to realize finally that he did have a difficult upbringing. When I saw what shaped him, the "whys" and the "where for's," it helped me to say: "You know what, he's a flawed human being like the rest of us." I could look at him and say: "He's trying to make it too." He took me baseball playing and beebee gun shooting. He taught me to ride a bicycle. He was a much more attentive father than I was!

Some fathers are purposefully cruel and plot it out. I've always thought that's pretty evil. I saw a father once, sitting in the stands. Every time his son missed a shot, he would clap! He was utterly malicious. In contrast, when I lost and Dad was coaching me, he would say, "You did the best you could out there."

Richey, Inc. had one rule of engagement: you'd better give it everything you have. Never lose through lack of effort. Maybe Dad took his frustration out on Nancy and me. But he was never trying to plot to make me miserable. Dad didn't set out to hurt people. He never did that on purpose. He just had a stubborn, iron will—about his opinions and everything else.

There came a phase where I didn't want him around that much. My biological family was suffocatingly close. You reach a certain age when you want your own identity and want to try to be out on your own more. I felt like he didn't know what I was going through. I think once clinical depression reared its ugly head, my relationship with my dad became more difficult because he had such set opinions on things. There are certain areas where I never failed to consult him, like finances. But in recovery, I tried to get through the codependency for the first time, so that I could be my own man. I tried to change the part of the equation I could.

Dad was such a paradox. He was the worrier of worriers. I would kid him. I'd say he was too negative. And yet if I had a problem I was really grappling with, he'd probably have a fairly creative solution and that was comforting. He was a smart guy, and he'd give me his best shot. Some of it was biased. But he taught me to look at a problem from several different sides. He was always looking for creative ways to get something done. Everything was doable.

That attitude is a pretty neat gift to give a kid. You can flip any situation on its side, get a new point of view. My kids have told me that they watch the way I tackle certain problems. I'll go in the side door if I can't get in the front. I learned all that from Dad.

I told Dad I love and respect him. He taught me lessons that are invaluable. We've been in the trenches together. I was fortunate to have a father who instilled in me the idea that you could win at any level. You didn't have to be satisfied with just the state championship. Take it national, man. Hell, you can even take it global if you want to! If we were willing to work hard, his message was: "The sky's the limit. Follow your dreams."

It's pretty neat to be able to say: hey, we survived it all. He was my best friend. He was the No. 1 guy. Pro was truly one-of-a-kind.

I buried my father with a tennis racquet in his coffin. I'm sure in heaven he's playing tennis even better. This time, maybe he is playing with his natural arm. . . .

CHAPTER FIVE

High School Drop-Out

I was raised by a father who basically scoffed at the idea that schooling was everything. Thank goodness I had a supportive family. When I dropped out of high school to pursue a tennis career, I did so with my father's blessing. Some players might have had to deal with being disowned for that kind of decision. Of course there were people who looked askance at the fact that I dropped out of school. That really used to tick Pro off. But then, Dad never reacted well to any criticism of the Richeys.

I considered myself a nerd in high school because I didn't really fit in. They used to hold these pep rallies. I hated them. They seemed so silly. My career had already reached the national level. They were talking about some district game. They would give the team "victory apples." It was so corny. I was definitely the odd one out on that deal.

As a teenager, I first started to wonder if I might not be normal. I can remember feeling not depressed necessarily, but just real melancholy feeling, real blue. I was playing against men players at the age of 15. In my early teens, I felt extreme anxieties, severe highs and lows. I was moody and volatile. But the depression was not bad enough yet to be a shackle.

I was already predisposed to clinical depression genetically.

Growing up, with my personality bent and nervous structure, my anxieties were soothed by each tournament win. I could never fully rub out the anxieties, but winning was the antidote I used against them. Winning was like antidepressant medicine early on. I used tennis as a salve for emotional pain.

In Dallas, the school honestly tried to cooperate with me. They allowed me to miss days to play tournaments. Highland Park High School was almost like a private school in that regard. They tried to persuade me not to drop out. They said, "We'll do whatever it takes to keep you in school, because we understand how important your tennis is." That school was great. They understood I was exceptional. In 1962, I won the USTA National Boy's 16s Championships in Kalamazoo, Michigan at age 15. From 1962 to 1964, either Nancy or I was in the paper, on average, every third day.

Geometry. I never did take a full year of geometry. Since Nancy was playing the U.S. Championships at Forest Hills, which ended in September every year after school had already started, I was always beginning geometry a week late. I didn't feel like a failure when I failed geometry, even though it happened two years in a row. Geometry was like Greek to me. I wasn't interested and didn't care. Geometry was just irritating. My mind didn't work that way. I dropped out of that class because I was hopeless at it!

My mother wasn't too keen about my not finishing high school. Mom didn't like the idea. It was unorthodox. Her upbringing valued education more than dad's. She cared more what people were saying. That bothered her more than it did him. But he was the man of the house. Hers would have been the dissenting vote, but she wasn't going to cross him. That wasn't the only time she got overruled. . . .

There at the end in high school, I'd make it only to about midday. I'd call Dad and say, "Come get me." All I wanted to do was play tennis. I wasn't worried about my grades. I don't remember if I feigned illness or just didn't show up for the next class. Right before

I dropped out, I remember attending this one class. It might have been math of some kind. We were supposed to cover our books. The teacher came around to inspect the job we'd done. I never was too good at that. She came and inspected mine. She didn't like anything about it. I guess maybe I must have known I was getting ready to drop out of school. I just closed my book, grabbed all my stuff, and walked out of class. In my mind, at least, I quit high school that day.

I felt like I had leeway to be that defiant to my teacher. My parents and I had already talked about it. I had just won the USTA National Boys' 18s Championships in Kalamazoo at the age of 16. I had also won the Texas Men's Championship that summer. My career was really starting to take off.

The strongest criticism against my decision would have been if I had not made it as a player. But, even there, we had our bases covered. My plan was to be a club pro like Dad. And that was an honorable profession. I was the shoemaker's kid who was going to become a shoemaker. The only thing I never learned that I would have had to do at a pro shop was how to string tennis racquets. Pros these days are more businessmen than they were back then. Dad gave lessons, strang racquets, maybe ran a tournament or two a year. There were no leagues in those days. The job only required minimal accounting. I could add and subtract, at least enough to sell racquets and gear. The rest of my schooling for what I wanted to do had already taken place. We saw those who criticized that decision as being a little bit arrogant. . . .

Ham Richardson was a guy I practiced with a lot at that time. He was a top player who had spent time in England as a Rhodes Scholar. One night at his house, at a party, some guy asked me what field I was planning to go into. I thought he meant, like, maybe a corn field! I didn't understand. The bedrock of what we tried to do as a family was that I could always teach tennis as a fallback if I had to. Even some of my extended family didn't understand that. I always did have a Plan B.

In 1965, I won the Dallas Invitational at the Dallas Country Club, one year after dropping out of school.

I would not have wanted to start playing the tour at the age of 21 instead of 17. That might have eliminated some stresses but created others. It takes five to six years to build a good tennis game. That's a pretty substantial investment. Like going to college and then on to grad school for a master's degree. You're going to get out of it what you put in.

I was lucky that open tennis came in when it did. The "Open Era" of tennis, when pros were allowed to compete against amateurs, began in 1968. When I dropped out of school in 1964, I didn't know my timing would be so good. But even if it hadn't been, I wouldn't have cared. I was ready to go to the other school —the world tour school. I played the world amateur tennis tour for the next four years.

There is something called the prodigy syndrome. It's not that I necessarily considered myself a prodigy, but when you're told that often enough, it kind of sticks. The newspapers were constantly calling to interview us. We had major articles in magazines: *Look, Time, Life, Sports Illustrated.* We were good very young, but then also we didn't flame out. We were child prodigies who continued on into our 20s and even 30s. In fact, Nancy just kept getting better. She never won the national girls' championships like I won the boys' title. But she did win the women's titles as a teenager. At that time, she was probably ranked in the top five of the nation. When you put it all together, she had a fairly long career. Her last big win was over Martina Navratilova at age 33.

When you're a prodigy, nothing about it is normal. We didn't even try to make it that way. Maxwell Maltz once said (in his book *Psychocybernetics*) that people are afraid of success because they might lose their friends if they stick their heads above the crowd. I didn't have any friends, so I had nothing to lose! It's not the most normal thing for a teenager already to know exactly what he wants to do when he grows up. To be working every day to become the best. There's not a lot normal about any of that, when you get right

39

down to it. But if you strive for excellence in any field, your life isn't going to be normal. If excellence were normal, everyone would be excellent. . . .

We were interviewed in the late 1970s for a book on prodigies. That author was very persistent. We turned her down a couple of times, but then she came to San Angelo and interviewed Nancy and me. The woman didn't use names but when her book was published, we could pick out which parts had been written about us. The book was about kids and their families who produced extraordinary excellence. The Richeys were a history-making family. The author was trying to identify ingredients for super-successful offspring. Is there a formula? I would say no, but there are some common denominators. You can create an environment conducive to germinating success.

There's a myth that more sports heroes come from poverty because they have such a drive to succeed. There may be something to that. It would be easy to say that to become great, you have to grow up in a one-room house on Elser Street like I did. But I don't think that's right. I think you can come from any economic background. There's just a huge difference between the mentality of having sports be an "activity" or making it into more than that. There's nothing wrong with its being an activity. That's the norm. But it's different. And the rich people think they can buy it.

You have to have raw talent. I think dysfunction also sparks a drive to succeed. It's some combination of those ingredients. As a family, we probably did err on the side of "nothing but boot straps." But we never wanted to err on the side of thinking you could throw money at a problem to solve it. If I have to err, I still want to err on the side of boot straps.

I was in the unusual position of having a sibling who was also playing tennis at the highest level. There would be many times when I would have an off day at a major tournament, but she was playing a match on that day. So we as a family would still be geared up for her match. We hardly ever took a day off.

I always competed with Nancy, but I did not feel inferior growing up in her shadow. I was just off doing kid things. There was a couple-year period where I guess I felt like I was having to prove myself. She was a girl, but she practiced against men players and beat a lot of them. She was beating some of Dad's Rice boys. So it wasn't like I was the only one it was happening to. Just because she was a girl didn't mean you couldn't lose to her. It probably would have been worse if I had had a brother. She and I had a race to see who would win the first national title in the family. I beat her only by a couple of days! We used to hold little competitions like that, but it was fun.

Our parents did treat the two of us differently. Dad always felt like he could be a little harder on Nancy, more demanding. He felt that she had, in a way, a little more substance to her. I was more fragile. If he rode me too hard, maybe I wouldn't hold up under it. She was perhaps a little more lazy. He had to light the fire under her more than me.

It hurt Nancy at times that he would say after watching her practice, "Those were good shots, BUT. . . ." It was like this perfectionism of his that could never be satisfied. In practice sessions, he clued in on the negative too much. A perfectionist tends to be that way. His temperament was hard on Nancy. There was lots of pressure. In tournaments, it's a wonder she could ever hit a ball! He would react visibly when she missed one, wincing, with white knuckles. He was harder on her than on me.

I suppose we vied with each other for Dad's attention. Dad never showed favoritism. He just felt like we were different, personality-wise. So he never even went through the motions of treating us the same. He was open about the fact that he handled me with kid gloves. He was gentler with me. He sensed that I couldn't take as much of the hard-hitting verbal demands.

Nancy used to make fun of me when we were very young kids.

We'd have a silly argument. She'd go "cheep, cheep, cheep" to taunt me when I was trying to make my point. That just used to drive me nuts! My sister, in her way, is every bit as competitive as I am. But as we got older, it wasn't a nasty thing. More like cheering each other on. Whenever I accomplished something, she was happy, and vice versa. I cried in the locker room after she won the French Open in 1968 because I was so happy for her. We had some knock-down, drag-outs on the practice court. We weren't ashamed of trying hard and competing. But there was no bad blood or wishing each other bad luck. It also helped that since we were not of the same gender, we knew we would never have to play against each other in a tournament, like the Williams sisters—Venus and Serena—had to do.

There were times when I helped her. I'd warm her up. I'd consult on the particular strategy she should use against a specific opponent. If Dad wasn't around at a given tournament, I would actually be in the stands coaching her. If I had not been there, she would not have won the French Open. She, in turn, helped me with my serve the night before my famous match against Stan Smith in 1970. She probably put in more time helping my career than I put in helping hers. Coaching was illegal from the stands, but everyone did it regardless.

We were enormous support for each other. There were parts of life on the tour that were easier for us to talk about with each other than with Dad. Not the playing of the matches so much. More along the lines of stresses that go with being that many weeks on the road and the absorption of that much competition. There were parts about that which Dad just didn't have firsthand knowledge of. In some ways, his nervous system absorbed things we didn't have to, like sitting in the stands with his hands tied. So he had unique stresses too. Nancy and I also knew about that, though, because we coached each other when he wasn't around.

There were times on the practice court when we would get irritated with each other. She never wanted to drill for as long as I wanted to. I liked a drill called "down the line and crosscourt." My objective with each shot I hit was to go down the line, while she would go crosscourt. The idea was to make each other run. To keep it up for long requires extreme discipline. It teaches you to feel the corners of the court. After a while, she would want to move on. With my obsessive/compulsive stuff, I'd still be stuck on that same drill. We used to get on each other's nerves big time!

I admit I abused Nancy verbally on the practice court. We are very vocal people, all of us. We played very competitive practice matches against each other. We always talked to each other pretty tough and were pretty loud-mouthed. We didn't have a whole lot of couth at times. We both were so competitive that, well, she was my sister, yes, but I looked at her more as a fellow competitor. Ultimately, we became known as the greatest brother/sister combination ever in the history of tennis. I played her sets throughout our lives. Even when I started the senior tour, when she was 39 and I was 35, perhaps by then she couldn't beat me any more. But we never went out on the court and saw it as just for funsies. It was against the family religion to say, "It's just a game."

Nancy and I were competitive against each other on the tennis court, but we were very protective of each other when it came to anyone else. For being brother and sister, we got along very, very well. We didn't view each other as enemies. We felt like we were on the same team. It was a huge advantage to have a built-in practice partner. The players today have partners to travel with them who are on call to do nothing but practice sessions. We were coaches and practice partners for each other, all wrapped into one. Nancy catered to my needs much more as a nurturer than I did for her. I was the baby brother. I asked her to do more off-the-court things, such as my laundry. She never asked me to wash her clothes!

Probably of anyone else in the family, Nancy and I saw eye to eye on most things. We were the subordinates to Dad's alpha position. He was the boss. We suffered tournament losses we had to

My sister Nancy and I saw eye to eye on most things. Here we are at the Western Championships at the Town & Tennis Club in Milwaukee, Wisconsin.

help each other get over. We could cry on each other's shoulders and commiserate. We were a consoling mechanism for each other. We held onto each other for comfort.

One of my regrets is that at Wimbledon in 1968, Nancy had reached the semifinals for the first and what would ultimately be the only time in her career. I had lost earlier in the men's tournament. I was always looking forward to preparing for the next event. I wanted to get back and get used to the hot weather again prior to the U.S. clay court season. I selfishly left London as soon as I was out of the tournament, leaving her to fend for herself. She had been used to my being there and helping her. It really affected her emotionally. I could have stayed and seen her through that battle. But I didn't. In hindsight, if I had it to do over again, I would stay. That was selfish. I was excessively dead-set on my career. And that happened more than once. I was just so self-absorbed.

We were Intense Personified. We probably were a little too intense. If just trying hard could get you success, then everybody would be successful. That was one bad thing the Richeys did: if we prepared hard enough, long enough and properly enough, we thought we could ward off the pain of losing. Pro always criticized the errors and didn't praise us enough. He taught us to seek perfection. That's a fallacy. Don't buy into that system. Excellence should be the goal, not perfection. But it was easy to buy into that perfectionism during early successes that came so easily. The way Dad coached, whether he knew it or not, that was insinuated. We absorbed it through osmosis. It created extreme anxieties.

My lack of friendships could not really be attributed to depression or Richey clannishness. I don't think it's that simple. The tour lifestyle is not conducive to friendships. You're tired all the time. You don't feel like doing a lot. I'd be the first to say that Nancy and Dad and I were pretty critical of other people. We were loners. That's not conducive to making friends. In my particular case, it was a confluence of events: career path and life circumstances. I didn't have any close friends for several different reasons.

Our family was not geared toward friendships, and neither was our lifestyle. When you're traveling on the tour, you're not home much. There was no social life for us. No normal life of teens. During our tennis years, we stayed away from other players too. We were encouraged not to get friendly with our opponents—literally not to speak to them before a match. I think that's too negative. It's not productive. I would do that differently now.

I never had much of a social life. I never really dated very much. We did some social things on some of the tours. For example, in 1965-66 in Australia, we would sometimes at night play cards or charades, so it wasn't totally lacking. But on the tour, you don't put that much of a high value on close friendships.

It's not like we didn't go to social functions, and there were plenty of them to attend. But we were not good socially. To cover that, the defense mechanism Dad used was to scoff at anything that smacked very much of being social. One time I got all dressed up to go on a date. My family made fun of me, saying I should wear a jacket. I got to the party and, sure enough, I was the only guy with a coat on. I looked like the dork of all dorks! I was so mad.

In 1965, the second year I played the tour, an icon in the world of sports reporting, Frank Deford, wrote this feature article about us in *Sports Illustrated* called "The Highest Ranking Family in Tennis." We didn't like the article. He chose photos of us where we had grim faces. We felt at the time that it was a hatchet job. In hindsight, though, it was probably fairly honest.

Dad did congratulate our opponents in the locker room afterward if we lost, but we were ahead of our time with our approach of wanting to win. That was socially unacceptable back then. I'm not sorry we ruffled anyone's feathers, but how much better it would have been if I had had a little more of a smile on my face! I might have gotten further in my profession if someone had taught me to smile and be nicer—to be a little warmer or more "fuzzy." Yeah, that was a big failing we had. We alienated people. I'm not saying we didn't deserve to be criticized. A lot of the criticisms were justified. We were a professional little Richey, Inc. unit that moved from town to town. In that pre-Open era, the tennis world was not ready for us yet.

Country clubbers. Sons of bitches. I don't like 'em. The country clubbers would pay for a $5 lesson with a $100 bill and ask for change, just to throw their weight around. The Richeys scoffed at country clubbers who thought they could buy a tennis game. Our attitude was that it cannot be bought. There is no easy, short-circuited route. I'm not too impressed with anything I can buy as a status symbol. The only thing that impresses me is talent.

We scoffed at going to cocktail parties. A party was a waste of time. That was what losers did. I wasn't kept from going to the junior prom. I didn't want to go. When I was 17 or 18, I played the U.S. Clay Court Championship, which was held at the Milwaukee Town and Tennis Club. The members there would host a tournament cocktail party. The clubhouse overlooked the tennis courts. We would be the only ones out there on the courts still training while they were up there having a party. That was an example of our rubbing it in the noses of the cocktail party crowd. It was very "in your face." They would be up there watching us, holding their martini glasses. We didn't have time to attend their party. We were out there to win —to beat the cocktail party crowd!

Our critics got so vitriolic, angry, and negative that people who considered themselves to be "civilized society" inside tennis lied about something the Richeys had done and were found out. The Dallas Tennis Association, the local branch of the U.S. Tennis Association, gave Dad expense money to take me to national tournaments in the summer time. When I got back, I wrote the tennis association a letter thanking them for the funding. Someone in the association lied and said we were so ungrateful that we didn't even thank them. But the wife of my practice partner, Ham Richardson, had actually seen the letter. The guy who was responsible for circulating that rumor came up to Dad 20 years later in Dallas. After all that time, he finally apologized.

At Wimbledon, there is a placard over the entrance to Centre Court that reads, "If you can meet with Triumph and Disaster . . . treat those two impostors just the same." The lines came from a poem by Rudyard Kipling. We used to scoff at that. We approached tennis from a professional point of view even when it was still just a "shamateur" game. The country clubbers were out there in their dainty little whites. Tennis was a high-class sport that originated in France and then drifted over from highbrow England onto the eastern seaboard. But we saw it as a hard-nosed sport. It did matter if you won or lost. All these years later, I'm more in agreement with that sign. I think I understand it better now.

The Richeys took losing pretty personally. For us, tennis was about the closest thing to actual warfare that you could get. It was very traumatic when we lost. Too much so. Andre Agassi always made the comment that to him, it was all about the process. Preparing, giving it your all. If you win, you win. Leave the end result up to the tennis gods. Competition is a great teacher. It brings out what you need to work on. But be sure to keep it fun. Not deathly serious. It's all about the process.

The up side of Richey, Inc. was the extreme closeness it fostered for relationships within our family. There were times when Mom didn't feel like drilling me on the court. But day after day, she would spend an hour and a half feeding balls to me. The most important thing inside the family was to win. Both of my parents, in whatever capacity, were always there for us. It actually was a little bit dangerous in some ways for Mom to feed me balls when she was 50 and I was 25. She'd be standing at the net while I stayed at the baseline. There came a point where Pro didn't want her to because I could have hit her pretty hard if I had accidentally misfired. But I think she was still drilling me even when I was in the seniors. She was nearing 60 at that point. Our parents were very generous. There was never a thought of her saying, "I don't feel like it today."

Even the members at the clubs admired the closeness of our family. They would conveniently find ways of leaving their kids at the pro shop all day long, partly to keep them out of trouble, but also to let them be around us. They wanted their kids to hang around at the tennis shop just to soak up some of our discipline. Those parents who had earned their money themselves didn't like the fact that their kids were becoming soft and lazy from the country club atmosphere.

Richey, Inc. was my life. But is anybody's life gonna be perfect? It damn sure wasn't. I was still in the amateur game and not making very much money, so I had to live at home. But I would be the first to admit that I had also still not severed the apron strings. It was all intertwined. Parents, coaches, practice partners, you name it. You become emotionally involved with all that beyond the norm.

I do not blame my family for my depression. No. I don't blame Dad or Richey, Inc. On the contrary, I can honestly say it was the roller coaster of the career combined with my genetic predisposition. For anybody who is already fighting emotional illness, the all-out, totally hyper-nervous family that we were—yeah, that's bound to exacerbate the depression. But it's more of a "group think" and not any one person I would point to.

That's what I think sometimes. But other times I think: aw, hell, my family was a frigging Iron Curtain! I have a hard time calling things abnormal. The way we did it segregated us from the rest of society. We didn't mind being antisocial with our actions, with our viewpoints. Author Maxwell Maltz had the theory that there are some people who are afraid of success because it segregates them from the rest of the population. You know you're gonna be different. And some people don't want to "stick out."

It would have been very difficult with Dad's personality for us not to play tennis. I don't know what else we would have done. It was certainly the path of least resistance. It was hard-wired into our system that tennis was what we did. Some of this closeness, I had had enough of. Since my coach was my father, I couldn't really fire my coach! That's what I call built-in dysfunction. But a lot of success is born out of dysfunction.

Codependency is another word for a lot of different words. The lines inside of a family sometimes become very blurred. When you still have a father who's as close to you at age 23 as at 14, there's a real blurring of the lines. Nancy said over and over, "I don't want to have kids." She said her career had been too confining. Her husband couldn't give her kids because he'd had a vasectomy. But that was just fine with her.

49

I think I rebelled with my own children against the close unit of Richey, Inc. That's apart from the depression, the anxieties, and what not. Once it came time to have my own family, I said: "enough." My children suffered because of the unusual tight-knitness of Richey, Inc. I was tired of moving in lockstep with three other people.

The butterfly starts in a cocoon. Richey, Inc. was our cocoon. We were kept in a hot house, a sterile environment, and then— at the right moment—turned loose on the world. The reward for enduring the hot house was the strong wings I developed. I had a great support system all throughout my tennis career, and through my depression. For the most part, they were the same players: my family. Dad would call me every morning in depression just like he used to go out and hit tennis balls with me.

If I could go back and tone it down a little bit, I would. But if everything had been a little softer and more comfortable, less dramatic, I'd only want that if I could still have had a good career. I can criticize because I was part of Richey, Inc. I would deeply resent anyone else criticizing us. After all, it wasn't their family, it was ours. We were the ones who lived it. They did not.

CHAPTER SIX

The Old Shamateur Game

The irony is, I quit high school to play pro tennis before there was much pro tennis to play. In 1964, tennis was still primarily an amateur sport. Prior to 1968, all of the big tournaments in the world like Wimbledon and the U.S. Open were still amateur events. The only real pro tennis events in those days were these one-night stand, "barnstorming" exhibition matches. There were only four to six guys in the world who traveled around and did that.

One of the grandfathers of the game, Jack Kramer, organized about 120 matches per year. It was known as the Jack Kramer Pro Tour. It was kind of like the Harlem Globetrotters—or maybe the circus! The incentive to get people out to watch those matches was that the previous year's best amateur would be induced to sign a pro contract to play the defending pro champion. The players did it to make money. They were offered a nice sum—in fact, so much they couldn't refuse. My plan was to win a major amateur event or two and then sign on with Kramer's pro tour.

The guys who played that tour were the real pioneers of the game: Pancho Gonzalez, Rod Laver, Ken Rosewall. But the moment they signed with Jack Kramer, they were excommunicated from the amateur circuit! It was a real devil's bargain. They could not play

Wimbledon or any of the major tournaments. They were barred from playing mainstream events, since they were now pros. They were out there in the boondocks—in the hinterlands—excommunicated from the game during their prime playing years. Laver is the only player ever to win two Grand Slams (all four of the majors within the same year). And he won them seven years apart! The reason was that he was off the main tour for five years. The first of his Grand Slams was in 1962, when he was still an amateur. Then after the game went open in 1968, he won the Grand Slam again in 1969. At least he was still young enough to do it. Open tennis came in too late for a guy like Pancho Gonzalez.

The world amateur tour looked totally glamorous to me at that point. The last stop on the Caribbean Tour was the Dallas Invitational—a tournament that I played while in high school. When those guys would come to town, it was like: "Wow, how glamorous is that, to be able to play the world tour!" The main thing for me at that stage was to do well. I just had this belief that if I played well, eventually the money would come. It only came in later, with open tennis. Before that there was very little official prize money.

I had already won the USTA National Boys' 18s Championship, but pretty soon I started having some very good results in the men's division too, even though I was only 16 years old. I won the Texas Men's Championship and the Pittsburgh Indoors. I won the Sugar Bowl Invitational in December of 1964. The next step for me in my tennis career was playing the Caribbean Tour. It started in Florida and then went on to Puerto Rico, Colombia, Caracas, St. Petersburg, Houston, and Dallas. In 1964, I played some events on that tour. We went to England in April of that year. My first tournament ever in Europe was in London at the Hurlingham Lawn Tennis Club. We then went to Rome, Hamburg and on to Lugano in Switzerland.

At the height of the Cold War, we played an event in West Berlin. I was with my buddy Roger Werksman, a Jewish tennis player, Nancy, and a couple of other guys. We decided to drive over into East Berlin, where we crossed Checkpoint Charlie. We saw the Brandenburg Gate and the Berlin Wall—from the other side! It was scary for Werksman because of the Nazis' history of killing Jews. We went into a restaurant/bar where everyone knew we were Americans. Werksman kept saying we might never get back and that stranger things had happened. Not many people during that time could say they had visited an Eastern Bloc nation. We only went over for a few hours, but I was a little scared. You felt like you were going into a prison. The whole atmosphere was frightening. It was not the smartest thing to do. The East German police could have arrested us and we might never have been heard from again.

In 1965, I was named to the U.S. Davis Cup squad at age 18. Davis Cup is an annual worldwide national team championship. It was a huge honor to be asked to represent my country. They play the national anthem at Davis Cup matches and wave the United States flag. I flew to Los Angeles to practice with the great Pancho Gonzalez, who was then our Davis Cup coach. When I say he was our coach, I do not mean that he was our captain. At that time they had a system whereby the USTA got to name an official Davis Cup captain who was a non-playing political appointee. This makes no sense, because Davis Cup is the only competitive tennis ever played which allows the captain to coach during matches. When I won the Davis Cup in 1970, I had a terrible captain coaching me in the final match: Ed Turville. At least as far as tennis goes, that guy didn't know his butt from a hole in the ground.

Anyway, the first year I played Davis Cup, the captain was George MacCall. MacCall was a good regional player from California who became a businessman. He got involved with the USTA, which administered the domestic amateur tour and was in charge of naming the Davis Cup team. MacCall had the idea for the Davis Cup squad to travel together year-round. The legal payment to players for the USTA was $28 per day at tournaments—barely

In 1965, at the age of 18, I was named to the U.S. Davis Cup team and competed around the world, including in Australia, photographed here at the Kooyong Tennis Club in Melbourne.

enough to cover expenses. MacCall proposed that we receive $20 per day even when we were not playing tournaments. So for the three years I played Davis Cup, I received an average $23 per day, year-round, plus air tickets. In effect, we were on salary from the USTA to play a so-called "amateur" tour. That's why we called it a "shamateur" game.

There was a huge amount of intrigue that developed between the Richeys and George MacCall. At the French Championships in May of 1965, early in his captaincy, I ran into the fence on a clay court. I slipped and sprained my thumb. I sliced it open on that wire fence. MacCall took me to the American hospital in Paris, where the doctor put DMSO (demethyl sulfoxide) on it. I called Dad almost daily, even overseas, so he was apprised of the situation. Dad found out that DMSO was a drug used more commonly at veterinary clinics. Typically they put it on race horses with swollen joints. It was considered a miracle drug because it reduced swelling very rapidly.

Not liking the idea of his son being treated like a race horse, Dad hit the panic button. He found out that DMSO had not been approved for human use in the United States. He then overreacted and claimed that MacCall didn't take good care of me. It became the Richeys vs. MacCall and that whole world. I pulled off the Davis Cup team after that flap. It became a public fight. It was in the press for three months: the Richeys against the Davis Cup's George MacCall.

A month or so later, the United States played Mexico in Dallas. It was surreal. I was watching a Davis Cup match, but I was off the team. To make matters worse, I was a Dallas boy—I even lived there at the time! The newspaper published a cartoon of me standing on a stool, looking over the fence onto a tennis match. All of a sudden I found myself an outsider looking in. It was a terrible feeling.

Later that fall, I wanted to go on the Australian tour. I asked the Australian Tennis Association to help defray my expenses. It didn't

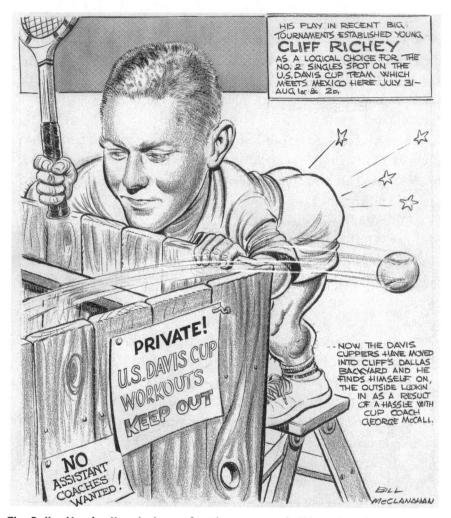

The *Dallas Morning News* had some fun at my expense in this cartoon in the sports section in 1965.

work. The only way to go was to make peace with MacCall and get back on the Davis Cup team. Dad didn't want me to. I stood my ground: "Dad, I'm going to Australia."

When Dad saw that it was a *fait accompli*, he said, "Oh no," and tears came to his eyes. That was the first time I ever crossed him. I was 18 years old.

I wasn't defying Dad on purpose, thinking I had now come of age. The Australian tour just seemed like a logical next step for my career. The mindset of Richey, Inc. was always that you do whatever it takes to "get there." So actually, I was just following through with something I had learned originally from Dad.

It was a little tense in Australia living with George MacCall, knowing that Dad didn't like him. It was like this epic battle of the two Georges. But MacCall and I got along all right. I just hated to feel caught in the middle.

Probably my most memorable Davis Cup match was in Ecuador, two years later. MacCall was still captain. Like in Europe, all the courts in South America were clay courts—not the most conducive surface for Americans. I was named to play singles against their top two guys in matches that were the best three-of-five sets. Davis Cup consisted of three days of matches: two singles on the first day, one doubles on the second day, and then two singles again on the final day. Arthur Ashe was also on the U.S. team and I certainly considered myself a better clay court player than him. In fact, we were worried about Arthur on clay. Clay was a good surface for me and we weren't concerned about the doubles since Marty Riessen and Clark Graebner were the No. 2-ranked doubles team in the world at that time. We figured, "We can't lose the doubles." The Ecuadorian players were not favored to win; but then again, they were playing on their home turf.

That week we stayed in a nice hotel in Guayaquil, the coastal Ecuadorian city where the matches were played, arriving a week before the matches to prepare for the conditions. We were being hosted by the Ecuadorians, so they assigned the practice courts at the tennis club. The only problem was, they gave us the very back courts. In fact, we routinely got a court which was situated next to a house with a pet mynah bird in the back yard. That darn bird laughed at us all week! We thought it was on purpose that they assigned us to that court.

Most of our practice sessions involved drills with some match play. Back then, the tennis balls came in boxes, not cans. The boxes were not pressurized so the balls went dead much faster. But at least all the pro shops would have stacks of empty boxes we could use for drills. We would take the empty boxes and put them in the corner of the court. The idea was to try and knock over the boxes. No one on the team liked to do drills except me. To convince Graebner to do drills, MacCall would give him 50 cents for each box he hit.

When the first match day came, the Ecuadorian crowd was very excitable—they sure liked their beer. The Guayaquil Lawn Tennis Club had thrown up temporary stands made of wooden planks able to hold 2,000 fans. I was the first to take the court and played my first singles match against Pancho Guzmán, the No. 2 player from Ecuador. I beat him in four sets to give us an early 1-0 lead. Arthur then followed to play Ecuador's most veteran player, Miguel Olvera, who was not as feared as Guzmán, a guy already in his 30s, but still a decent player. Surprisingly, Olvera took out Arthur, winning three straight sets after Arthur won the first set. So after the first day, it was tied 1-1. The crowd was rowdy, but under control and not too bad. The next day, Graebner and Riessen played Olvera and Guzmán in doubles. Our team was favored to win big time, but crazy stuff can sometimes happen in Davis Cup and we lost 8-6 in the fifth set. Now our butt was really in a crack. We were down 2-1 to little ole Ecuador.

The first match of the final day was Guzmán against Ashe, followed by me against Olvera. Arthur had to beat Guzmán in the first match to keep us alive. Then my match with Olvera would be the decider. As Arthur was playing, I had the radio on at the hotel, listening to his match. Guzmán's main weapon was a real good forehand. So as I was listening to this match in Spanish, I kept hearing "bueno forehand." I was hearing "bueno forehand" much too much for my liking. I could tell what was happening: Guzmán was beating him. At one set all, I hailed a cab and went to the stadium. Just as I got there, the crowd went into a roar. I walked to the locker room and asked what had happened. Arthur had just lost the third set, so he was two-sets-to-one down. Everyone was in the locker room during the 15-minute break held between the third and fourth sets. I saw Arthur sitting in front of his locker, dazed. MacCall stormed in, punched his hand through a metal locker and said, "If we lose this goddamn match, I'm going to eat that fucking clay!!" Arthur was almost comatose. I knelt in front of Arthur and got his attention: "Art, he's clocking forehands down your ass and you're losing." He agreed. I coached him not to come to the net; instead, he should try and out-rally him at the baseline. When play resumed in the fourth set, Arthur took my advice and didn't come to the net one time—and won the fourth set 6-0! He did exactly what I told him to. He played a defensive game. At two sets all, as they went into the fifth set, I was on the side of the court, watching. I was anticipating that I would have to play the decisive match with Arthur holding the momentum. But Arthur went back to his old-style game and proceeded to lose 6-3 in the fifth. I asked him in the locker room later what happened. He said he didn't think he could finish him off with such a defensive game. Guzmán won the match by the curious score line of 0-6, 6-4, 6-2, 0-6, 6-3. Ecuador had beaten the United States in one of the biggest upsets in the history of the event.

After the last point, the crowd went into pandemonium. The Ecuadorian captain tried to jump the net to hug Guzmán. He didn't get enough air and his foot caught in the net. He fell and broke his leg. He came back to coach during my match wearing a cast. So we had an American coach with a busted hand and an Ecuadorian coach with a broken leg!

Despite the result of the match already being determined, I had to play the fifth, meaningless match. With no tickets left for the matches, Ecuadorian students, who wanted to be part of the scene and celebration of the upset win over the Americans, were trying to break into the stadium. The students proceeded to throw rocks onto the court as I was playing. Rocks began raining down from everywhere. The crowd nearly rioted on changeovers. It then became apparent that Olvera started "tanking" the match to me (throwing it away). I sat down on the bench during the break and said to our captain: "George, he's not trying. I don't understand—why?" Mac-Call said evasively, "I'll tell you when the match is over." I demanded, "No, I want to know now." My captain admitted ruefully, "He's afraid if he beats you, there will be a riot. He just wants to get out of here. When the match is over, don't come back over here. Run straight to the locker room and I'll bring your stuff." I beat Olvera 5-7, 6-4, 7-5, 4-6, 6-0! He was tanking. No telling what could have happened if that match had lasted very much longer.

That United States vs. Ecuador Davis Cup match was as messy a competition as you would ever want to get involved in. Rocks flying, mynah birds calling, captains with broken body parts—this wasn't the glamorous world tour I thought I had signed on for!

Meanwhile, my anxieties were mounting. I said in a letter I wrote to the folks back at home: "I had one of my anxiety weeks last week (sort of nervous all week) . . . that old inspiration wasn't there. I'm trying to relax & talk myself out of my anxiety. I guess the only difference between me and a bum is: I have money and can hit a tennis ball." Not exactly the shining self-image you'd expect for an up-and-coming, world-class athlete!

That was 1967, the year just before open tennis. Both mentally and career-wise, that was right before my floodgates burst apart. . .

• CHAPTER SEVEN •

Boycotting Wimbledon

I n 1966, the city of San Angelo began building us a tennis court. We had been living in Dallas since 1961, when Dad got over his skin cancer scare and took a job teaching at the Brook Hollow Golf Club. Dadda (Roy Richey) had been getting older. He was in his 70s and not in good health. He wanted us to move back to San Angelo. Ever the salesman, he brokered a deal by which if we would move back there, the city would provide us with a free tennis court, a new house at cost, and even a small stipend for Dad. San Angelo felt that we could give the town a lot of publicity because of our name. We were from there. We were all born there. So in 1966, Dad quit his job in Dallas and Richey, Inc. relocated to San Angelo.

At Wimbledon in 1967, after that fiasco in Ecuador, I played the great Aussie Tony Roche in the first round. I beat him 3-6, 3-6, 19-17, 14-12, 6-3. It lasted four hours and 40 minutes—and 89 games. It was one of the longest matches in the history of tennis.

At Wimbledon, officials wouldn't let us practice on the tournament courts. We had to go find practice courts 45 minutes away. But at least those courts had nets! One time in Sasiri, Sardinia, we had to use a garden hose for a net on the tennis court to practice after the tournament. In the final match of that tournament, I beat Herbie Fitzgibbon. They were in such a hurry to get us off

61

the court, they started wheeling out the trophy. Herbie was like, "C'mon, give me a chance, here, it's not over yet!" Ah, yes, the good old shamateur days.

At the U.S. Championships at Forest Hills, we could practice on the courts at the West Side Tennis Club, but to get to the club we still had to take the subway. There were no limos in those days. I often carried six racquets, plus heavy bags. Meanwhile, we would have to haggle with the tournament director each week on the tour over our appearance fee. We didn't play for prize money. We were paid under the table. The last amateur check I got (in Phoenix) was for $750. That was technically more than the rules allowed. The amateur officials all knew we were making money on the side. That's why we called it a sham. It was a mess. But that's just the way it was. The first five of the 15 years I played the regular tour were under that old shamateur system.

When Nancy won the Australian Championships in January of 1967, I was not there. I had already left town. I played the quarter-finals against Tony Roche and lost in five sets. Afterwards, I started drinking some Foster's Lager in the locker room. We found some more beer back at the hotel. Rosie Casals, an American woman player, was there. I ended up getting smash-faced. I drank plenty, man. I took Rosie out on the beach that night—the Glenelg Beach. I actually ended up proposing to her! I laid on her some long story about why it'd be a neat idea. Nancy was staying at the same hotel. The way the tournament progressed, she had already won her semifinal match and was set to play the final the next day. I woke up in the middle of the night and came to, out of my drunken fog. I thought, "Oh my God, I've proposed to Rosie Casals, and I think she thought I was serious!" I made my plane reservations to fly out of the country immediately. As I was leaving the property, I had to pass by the lobby/breakfast area. There was Rosie. I hopped a cab and hid between the front seat and the back. I told the taxi driver, "Get the hell out of here as fast as you can." That story got out.

Three-time U.S. Open champion Ivan Lendl still teases me: "Cliff, tell me the story about you and Rosie."

The next time I saw Rosie, it was embarrassing. In hindsight, I didn't have enough feeling for what that would do to Nancy— my leaving right before her playing in a Grand Slam final. It was a replay of that other time I left her in London. Can you see a pattern starting to develop here? It's even more of a credit to Nancy that she could still go out and win the match.

Open tennis came in 1968. How did open tennis come about? Wimbledon finally woke up one day and had no top players. All the top players were signing pro contracts to play for Lamar Hunt's World Championship Tennis (WCT). Once Wimbledon decided to open up its event to all eligible players (both professional and amateur), the other big tournaments in the world eventually followed suit. And that is how the "Open Era" of professional tennis was born.

It was such a huge sea change. Tennis was now a professional sport that could be sold to the TV networks. Earlier that year, in 1968, when I played the U.S. Indoor final, it was televised nationally on the PBS channel. Mom and Dad drove over to Georgetown, Texas and got a hotel room just to see it! TV "made" every pro sport. The amounts of money involved increased exponentially. TV was the driving force behind this inflation.

Endorsements were legal now. Nobody prior to 1968 had endorsements (at least not officially). In the old days, our family was paid $3,500-5,000 a year to use Bancroft racquets. The money was paid to Dad since it was technically illegal for us to accept it. It was like an under-the-table endorsement. But with open tennis, all of that changed. The endorsement checks could finally be made out in our names!

In 1968, Nancy won the first French Open in what was the first major tennis tournament open to pros and amateurs. That was still a transitional year, though. The USTA did not allow Americans to play for prize money. The reasons for that were complicated and political. That same year, Arthur Ashe won the first U.S. Open, but due to the USTA ruling, he didn't even get the money! Instead the first prize—$14,000—went to Tom Okker, the runner-up, because the Dutch did let their guys play for cash. Although the game was already technically open, the USTA had not kept up with the times. That period was chaotic, but that's what happens, I guess, whenever major changes occur within a relatively short time. In 1969, open tennis finally became official for the American men as well. It was only then that we were allowed to accept prize money.

In March of that year, I played my first pro match at Madison Square Garden against Rod Laver. I still believe the "Rocket" is the greatest tennis player of all time. Amazingly, I won that match. The first pro tournament I won was in Cincinnati that July. The prize check was for $5,000. It felt good finally to be a real pro. That helped my self-image some. At long last, we could play for purses instead of under-the-table guarantees.

Between 1968 and 1973, there started to be some talk about the players forming a union. I think it was Jack Kramer's idea. Our purpose in doing so was to protect the players' interests in the new open game. We did it so we wouldn't just get trampled on. We were the new product being sold. We had to put some limits on how much profit the tournament directors could make off of us, how much they could pocket. We formed the Association of Tennis Professionals, the ATP, underneath the grandstand at Forest Hills (where the U.S. Open used to be played) in September of 1972. I'm proud to be a founding member of the organization that still controls professional tennis to this day.

The second week I played open tennis, after playing Laver at Madison Square Garden, I went to play the South African Open in Johannesburg. I did not know then that I would go back ten more times. I was real young, 22, but I was dimly aware of how they treated black people in South Africa under apartheid. However, I had no idea how bad it really was. I remember picking up the newspaper and seeing that white police had arrested black men and put them in the back of a paddy wagon. They had stuffed so many in there that several of them had suffocated and died.

In those days, some players stayed in private homes and that was offered to me as an option. I stayed in several private homes in South Africa. I found that South Africa was a very wealthy country. Some of the white ruling class down there who were of Dutch descent spoke Afrikaans. You could practically classify some of them as slave owners. They had black waiters and servants who would still call you "boss." They would still be in that subservient role.

Even though I came from the South, traveling to South Africa was like going back 100 years in time to the plantations. It was a far different atmosphere from the United States—a real eye-opener. At that time, the apartheid government didn't even let Arthur Ashe into the country to play tennis because he was black. At a restaurant one night, I saw the Minister of Sports for South Africa, who was a government spokesman. He asked me about Arthur and I said, "We've just finished our indoor season. He hasn't had any sun for a while. He's turned so white, you could even invite him here!" I enjoyed sticking it to that pompous official. He obviously didn't know what to say.

As tennis players, we didn't even see color in the locker room. That was truly one atmosphere that was color-blind. I loved South Africa, but I wanted my fellow American and Davis Cup teammate to be allowed to play there.

Of course, the United States still had racial problems of its own. Every year, we used to play the River Oaks Invitational in Houston, an old tournament that had been around for 40 years. The name says it all: it was an invitational. They had never invited Arthur because of segregation—and he wouldn't have felt comfortable there anyway. It was one of the poshest country clubs in the southern United States. When tennis went open, it became a pro tournament with prize money. In 1971, the event became a stop on the World Championship Tennis (WCT) circuit. Arthur, by contract, was on the WCT tour that year and River Oaks was an official event on that tour. So they had to invite Arthur, whether they wanted to or not. They would have faced lawsuits if they had tried to bar him from playing. Well, when the club managers found out Arthur was coming, we suddenly found ourselves no longer in the main clubhouse locker room. They put us in the pool locker room instead! I mentioned something to the tournament people about it. They gave the excuse that the pool locker room was closer to the courts. Bullshit! That's the kind of stuff Arthur had to put up with.

In September of 1969, I was eating lunch in the clubhouse at the Berkeley Tennis Club. Jack Kramer and Vic Braden were sitting in the booth right in front of me. Jack was the same guy who had sponsored those one-night barnstorming events before the game went open. After the advent of open tennis, he became powerful within the USTA and was one of the movers and shakers in the sport. As I was sitting there eating my sandwich, I couldn't help overhearing part of their conversation. They were hatching the idea for a Grand Prix! Vic used to help Jack run his old exhibition tour. I got up and went over to their booth. They didn't ask for my opinion, but I (in typical fashion) gave it to them anyway. I objected that it sounded like too much travel. I told them the players would get too worn out. The proposed "World Point Title" was conceived as a world tour. I would have preferred a Grand Prix contest based primarily in the United States. But at least Jack and Vic were trying to grow the young open tour. That was a good thing. I was certainly all for that!

Even after the Open Era, there were vestiges of the old shamateur game. In the 1970s, Ilie Nastase's mentor, Ion Tiriac, asked me if I wanted to play in Buenos Aires. He helped promote that tournament by signing up good players. My guarantee was $5,000. He came up to my hotel room and peeled off 50 hundred-dollar bills.

It felt like the mafia or something. That seemed like a lot of money at the time! I had to get on the airplane carrying that much cash. I deposited it in the bank (and did pay taxes on it, for the record!).

After the game went open, another factor that did not change was that Davis Cup was still not played for prize money. You did it only for the love of the game and for your country. You received barely enough money to cover travel expenses. In 1970, I was the Davis Cup MVP in Cleveland when we beat West Germany. The next year we played Romania in the Davis Cup final in Charlotte, North Carolina. The USTA was in charge of designating where the Davis Cup matches would be played. Like everything else involving the USTA, that too was political. When we defended our title in 1971, the USTA gave the event to the city of Charlotte, which had clay courts. Everybody knew Romania was best on clay. The USTA could have picked a city with a better surface to favor our team. I said, "The USTA is unconcerned about whether we win or lose. We might as well be playing in Bucharest." I boycotted and refused to play.

By doing so, I was risking my endorsement contract with Wilson Sporting Goods. Jack Kramer came up to me in the Forest Hills locker room as a father figure and asked me if I really wanted to fight this battle. I refused to reconsider. The USTA was feeding us to the wolves. It got nasty. But I'm not sorry I stood my ground. I was interested in winning, not the politics of the game. Now, within the last 20 years, the Davis Cup captain and the USTA have picked the court surface each time which will be more conducive to an American victory. So I feel like I have been vindicated. That was the last time I ever played on the Davis Cup team.

As it turns out, I actually ended up boycotting Wimbledon as well. After we formed the ATP in the fall of 1972, we as a union had something laid into our hands the very next year. One of our fellow members was a Yugoslavian player named Niki Pilic. He got into a dispute with his Yugoslavian tennis association regarding some of his Davis Cup play. He was suspended from the Yugoslavian federation. Because of that dispute, the International Tennis Federation (ITF) said they were going to honor the Yugoslavian federation's suspension of him. Therefore, he would not be allowed to play Wimbledon. It then got into a legal hassle. Pilic's stance was: "I'm a professional tennis player; I want to play Wimbledon; the ITF is depriving me of a way to make a living." He took it to a British judge. The judge upheld the ITF's stance. The ATP guys met at the Westbury Hotel in London, in Jack Kramer's room. Kramer, who was our executive director, said to us: "Guys, we have a problem. We should demand as a union that if Pilic doesn't get to play, none of us will."

We all boycotted Wimbledon in 1973. That went a long way toward establishing our legitimacy as a group. When we stood our ground, the ITF and the rest of the tennis world saw for the first time that we were a force to be reckoned with.

I was enough of a rebel to want to stick it up Wimbledon's ass. Being a red-blooded "muni" guy, I never really liked the blue-blooded attitude of the Wimbledon officials. Their attitude was, "Come in the back entrance, and we might give you lunch today." If we had not banded together to boycott Wimbledon, the ATP might not have survived. Who knows? The modern game of tennis might have taken an entirely different direction.

We paved the way for the young stars playing today. We played more tournaments a year than the young ones play now. Anytime you pioneer anything, you have to just go out there and do it. With the year I had in 1970, my best year, I won $97,000. That same year today would easily be worth millions. In the semifinals of the French Open in 1970, I won $3,000. That same thing today would be worth $250,000. That's quite a rate of inflation! The U.S. Open semis in 1972 was worth $5,000. That again would be worth a quarter million now. Dramatically different as well would have been the endorsement structures. A racquet endorsement today would be worth a half million dollars a year. I probably maxed out at $15,000 for that.

When I look at the young guys today, I'm not resentful of their spectacular financial success. I feel no jealousy. I'm not one of these old fuddy duddies who moans about how they're making more money than I did. The reality is, there are better athletes playing now than in my time. The coaches have also improved their training techniques. I enjoy the heck out of watching the matches on TV. However big the game gets, I'll be cheering it on and loving every minute.

Most of the young players wouldn't believe it now if they heard there was a time when we actually had to boycott Wimbledon. That episode just shows how I teetered on the cusp of the Open Era of professional tennis. My fellow players and I definitely pioneered the modern game. We were there at a crucial moment in the sport's evolution. That is something we ATP founders ought to be very, very proud of.

It's too bad I couldn't enjoy my role in making sports history while it was happening. It's too bad my days (and nights!) were so anxiety-ridden. Around about this time I addressed a letter home to: "The Richeys (World-Renowned Tennis Greats)." On the back of the envelope, in the space for the return address, I wrote: "The Gypsy. Parts Unknown (a Zoo if I don't take care!)."

As I look back at that letter now, so many years later, I wonder how much of it was self-consciously meant as a joke. Obviously, I was trying to be funny; but was I also crying out for help? Did I realize even then that I was quickly degenerating into a nut case—if not exactly a caged animal at the zoo, then (at least potentially) a suitable resident for the psychiatric ward?

In all honesty, I don't think that had dawned on me yet. Believe me, in such cases, ignorance truly is bliss. If I had had even an inkling of what was in store, I might not have rushed headlong into a desperate love affair.

CHAPTER EIGHT

Uptown Girl

I didn't date many girls. I can't remember going out on a double date with anyone, ever. My first girlfriend was Linda Barry. I was 14 and had raging hormones. She took a shine to me, and I to her. Sometimes Mom and Dad would go home from the club for lunch, leaving us alone at the tennis shop of the Brook Hollow Golf Club in Dallas. Linda and I would hide somewhere and play smoochy face in the closet.

I did sort of have a girlfriend in Australia for a while. I was 18 and she was 15. She was a native Australian who was playing some of the tournaments down there. I asked her out. I even went to her house in a suburb of Sydney to eat dinner with her parents. I might have kissed her once. Once I got home, we wrote letters back and forth. It should have made me suspicious when her mother started answering my letters instead of her! But I was pretty thick. When I got back down there to play the Aussie tour again the next year, her father picked me up at the airport. He said she was out on a date with Tony Roche. That was a rude awakening for me. I guess I should have seen that one coming.

That was about it in the way of girlfriends (the thing with Rosie on the beach doesn't count). Back in those days, the only kind of "love" that formed a part of my daily vocabulary was the one that means "zero" (from the French *l'œuf*, or "the egg") in a tennis game.

That is, until I met Mickie. In April of 1967 I played an event in Buenos Aires called the River Plate Championship. I went down to play that tournament with the Davis Cup team on our way to a match in Trinidad the next week. Our captain, George MacCall, had us play the Argentina event as practice. "One Ball MacCall" was his nickname. That was because he used to be a navigator on an airplane. The story was, he was unloading some cargo and squeezed off one of his testicles. Behind his back we called him that. It had nothing to do with tennis balls.

I finished playing a match in Buenos Aires on one of the side courts (not the stadium, but still a grandstand). I think it must have been a doubles match because I was more open and friendly than usual that day. I had a different frame of mind for doubles than for singles. Winning doubles didn't matter as much to me. I heard someone call my name. It was Dr. Louis Girard, an ophthalmologist from Houston. He knew who my father was because he had graduated from Rice University, and Dad used to be the Rice tennis coach. Dr. Girard said, "This is my daughter Michelle."

From a male's point of view, she was absolutely drop-dead gorgeous. I always liked women with full lips. She had very dainty hands and wrists. I sensed pretty early on that she was a beautiful soul and that she had the unbelievable combination of being an attractive woman and a beautiful person inside.

We chatted. We remarked how that week was the week I normally would have played the River Oaks Invitational in Houston at the club where they were members. The Girard family loved tennis. They were avid tennis fans. Mickie played club tennis and used to watch the River Oaks matches. Dr. Girard had probably even watched me play the final match of that tournament a few years earlier. But instead, this week, we were all in Buenos Aires!

Dr. Girard invited me to dinner and to go see some flamenco dancers. I had to play the semifinal or final match the next day. I said, "No, I have to play a big match tomorrow." I went back to the hotel—The Plaza, where in fact we all were staying and I was sharing a two-room suite with the Puerto Rican Charlie Pasarell, who was a real Latin lover. When I got back to the room, I told Charlie about meeting Mickie and the invitation I had received for dinner. He said, "Hey, Cliff, what were you doing? You should have said yes." I remember thinking, "You know, he's right."

I played the rest of the tournament. I thought, "I'll call her up before I leave town and ask her out." I called the front desk, but they had already checked out. I asked what room they were in and the front desk told me—it was the room right below mine! I thought, "Aw, man, I'll never see her again." I couldn't even remember her name.

I won the tournament. I was excited. As a team, we got into two taxi cabs at the Buenos Aires Lawn Tennis Club a couple of hours after the final match to go to the airport to fly to Trinidad. We had six or seven team members plus a captain and a wife or two. They filled two large cabs with people and luggage. Outside the club, there was some confusion over who should go in which cab. On top of that, we were running late for our international flight. At the last minute, I got into the opposite cab of the one I had thought I was going to take and we were off to the airport, driving caravan-style. A train came down a train track we had to cross and one cab was able to cross the tracks before the train came through, but the other cab didn't make it. Lucky for me, I was in the cab that made it across. As it turned out, the people in the other cab never made the flight.

We, none the less, barely made it onto the plane—jumping on board just as the flight attendants were closing the doors. It was a day from hell. You can only handle all this if you're 20 years old. I stepped onto the plane, and there were Dr. Girard and Mickie. I would have expected to see Jesus before them!

When I had talked to the front desk at the hotel, they had

already left for Montevideo, Uruguay. This flight had originated in Montevideo and was going on to Rio de Janeiro. Mickie yelled out, "Cliff!" and I thought, "Crap, I don't remember her name." I sat down in the back of the plane. I found out later that she whispered to her father, "Watch me go get a date with Cliff." She got up and made her way to the back of the plane. All of a sudden I looked up, and there she was.

She put the moves on me. She seduced my ass. Of course, I was a 20-year-old stiff one, so it didn't take much. . . . It was late in the day already. We stopped over in Rio to catch a flight to Trinidad the next morning. The Girards were due to stay in Rio for a while. They were in the middle of a month-long trip. The flight landed close to midnight. Mickie was staying at the Copacabana, a fancy hotel, while I was staying someplace decidedly less fancy. We agreed to meet somewhere after the flight. We walked down to the beach. We saw a couple lying there on the beach as we drank screwdrivers at a little bar with a view of the ocean. We played kissy-face on the beach as the rats scurried along the boardwalk.

I don't like goodbyes. I really didn't think we'd see each other again. But it seems cheap to me to kiss somebody on the beach for three hours and then abruptly say, "Goodbye." It would hurt me to do that. It used to bother me to say goodbye even after sitting next to some random person on an airplane.

When we got back to the hotel, a security guard went with us to her floor. He watched to make sure I didn't try to stay. I gave her a kiss as he watched. It was just a peck. I said, "I don't like goodbyes. I'll see you down the road."

From very early on, I knew I really liked her. We bonded that night, two Texans in a strange land. Mickie wanted to speak English with someone her own age. But we went our separate ways. I went to Trinidad to play Davis Cup, where I won both of my matches. She continued on with her father, who was giving a lecture tour. Mickie had taken a month off from school at the University of

Texas to travel around South America with her dad.

Right after Davis Cup in Trinidad, I played a tournament in Atlanta. I must have been lovesick, because I lost in the final to Marty Riessen on clay. I never used to lose to him on clay! I was thinking about Mickie and decided: "I have to find her." There was a tennis player named Lew Gerrard from New Zealand, so it was easy for me to remember that since her father's name was the same as his. But that still left one problem—I didn't know how to spell it. I called the Houston information line and said, "I'm trying to find this girl. I need to find a Dr. Lou Girard but don't know the spelling." The operator was sympathetic and tried to help me. She found a Dr. Louis Girard on Del Monte.

At the time I called, Mickie was having dinner with her family. She couldn't talk long. They had just returned from their month-long trip. She was leaving the next day to go back to school. We agreed that I would visit her in Austin, where she would be returning to UT, where she was a junior psychology major.

I went to visit her in Austin during the first part of May. She came to pick me up at the airport in a friend's old beat-up Volkswagen. She ran out onto the runway and greeted me with a kiss. (They didn't have the same level of security at the airports then as they have these days.) I stayed for three or four nights and slept in a room by myself at a little motel just off I-35, behind the football stadium. To keep my tennis game up, I practiced with the UT tennis team. The Davis Cup squad was getting ready to go down to play in Mexico City so I needed to keep my game sharp. Somehow the local newspaper reporters found me. Mickie was impressed. They interviewed me and did a nice story. They mentioned in the article that I was there to visit Michelle Girard. Our courtship was chronicled on the AP wire! I told Mickie she'd better get used to living her life in a fish bowl. . . .

Following my visit to Austin, I went to Mexico City with the Davis Cup team, where we beat Mexico 4-1. We had to arrive the week before just to get used to the altitude. I lost to Rafael Osuna in the opening match which ended up being the only loss for us all weekend. All told, I only lost two other Davis Cup matches out of 13. The thing I remember most about that week was the famous red-headed movie actress Maureen O'Hara who came to watch our matches. She was already old, well past her prime, but her presence added to the excitement.

After our match with Mexico, I invited Mickie to come with me to the Tulsa Invitational. I paid for her ticket. She didn't know at that time how much money I made or didn't make. I paid for her air tickets and long distance phone calls. She came from a wealthier family than mine but was on a tight budget while she was going to school.

Everything in the 1960s was fairly prim and proper. I wrote a letter to Mickie worrying about whether it was appropriate to take her to Tulsa. Ours was the last generation before free love. We were both virgins (although I will admit to some heavy petting!). She agreed to go because it was properly chaperoned. We stayed in a private home set up by the tournament committee with separate bedrooms. Still, it was an eyebrow-raiser to show up at the tournament with this gorgeous woman. We were some of the last people who did not live together before our wedding.

The Tulsa tournament was Mickie's one chance before she married me to see what our life was like—to see how the Richeys moved as a unit. Both Nancy and I won the tournament with me beating Clark Graebner in the final and Nancy winning against Carol Graebner (Clark's wife). All the headlines trumpeted: "The Richeys beat the Graebners."

I wanted Dad to meet Mickie because I wanted his approval. Dad was completely taken with her. He said, "Unless she's the best actress in the world, she's a terrific person. Marry her." It was so ironic because Dad had always said, "Never marry a River Oaks girl." Mom, in turn, had always said, "Never marry a Catholic."

Mickie was both! Dad had told me fairly early on, when I met the Girards, that he had heard from people in Houston that Dr. Girard was a real social climber. While the Girards were living on Del Monte in River Oaks, we were living in a one-room shack on the north end of town. Heck, I had slept on the couch until I was 16! I remembered then how I used to ball boy at the River Oaks Country Club when I was 10 years old. We used to drive to the other side of town, and I just couldn't believe the opulence. River Oaks was the epitome of country clubs. Our marriage was like "North Houston meets River Oaks"—or like that Billy Joel song, "Uptown Girl."

On the non-romantic side, I think both of us were looking for someone to escape the other situations in our lives. She was not looking to get married, necessarily. She had always planned to finish school, but she wanted to escape from the Houston social scene. I had been on the tour since 1964 and had already traveled the world. After three and a half years, I was tired of being alone. I never really had a chance to date. I was still a kid with a crew cut, pimples and poor social skills—but I was looking for a mate. We were probably drawn together by . . . not all the right motivations. The Richeys were emphatically not country clubbers. We catered to country clubbers from across the counter.

All of our "dating" was done between tournaments, and that only lasted for about three months. I never even told her I loved her. One day, I asked, "I-love-you-will-you-marry-me?" Just like that. All in one sentence.

Her family disagreed with our decision to get married. Her stepmother Lorraine wanted her to marry an older Dallas society guy. The first of many clashes I had with Dr. Girard was when I announced that I had designs on his daughter. I went up to his office. The conversation was based around whether I could afford it and what I was planning to do with my life. He never once asked me what my morals were. It all revolved around money. I didn't think he even came close to hitting the mark as far as what was important. I told him I was on salary with the USTA, all my expenses were covered, and I could afford to get married. I also told him I could fall back on teaching at a club if I needed to. I thought it was funny that he didn't ask me other questions about values, or integrity, or something like that.

Another thing that bothered me was, going into the deal, he had basically jumped through hoops to come and meet me after that tennis match in Buenos Aires. To be fair to him, I will say that even though he had those reservations about me, once we got married, he still supported my career. When I reached the semifinals of the U.S. Open shortly after that, I remember getting a telegram from Dr. Girard which said "GO GO GO GO GO" about 40 times. It was like he was on my team. I got the feeling that he and Lorraine liked to show me around at their fancy parties, but he saw me as somebody who could entertain them with my tennis, or perhaps someone he wanted to meet so he could drop my name later in conversation. That did not mean I was good enough to marry his daughter. . . .

The evening we got married, I had been out on the tennis court all day—with no sunscreen. I had just gotten a terrible haircut. Mickie was horrified. It totally ruined the wedding pictures. My gold ring cost $25. She bought it with her own money. That night we stayed at the Warwick Hotel. The next day, we flew to the U.S. Championships at Forest Hills. We got married on a Wednesday. Forest Hills used to start the tournament on a Wednesday (it was a 10-day tournament) so I called the USTA and requested not to play until Friday. The tournament organizers were kind enough to agree.

Mickie experienced a real culture shock, coming into my environment. That first week after we were married, I was practicing on the grass courts at the West Side Tennis Club. Mickie must have gotten hungry while I was hitting. I came back up to the clubhouse and saw her eating lunch. I had to say to her, "You can't do that." The players all ate fast food. We had enough money to live on, but

Mickie put the moves on me from the beginning and seduced my ass. Here we are after I won the 1968 U.S. Indoor Championships in Salisbury, Maryland.

we had to watch every penny. We couldn't even afford a $3 lunch at the clubhouse.

Mickie's mother had always told her, "Don't ever wear curlers to bed, or your husband will divorce you." So that week, heeding her mother's advice, Mickie went to get her hair done at a salon. That was the last time she ever had her hair done by a hairdresser. We couldn't afford it. From then on, she had to wear curlers to bed. . . .

Mickie's mother was schizophrenic. She later committed suicide. We didn't talk about the mental illness in her family much before we married. I did know how absent her mother was, always in and out of hospitals. It wouldn't have mattered to me anyway. It was not a theme we bonded over, since I didn't realize I had depression yet. My own particular brand of hell was on its way, but at that point, clinical depression was still in the future. I had mentioned something to her about my own mother's nervous breakdown. Neither one of us was freaked out by it. That was probably another thing we had in common.

We went to meet Mickie's mother Bonnie on Long Island after I lost to John Newcombe in the third round at Forest Hills. We liked each other right away. She really loved my fighting spirit. The second day after Bonnie met me, she said to Mickie, "He has just the right mixture of confidence and shyness." Almost from the beginning, Mickie was under a lot of pressure from being pulled between her father and me. From early on, there was this tug of war. In light of all that, her mother advised her, "You should always stick by your husband."

Right after we got married, George MacCall still had the Davis Cup squad being paid a per diem. He arranged for us to do a tour in Texas, playing exhibition matches against the Australians. We played in Midland and then flew to McAllen in a private Lear jet. Mickie and I both thought that was fancy. Then in the fall, we did a six-tournament tour of South America: Buenos Aires in Argentina, Porto Alegre, Curatiba, São Paulo, Rio de Janeiro in Brazil, and finally Lima, Peru. The highest number of tournaments I ever won in a row was three. On this tour, I won the first three events. After I won Curatiba, when I got back to the hotel room, Mickie had made a sign that said: "3 in a Row, Way to Go." Back in high school, she used to be a cheerleader. Somehow that seemed appropriate.

It might look on the surface like we were oil and water trying to mix; but actually, we had a surprising amount in common. She had traveled the world more than most young women her age. We were both skeptical of the country club scene and didn't really buy into all that. She was sympathetic toward my discomfort with all the fakes. She was looking for an escape, and I provided that. She was tired of dating boys who were slick, superficial, and dishonest. I was refreshingly "real" to her. She had been required to do a lot of dating in the sorority and in her two years of debutante life. She used to say all those boys came out of the same cookie cutter. I was different from anyone she had ever met. She thought I had a cute crew cut. She said I was shy, not arrogant, and not at all preppy. I was everything those fraternity guys were not.

She traveled with me most of the time during the first few years we were together, but for some reason one time she didn't go to Wimbledon. I can still recall the last few words of a love letter she wrote to me which I received while I was playing there. I still remember the last nine words: "I need you. I want you. I love you."

• CHAPTER NINE •

Pressure Flakes

From 1964 through 1970, I didn't worry about my skills too much. Success is as intoxicating as a drug. It just feels great. You get instant approval. The crowd hollers. They give standing ovations. You walk away with a trophy. You go back to the locker room, and everyone congratulates you. You get headlines in the next day's newspaper. You have confidence in yourself. You're on a roll. It's all the affirmation that kids (and later, adults) want in life. There's an adrenaline rush. It's a real thrill. It feels like drinking about eight cups of coffee. Ecstasy would be putting it mildly. You feel lit up. You can't turn off your motor. It's revved up and it stays revved.

Once you've felt that, you want it again. You start chasing that next victory. Society puts its stamp of approval on winning. I've heard other athletes talk and they say once they retire, they can never find anything to match the thrill of the ball field. The cortisol, the "fight or flight" hormone, actually changes your brain chemistry. It also makes you more prone to disease: heart trouble, cancer, hypertension. You ride that crest during the "up" periods of accomplishment. You get addicted to the highs like a drug. I would like to know the percentage of how many ex-athletes become drug addicts and alcoholics.

I was elated to win the U.S. Indoor Championships in Salisbury, Maryland, but then crashed very hard, very fast.

At the start of the season in 1968, I pulled a rib muscle. It took a full month to heal. Once I could play again, I only had ten days to prepare for the U.S. Indoor Championships in Salisbury, Maryland. I beat Jan Leschly, Stan Smith and Clark Graebner to win the title. It was a huge win.

But after winning the U.S. Indoors, I crashed very hard, very fast. It almost didn't seem possible to sink that low after being so high. I've always experienced volatile emotional content. One of the problems with depression in general is that rather than recognizing it as a disease, you rationalize it as, "Oh, I'm just going through a difficult time right now." That's what happened with me after the U.S. Indoors. I would come back from a tournament, and it would take me 10 days to feel normal again. In hindsight, I think some of that was low-grade depression. Dad used to say: "As fit as you are, there's something wrong if it takes you that long to recover."

By the laws of physics, what goes up must come down. The cycle of competition and gearing up for a tournament fosters a crash after it's over—much more than, say, a typical 9-to-5 job. There are performance anxieties, stage fright. With my drive and type-A personality, there was probably also a touch of bipolar there. When you lose a match, that insecure, anxious feeling takes away your self-esteem completely. You feel worthless. My drive for success on the court was in part a desperate attempt to ward off recurrent bad moods. I lived from one victory to the next.

I did let myself enjoy some of my victories on the tennis court. At least, I think so. But one of the bad things about any tour is, if you play more than just a few in a row, you're never able to sit back and enjoy it as much as you'd like. You certainly can't enjoy it for very long. You know you have to get back to business, to begin training for the next one. I was always already thinking about the next match.

Normally, for a tournament, we had either a 32- or 64-man draw, so you had to win either five or six matches to win the title. That means you only had a few hours to enjoy each win. In that setting, if you don't start immediately preparing for the next match, you'll fall flat. Your job isn't over. You have to play another one the next day, so you have to be disciplined. You don't have time to gloat. You'd better not be thinking about your last win too long or too hard, because your matches only get tougher as you go.

"Adverse pressure" is the term Dad always used to describe the pressure to produce again once you've already succeeded. You can win two tournaments in a row and go on to the third and still have someone ask you, in essence, "What have you done for me lately?" It's like what I used to tell Jimmy Connors. Much later, in 1975, when we were practicing a lot together in England leading up to Wimbledon, he was feeling stressed out about defending his Wimbledon title. One evening over dinner I said, "Jimmy, here's what you've got to do. You won it last year, and the trophy is in your trophy case. Now to win it this year, you have to psychologically take that trophy out of your case and put it back on the common shelf. You ain't defending shit! The day Wimbledon starts, you're competing for it all over again just like everybody else."

The up side to anxiety, if there is one, is that it drives you toward success. The moderate down moods even help too (they call this dysthymia, or low-level depression) by motivating you to get out there and succeed in order to feel better. You learn to counteract pain with the tonic of success. When dysthymia hits you, it drives you on. It tells you that you aren't very good. You try to smother feelings of inadequacy by being creative and successful. Even when you win, that insecurity keeps telling you: "You still aren't good enough." It propels you into wanting to become even better.

I had no bad depression before the age of 22. Perhaps that was at least partly due to the fact that up to that point, I had experienced very few losses. I still won most of the time. In 1969, I had some depression and some anxieties that were just awful. The absolute stark depression wasn't there at the beginning, but there were some early warning signs: nervousness, extreme highs and lows, severe irritability.

It was a good year, play wise. In fact, it was the second-best year of my career. Winning the Canadian Open—beating Butch Buchholz in the final—was the highlight. The entire year was pretty much around-the-clock training and playing. If you're playing well, you're playing five matches a week. I always liked to be on the go. I'm an A-type. I have a lot of nervous energy. I think people with type-A personalities are, in general, more prone to depression. I have the agitated kind of depression, where your metabolism actually speeds up.

I also bite my nails. It's a nervous habit. All the stress I was experiencing that year started to manifest itself in my sleep. I used to have very vivid dreams of winning one of the four Grand Slam tournaments. They felt so real that when I woke up, I was disappointed. I used to have a recurring dream where I was in the locker room, getting my court bag together. I was in the process of putting my tennis clothes on, or maybe taping a finger. All of a sudden, it would be just before the start of the match and I couldn't get out of the locker room! They finally had to default me. That was one of my frequent anxiety dreams. In all probability, it was during those sorts of dreams that I first started grinding my teeth. It was during that period that I was diagnosed with temporomandibular joint syndrome, a jaw disorder known as TMJ. I clenched my jaw so hard, it started to crack my teeth. I had to get crowns. I sustained a lot of dental damage before it was properly treated. Most of the teeth in my mouth are cracked.

During the daytime, when I played tennis, the stress started to manifest itself in other ways. When I'm excited, my eyes get so big, they look like they're about to pop out of their sockets. My eyes would dilate from the excitement of battle. I also tended to hyperventilate, another classic "fight or flight" response. Hyperventilation can produce leg cramps, because your system gets permeated by too much oxygen. I had those quite a few times in my career. Cramping is an awful thing. It can hit you out of nowhere and basically incapacitate you. Any type of inactivity, a 10- or 15-minute break, can make the muscles start to spasm. I learned never to go into an air-conditioned locker room during the break between sets, because the cold air can also make you cramp.

When I was in the excitement of battle, my eyes would dilate. I also tended to hyperventilate, which was another classic "fight or flight" response.

But just because I was cramping, that didn't mean I gave up. Only once did I not keep playing and finish the match even though I had muscle cramps. That happened in Paris. I was cramping so badly, I couldn't even stand up! Five guys had to lift me up like a piece of lumber and carry me away. A little later in my career, when I was in the process of winning a five-set final match in Fort Lauderdale in 1971, I started to get leg cramps during the fourth set. Someone suggested to me that I should try breathing into a paper bag. I followed that suggestion, and it actually helped. The newspapers had fun with that incident as one of the headlines read: "Richey Paper-Bags it to Victory."

A lot of amateurs think that if you put yourself under the heat enough times, eventually you get to a point where competition doesn't vibrate your soul. That you get to a point where you're not nervous any more. Well, guess what? It's not like that. I played 1,500 competitive matches in 500 tournaments over 26 years. You get "up" and nervous for every single match—out of fear. Each one is life or death. You're never immune to that pressure.

I'm a competitive person. That's what I do. It would almost be more surprising if I didn't scare people. You don't just turn into this nice, friendly, non-combative, congenial person during your off time. It's still bare-teeth competition. Mickie's kid brothers used to say I ate "pressure flakes" for breakfast. If I could have found some, I would have eaten them, that's for sure!

The tour was an escape mechanism, in a sense. It gave me places to go, places to run from my troubles and worries. Anxieties have a lot to do with constantly being on the move. That's the definition of anxiety. You constantly feel like you could be doing more. Anxieties also create self-doubt. I practiced more than most people because I constantly doubted my abilities. Insecurity is a double-edged sword: it makes you more productive, but it also slices you up into tiny little pieces. You're like a frog in a pot of boiling water. When the temperature is turned up, at first, you don't notice; but the next thing you know it, baby, you're cooked!

In addition to worrying about my own career, because of Nancy, there was the added strain of vicarious competition. My sister had just beaten Billie Jean King and Ann Jones to win the French Open in 1968. That was special. Dad wasn't there that year, so I had to coach her. In the semifinals, Nancy beat Billie Jean, the two-time reigning Wimbledon champion, 6-4 in the final set and then beat Ann, the No. 2 seed, in the final after being a set and 4-1 down.

Ann was a tough player for Nancy to play because of her style. She was a master of different spins and it was hard for Nancy to get into any rhythm against her. She was also a very smart player and a great competitor who would win Wimbledon the following year. I sensed that Nancy needed to do something different than her usual

In addition to worrying about my own career, because of Nancy, there was the added strain of vicarious competition. Here I am coaching Nancy in 1972 before she beat Chris Evert to win the Virginia Slims of Washington, D.C.

game. I also felt like Ann was getting tired. Just prior to that tournament, Ann had signed on to play a Jack Kramer-style women's pro tour where she played a lot of one-set exhibitions. From playing a lot of one-set matches, she was not accustomed to playing two- and three-set matches. She was a little out of shape, really.

I told Nancy from the stands to do some things she wouldn't ordinarily have done, like coming to the net more. I had to keep telling her to attack. I knew I would have to stay with her so she wouldn't fall back into what was comfortable. I was directing her from the stands. It was the next thing to my being out there playing myself.

It doesn't do any good to finish runner-up at an event, especially a Grand Slam tournament. Beating Billie Jean King in the semis was great, but now let's go out and win this damn thing! I was in it to the max. I was living and dying with every point. I knew what the big, important points were.

After Nancy won five games in a row and won the second set 6-4, the momentum definitely changed. When she finally won the match by a 5-7, 6-4, 6-1 margin, I was just spent but also absolutely ecstatic. I went into the men's locker room, into a bathroom stall. It was no more than a hole in the ground. I shut the door. I was so happy, I cried! I had to get away by myself. Richey, Inc. had just won our first Grand Slam title of the Open Era.

As early as 1969, I was asking Mickie's mother for the name of a psychiatrist. High anxiety is a kissing cousin to depression. But in our minds, at that point, my disease still went unnamed. Obviously I must have had enough of a psychiatric event to want to get help. Now, athletes of all kinds have sports psychologists or traveling shrinks. Things have progressed so much since the days when I played. I actually think a sports psychologist would have helped me, even though our family never sought help very readily.

I began self-medicating with alcohol. Free beer was easily available from tournament sponsors in the locker rooms. I drank my first beer ever at age 17 at Lion's Corner House pub in London. In Newport, Rhode Island, at age 19, I was out with Cliff Buchholz, and we got stinking drunk. One of the other times I remember getting just rotten drunk was when I was 20 down in Australia, after I lost to Tony Roche in Adelaide. However, I remember those occasions because they were so infrequent. In general, I set a "four beers a night" limit for myself and stuck to it. I was very disciplined about that. Drinking any more than that would have interfered with my ability to play well.

Mickie first noticed that I had a problem within the first few weeks of our marriage. Even though I was on my way up in my career, the mood swings became evident very soon. Poor Mickie didn't know where to go. She thought of herself as pretty capable and adaptable. But there's no place to go if you're sharing a small hotel room with someone and that person suddenly starts to go ape shit. She was caught between admiration and respect for my tennis accomplishments and being at a loss as to how to deal with the emotional aftermath. The seamy underside of the tennis tour is not pleasant sometimes. It's not pretty when you lose a match. You're out there and it's 90 degrees and the crowd turns on you. There's not much down time. It's like being in a vacuum. It's a pressure cooker. I always kept her at a distance. She was constantly walking on egg shells. Sometimes she would have to go outside and wander around just to get away from me. She wanted to crawl in a hole somewhere and hide. Even though we loved each other, there was this thing between us. We were in love, but there was all this tension. Mickie told me after we got married: "You scare me." I didn't do it on purpose. I was just so intense.

I was a failure as a husband for what Mickie needed. I was already so married to my career. It was unfair to ask her to get involved with that. Marriage was such a new concept to me. I didn't know how it would be after I got married. Team sports do not allow wives to travel with the team. Individual sports are different that way. The wives go along. It's like a very small sorority. The Richeys traveled as a family until Nancy split off with the women's tour. Mickie felt like an adult kid tagging along with this tennis family. She didn't know what to do to help. From her perspective, my mood swings and irritability while I was getting "up" for my matches were very difficult for her. Coming down after matches, even if I won, wasn't necessarily much easier emotionally than if I had lost.

There was only a small window left for our sex life, because all the time I was usually either getting ready for a match or coming down off of one. During this as well as all my subsequent depressive episodes, my sex drive was still normal. Thank God I didn't lose that! But tennis interfered. Before and after a match she would avoid me. I was arrogant. The competitive adrenaline creates an even stronger libido. There was no intimacy. She felt like she was there to service me. Sex for me was like stopping to get gas, little more than putting a hose in the tank. Everyone told her it was her fault for feeling this way. That made her feel lower than low. At one point after giving birth to our first child, she asked a gynecologist if there was anything wrong with her physically. She wanted him to fix it if there was. He examined her and pronounced her perfectly normal. Mickie is a passionate person. She's pretty darn good! I didn't understand this until much later. I led a very selfish existence. There was no time for romance. My hormones were coursing with competition. I was burning off sexually what I didn't burn off in my matches. I would chew her out, irritable about something unreasonable, and 10 minutes later want to have sex. She would say to me: "Cliff, I don't call that making love."

The 1970 year was my signature year—my best season. All that year I was up, up, up. Winning, winning, winning. I played 112 matches that year and won 93 of them. I lost only 19 times that year, not counting Davis Cup or exhibition matches. I won the first World Point Title (the Pepsi Cola Grand Prix) and was ranked No.

1 in the United States. I won the U.S. National Clay Court title and reached the semifinals of the U.S. Open and the French Open. I also led the United States to a repeat victory in the Davis Cup—while being named Davis Cup MVP to boot.

When I was named the Davis Cup's Most Valuable Player, it was a surprise. I don't know who decided it. I think it was the sports writers. I was as surprised as anyone. They gave me a trophy. I didn't even know there was an MVP award. Those kinds of awards never meant a whole lot to me, really, because I knew they were all so political. I don't like hoping someone likes you well enough to give you something. I'd rather earn it.

The press knew there had been some controversy over whether I would even be named to play that year. They had held a reception in Shaker Square (in Shaker Heights, a fancy neighborhood in Cleveland) for the purpose of announcing the Davis Cup draw for the final against West Germany. We all knew Stan Smith and Bob Lutz would play the doubles. As far as the singles players, it would be Arthur Ashe for sure but in the other singles slot, it was going to be Stan Smith or me. I would have walked out if they had named Smith to play. The previous year Donald Dell, the non-playing captain, had picked Stan over me because he was Stan's agent, not mine. But this time, it was my name that was drawn out of the Davis Cup trophy during the draw. Fred Stolle, the great Australian player and the coach for the German team, told the press I would be easy to beat. He predicted I would choke. He thought I wouldn't be able to handle the pressure of representing my country for the world team championship. As it turned out, I won both of my singles matches and we beat the Germans 5-0. So that might have helped me win MVP: I didn't choke as expected! I think I may have gotten a few sympathy votes.

It was kind of ironic that I won the first Grand Prix point title after objecting to the very idea of the whole thing. What used to be the Grand Prix is now the ATP Champions' Race that players

The 1970 victorious United States Davis Cup team, left to right, me, Arthur Ashe, Captain Ed Turville, Stan Smith, Bob Lutz and Coach Dennis Ralston.

like Pete Sampras and Roger Federer won many times. I won the first Grand Prix ever. Originally it was sponsored by Pepsi Cola, although other companies joined in on subsequent years including Nabisco and IBM. It started as a way to attract more world interest to the game. The contest began in May at the French Open and all the tournaments were worth points. That year, I "chased" points, so to speak. I played a lot of tennis that year. These days they have computers to tabulate wins and losses, but back in 1970, we just had someone sitting in a central office, keeping track. I remember being in Stockholm at the last point tournament of the year. I knew I was close to winning the title. I called over to London to the headquarters of the International Lawn Tennis Federation to find out how many points I had. "Where do I stand?" I asked. I was told that if I won one match in Stockholm, I would tie for the Grand Prix point title with Arthur Ashe, even if he won the tournament. I would be sitting pretty. If I won two matches, I would win the Grand Prix title outright.

I had lousy luck with the draw. I'm not saying they rigged it, but normally the best players are seeded so they're protected from each other until the end. In the first round, I played Andrés Gimeno from Spain, who had reached the semis of Wimbledon. He should have been seeded, but he wasn't. People fight over the draws in tennis. There are rumors of cockamamy excuses for why draws need to be redone. I was not a popular player. I really had to question why they had me playing Andrés in the first round. I beat him 21-19, 6-1. I clinched the point title outright in the second round when I beat Zeljko Franulovic of Yugoslavia 6-1, 8-10, 6-3. They had a point board posted at the tournament. There's a picture of me using my racquet to show the total number of points on the board. The point race was over before the tournament was even finished.

The reason I didn't like the idea of the Grand Prix in the first place, as I told Jack Kramer at the time, was that the players would get exhausted. And then I ended up winning the darn thing! But I had predicted correctly. The week after Stockholm, we flew to Tokyo for the Masters' Championship. I was so tired when we got there, I was sleeping 17 hours a night. I went to see a doctor in Tokyo who thought I might have hepatitis. He said I should not play the tournament. I went to the auditorium and hunted down Jack Kramer. I wanted to tell him personally why I couldn't play. He thought because it was an indoor, fast surface in Tokyo, I was backing out because I thought I might lose. I had always been known as more of a clay court player, but I had just won on two super fast surfaces! A few weeks prior to that, I had beaten Ken Rosewall in London on a lightning-fast court, right after he won the U.S. Open. The next week in Stockholm on another fast surface, linoleum, I also beat

This is where the rankings stood in the Pepsi ILTF Grand Prix at the Stockholm Open in 1970

Gimeno; so the idea that I might be scared of fast surfaces was a joke. I was just run-down and fatigued. In the end, as it turns out, I was right. I had just played 30 tournaments, spread out to the four corners of the globe. In the run-up to the Grand Prix, they played us to death.

The other funny thing that happened when I won the World Point Title was that I won $25,000 in bonus money, but no trophy. I always played for the trophy, not the money. The trophy was something more tangible. I said to Jack Kramer, "Why didn't you guys give me a trophy?" The ILTF took my complaint to heart. They actually presented me with a trophy a year later! I had to shame them into it. I wanted the damn trophy! They rustled one up a year later at the Masters in Paris. The inscription reads: "Pepsi Grand Prix 1970, Cliff Richey." To this day, it is one of only two trophies I keep on display in our home.

Sometimes when I'm feeling blue, I'll write down my five greatest tennis accomplishments:

1. World Point Title (Grand Prix)
2. Two-time Davis Cup Champion and MVP
3. U.S. No. 1 Ranking
4. 45 tournament wins
5. Legends Senior Tour Champion

Strangely, even when I write it down, it doesn't sink in. But at least three out of those five successes occurred in the same year, 1970. The No. 1 ranking was the last to fall into place, after that "Sudden Death" match against Stan Smith.

At that point, emotionally, I could be described as somewhat crazed. Arthur Ashe said he worried about me because he thought I would burn out too quickly. Those words of his turned out to be prophetic.

• CHAPTER TEN •

It Ain't All Autographs & Sunglasses

Celebrity. We overuse that word. We've worn out the word in our society to such a degree that we've now got self-appointed celebrities. These days our culture artificially makes celebrities, even out of people who have never accomplished squat!

It's not that I consider myself a big celebrity, necessarily. I have just lived a life that is not like most people's lives. I've been fortunate enough to live in a world of gift baskets and courtesy cars. It does warp you into thinking you're privileged. You even start to think that somehow you deserve it all.

I'm not as integrated into societal structures as the majority of people are. Most people have a 9-to-5 job. I don't. Even on the tennis tour, I had a schedule I chose. That's a lot different from having it imposed on you.

Success, by definition, is not a normal thing. It's just not going to be your average life. Very few people get so good at something that they are ranked No. 1 in the country. By virtue of that fact, you are already different. You have to think differently to get there. You have to go against the grain. But the rewards are so high, there's got to be a price somewhere. As hellacious as it was to go through, I still don't think it was too high a price to pay, considering all the rewards that I got.

The danger is, as one success follows rapidly upon another, you begin to think you're bulletproof and that you're invincible. When in reality, you're only one loss away from puncturing that bubble. . . . You're only as good as your last performance. This creates a unique kind of mental pressure.

It's not that my job is any tougher than, say, a doctor's. It's certainly a lot less important than performing surgery. But nonetheless, you know that most people don't have the discipline to do what you do. You become very critical of other people because in the first place, you're hard on yourself! You've had to say "no" to yourself, to make sacrifices. You never have time to go shopping or to the movies. Some of that is not healthy. But that is what it takes to make it to the top.

Celebrity has to do with the free enterprise system. There are not too many celebrities under communism. Tiger Woods used to make 90 million dollars a year. Is anybody really worth that? It's craziness, but that's how it was. He was worth that, because capitalism is a beautiful thing.

Capitalism says that if you are very successful, you will be rewarded. The celebrity feels he deserves that. It's not too far off the mark. Celebrities will immediately be seated at the best table in a restaurant. A lot of people will see it and resent that. They're jealous. But if you think about it, it's the barter system. The restaurant owner is receiving a valuable service from the celebrity whenever he arrives there and shows his face. The owner gets publicity for his business. It's a form of trading services.

My friends and I do get playing privileges at some of the nicest golf courses all over the country. Legends Trail Golf Club in Scottsdale, Arizona offered me free playing privileges in exchange for my celebrity caché. They wanted me to hang out at their facility. That is their primary advertising ploy. My dog even got free celebrity treatment one week at a pet resort! It had a TV, swimming pool, manicure, pedicure, you name it. I thought she might get a big head and stop licking me after that.

Now, close to 40 years later, as the faint memory of my stardom continues to fade, the question might legitimately be asked: was I ever a "real" celebrity? I've truly never seen myself as all that famous. I am definitely well known inside the tennis world. But people rarely recognize me when I step onto airplanes. A lot of people do recognize the Richey name, however, because of the double or even triple tennis career inside Richey, Inc.

Even at the height of my career, I wasn't ultra-famous. I didn't have the kind of face recognition that makes "real" celebrities lose their privacy. I acted as my own agent and Nancy's for endorsement deals. I actively sought them out and met with sporting goods representatives personally or negotiated contracts over the phone. I badgered Wilson Sporting Goods into giving me a bonus one time when I used their racquets on national TV to win the CBS Tennis Classic. I told them they would get four hours of everyone seeing their big red Ws on my strings. But I've never been in the fortunate position of being such a huge star that I could afford to turn down offers because there were so many. Instead, I've always felt like the outsider fighting my way in. I've had to shout, scream and tug at their coat tails to get attention.

At least in the local newspaper, back then, I had what was considered big-time superstar status because the reporters referred to me simply as "Cliff." I also used to receive fan mail with just my name on the envelope—no address, just the city. To this day I get periodic fan mail. My fans typically say, "I so admire your competitive spirit." Yeah, I was competitive all right. I was a raving *animale!*

In West Texas, you'd better be tough, or else you're not going to survive. The first few years particularly, the world press loved to call me a Texan because that name has such a mythical quality. They liked to call me a cowboy, especially if I acted up. I was known as a tough, brash Texan. It was a fair description of the way I acted. It didn't bother me. I've always been proud of being from Texas. I certainly never coveted being from the highbrow climate of the East. I never pined for that. I was proud of my roots.

I was fortunate in the sense that a lot of kids now get backers and sponsors to pay for them to go play their first few tournaments. By and large, I didn't have to do that. I went from the last week of amateur tennis (when I was paid $750 under the table plus expenses) to the first week of open/professional tennis, when I earned $900 above-board. That was literally the very next week. It was a fairly seamless transition. It just all sort of flowed together.

When open tennis came in, the game went gangbusters. It was a huge media circus. There were specific media ploys like the "Battle of the Sexes" at the Astrodome in Houston, where Billie Jean King beat Bobby Riggs. That was one of the events that helped make the game big in the 1970s. I made $50,000 the first year the game went open and $100,000 the next. My endorsements added a nice sum to my earnings in prize money. My endorsements for equipment were with Wilson, Converse rubber, B.F. Goodrich tennis shoes (the Jack Purcell shoe), Yonex racquets, and Dunlop Sporting Goods. As far as clothes, I was affiliated with Fred Perry, Lacoste, and Jantzen. When I signed with Jantzen Sports Wear in 1972 (a contract that lasted through 1977), in addition to my wardrobe, they sent free clothes even for other members of my family. My wife and kids used to have fun looking through the catalogues to pick out what they wanted to order. Jantzen called me back in 1983 and said they were coming out with a Davis Cup collection of clothes. They signed me on for three years again in the 1980s. I was also paid to endorse specific resorts and tennis clubs. I represented a place in Sarasota, Florida called the Colony Beach and Tennis Resort. In theory, I played out of Sarasota even though I didn't have a residence there. When I walked onto the court, they would announce me as "Cliff Richey of the Colony Beach and Tennis Resort in Sarasota, Florida." There was also a place on Lake Conroe, north of Houston, called the Wood Harbor Yacht and Racquet Club. They called

Jack Purcell was one of the companies I endorsed. Here I am looking coy in one of their advertisements.

and said they wanted the Richeys to represent their development. The deal was $15-20,000 a year for a three-year agreement. We did a tennis clinic for them at Memorial Park in Houston in the summer of 1973. But then their company went bankrupt and the facility never got off the ground.

With so many freebies coming in the mail all the time, it's extraordinary to think now about how many of them went to waste. I would routinely call up whatever company was supplying me at the time and say, "Send me six or eight or 12 racquets." I was always very particular about the balance point on a racquet. I wanted them medium-balanced. They had my specs at the factory, so they'd try to cull out the ones they thought I would like. I liked 13¼ ounces total weight for the racquet. The strings added another half an ounce. However, they couldn't always get it right. Out of each racquet shipment I received, I would pronounce up to a third of them "unusable." Up to a third of those racquets would be tossed out before I ever used them to play a single game!

I still refer to racquets or golf clubs as grown-up toys. Athletes in general are talked about as kids who never grew up. For competition, that's a good thing. Our expertise revolves around what other people do for fun. It's deeper than they understand. But youthful enthusiasm keeps you young. I like to think of myself as a 60-year-old kid.

If I still think of myself as a kid now, it's mildly appalling to think about my immaturity back in those days. When I met President Nixon at the White House, I was too young to take it all in like I would have later in life. After we won the Davis Cup over Romania in 1969, Donald Dell (the captain that year) informed us at the last minute that we were going to be received at the White House the next day. He had a reputation for doing things at the last minute. We were getting ready to board the plane to go to D.C. Donald almost missed the flight. We had to beg them to keep the airplane doors open so that he could get on. We were saying to the

One day after we beat Romania to win the 1969 Davis Cup title, President Richard Nixon hosted both teams in the White House Rose Garden.

stewardess: "Please, we're going to see the President!"

When we arrived, first we went to the old executive office building next door to the White House. President Nixon's executive administrator for sports, Bud Wilkinson, the famous football coach from Oklahoma, received us there. He or an assistant told us what was going to happen next. First we were given a tour of the White House. We received nice little presidential medallions and golf balls with Nixon's name printed on them. Then we went out on the lawn for a photo op. We were told exactly what to do. We all lined up. I was standing beside my teammate, Clark Graebner. He leaned over and said, "There's Henry Kissinger." He was standing on the back porch of the Rose Garden. It's ironic, given my later interest in politics, but back then I didn't know Henry Kissinger from a bar of soap!

The most unusual thing I remember was that Nixon would not allow any women at the ceremony. Women were not welcome.

Today that would be considered a colossal gaffe. Poor Mickie didn't even see the inside of the White House. She had to stay over there at that old executive office building the whole time.

Once we were lined up in order, you could hear somebody say, "Here he comes." The next thing we knew, Nixon came up. He had a prompter with him. He greeted each person individually. He would say a little something to each one. When he was about three guys down from me, it dawned on me, "What the heck do I say?" I panicked, man. What in the hell do you say to the President of the United States? What could possibly make any sense? He shook my hand. I said, "I've heard a lot about you." How stupid is that?! My insipid comment became almost funny in light of the Watergate scandal four years later.

If you could see me today, you'd never guess I had once graced the White House lawn. I wear blue jeans, a golf shirt, and tennis shoes. My normal accessories are a cowboy belt with silver buckle, engraved with my initials, and a ball cap which often gets stained with sunscreen. I usually need a haircut. The only luxury I allow myself is an 18-karat gold Rolex watch. I bought a 14-karat gold one in 1974, but two years later I bought the 18-karat one because, as they say, "the stars wear 18-karat." My best friend Ralph Terry, the former New York Yankee pitcher and 1962 World Series MVP, calls me a phony because I wear shitty clothes. He says at least he matches—he wears a shitty watch and shitty clothes!

In our family we have a saying: "It ain't all autographs and sunglasses." Dino Martin was the first one who said that. He was Dean Martin's son. Dino tried to play the tour in the late 1960s and early 1970s. We got to know each other down in Australia in 1975. He was also in a rock group with the son of Lucille Ball.

It's not all autographs and sunglasses, baby. That's our little inside joke. I call my youngest daughter Sarah "Hollywood" because she used to tease me. We would kid about my being a big celeb who has to wear sunglasses to ward off autograph seekers. Not exactly!

Sarah Hollywood used to call and remind me to carry my pens with me for signing autographs.

It's not all about just having this glamorous life. Yes, I was making a lot of money, but during Jimmy Carter's presidency in particular, I fell into the 50 percent income tax bracket. So there went half of my earnings! It was like going into business as an equal partner with the government. I will admit it's still hard sometimes not to resent that.

When Mickie and I met and then went through our whirlwind courtship and engagement, all of that was very romantic. It was glamorous for me to have this high-class girl on my arm. But it was tougher to continue the romance once we got married. I had to get back to my career. I've never been very good at multi-tasking. I'm actually surprised at how well I did at tennis while I was dating and getting married. I did win that tournament in Tulsa with Mickie sitting there watching. But I was unprepared for marriage. I was so young and selfish. Everything revolved around me. I didn't grasp what a culture shock it would be for Mickie just to walk into my world.

A certain amount of self-absorption is necessary for success. It's a very regimented life. Playing professional sports makes your life selfish. It's a lopsided, one-way deal.

There was both electricity and discipline in that atmosphere. It's not all autographs and sunglasses. It's work. Besides being a professional competitor, I'm a professional entertainer. When the people who go to the office every day want to find recreation, where do they go? They come to us—to our matches. We were out there trying to please crowds all the time.

There were some wives through the years who resented their loss of identity, being married to celebrity husbands. They didn't like playing second fiddle, being second banana. They had nothing to do. Not enough shopping, I guess! They resented the attention their husbands got all the time. In the old days, we didn't stay in the finest resorts. Only when open tennis came in did all that start. Then we began flying in much higher circles. But even with improved living conditions, some of the wives were still complaining all the time. I never could understand that. They weren't having to keep house or carpool. Still, they did nothing but bitch and moan. Mickie never did that. None of that spoiled syndrome. With 99.9 percent of the women I could have married, I know that we would have gotten divorced early on. I would have been a big reason why that divorce would have happened. It would have been every bit as much my fault as theirs (probably more). But it wouldn't have lasted long, I can tell you that right now!

Mickie had a lot of empty time on her hands. The time I spent in the locker room could drag on. There was a lot of waiting time. She took up needlepoint to pass the hours. She had taken care of her five brothers and sisters from a very young age. She was not used to just sitting there, twiddling her thumbs. Mickie wasn't employed outside of the family. She learned pretty quickly how to do the bookwork and pay the bills. I didn't make very much money at all in the early years of our marriage so it didn't make sense to get an apartment for a full year and only stay there for three months. We were on tour the rest of the time. So we lived with Mom and Dad and then contributed to their household expenses. That was a strain on Mickie, to be living with her in-laws. She was in charge of our laundry, although I washed my own clothes when she wasn't around. I traveled with seven or eight changes of tennis clothes. There would be days I'd go through three of those—and that's not counting street clothes! Most of the players did their own laundry in the bathtub. The turn-around time wasn't fast enough to send it out.

Mickie never really felt that she fit into Richey, Inc. She never found her place. From the Richeys' point of view, she was an easy fit for us. But I don't think we were an easy fit for her. We were pretty emotional people. One of the main cogs in the wheel was Mom. She held a lot of it together. She was pretty laid-back. The

rest of us were volatile and domineering. Mom had totally subordi-
nated herself to Richey, Inc. as far as becoming Dad's assistant and
travel agent. She had a calming effect on everyone.

In the first five or six years of our marriage, Mickie was con-
fronted with real problems. It was a different situation than she
ever could have prepared for. She had to start dealing with my
depression almost immediately. She was already handling the life of
an athlete and then on top of that, there was my depression. One
of the devilish things about it is that depression, by definition, is
abnormal. In addition to that, I didn't have a normal career. I was a
vagabond. I had no close ties except to immediate family.

I have led, by all appearances, a glamorous life, but there's a
seamy, gritty underside that people don't see or understand. Anybody who's been on the tour as long as I have will say that it shapes
you in kooky ways. It's a goofy life. It makes you neurotic. Being on
the road is difficult. It's lonely out there. It's tough even on a winning streak to keep going. It all happens too fast to enjoy it.

Touring is a nomadic lifestyle. I had raging hormones. A lot
of people wonder what really goes on in those hotel rooms. Ilie
Nastase used to walk through hotel lobbies with a girl on each arm.
Some guys would take two play bunnies up to their rooms at the
same time! The way I was raised, you don't go to bed with someone
unless you're married. But there were a lot of busted marriages on
the tour. There was a fair amount of drinking too. One time when
two of my fellow pros had a few too many on an airplane, they
started peeing into their sweaters. There was no bathroom on the
plane. Several times I stayed out drinking all night and left Mickie
in our hotel room alone. That was just gross, negligent behavior.
There is simply no excuse for that.

There were always a lot of women hanging around. You could
take advantage of those situations if you wanted to. And a lot of
guys did. I won a tournament in Bretton Woods, New Hampshire
in 1972 and after the final, I went out and played golf with one of

the other pros in the tournament. Needless to say, he had a "repu-tation" on the tour. After nine holes, he said he had to go up to his room to get something. He was gone 20 minutes. (That's not normal in the middle of a round of golf.) When he returned, I asked what had happened. He said, "I ran into a little camp counselor in the hall." I realized then that he had knocked her off at the turn!

There were certain tournaments like the U.S. Indoors in Salis-bury, Maryland where some pretty scuzzy-looking women would show up every year. They had a lot of parties. A lot of goofy things you could get involved with if you were so inclined. In 1972 at a tournament in St. Louis, I remember seeing one of the players in the hotel elevator. I asked him, "Well, are you going to last the week?" He smiled and whipped out his pecker. It had blisters on it. That was some kind of wild party going on up there!

That same week, Tom Okker and I were invited to a tournament party at a private house. We went over there, but it was too early. The party hadn't started yet. So we went back to the hotel. We bagged the party idea. We decided to go to the hotel bar instead. There were a couple of women there who were real icky. They started to drape their arms around us. One of them said there was another player in one of the rooms who had a private party going on. They invited us. I declined. I went back to my room. Then, the phone rang. It was a woman. She said, "Why don't you come on over now?" I thought it was the woman from the bar. I said, "You dirty whore! I already told you, I'm not interested," and hung up. I didn't find out until a year later that it was the society woman from the tournament party!

In my generation, that I knew of, no one did heavy drugs. There were rumors of people smoking some marijuana, but nothing heavier than that. In the late 1960s, I went to a party in Los Angeles where I had maybe four or five beers. Somebody had a marijuana joint and offered it to me. I took a couple puffs. That's the only time I ever even saw an illegal drug. Of course, like Bill Clinton, I didn't inhale!

In the next generation after ours, some characters were known to take heavier drugs. Vitas Gerulaitis was one player who was alleged to take drugs. Vitas was fortunate enough to have won a major, the Australian Open in 1977. He was seven years younger than I and a real nice guy with great talent. He was gregarious and everyone loved him. In my opinion, he suffered from depression. I think it may have been drug-induced. He played in a benefit tennis tournament we organized in San Angelo in 1992. I asked him how he was feeling. He said, "Most of the time, the world is gray."

Drugs really only became part of the tennis scene during the years when I was playing the senior tour. I got on an airplane the day I won the Sarasota senior tournament in February of 1986. The final match was televised nationally on CBN—the Christian Broadcasting Network—and one of the their TV production people was on the plane with me. He looked at me and asked, "Do you have any candy?" I asked, "What do you mean?" He said, "You know, nose candy." I said, "No, sorry, I've never been into that."

What makes pro athletes think they can take drugs and get away with it? Celebrities are just treated as these special creatures all the time. A night out on the town and a drunken spree is viewed differently if it's done by a celebrity than if it's the town bum. The ticket out of jail is the success you have had. You start thinking you're bulletproof. A lot of that mindset is just not healthy at all.

I had a cop stop me once for doing 55 in a 30. He saw the name on my driver's license and let me off with just a warning. I carry four or five of my sports trading cards in my wallet all the time because I give them out as business cards. I like to give them to people at golf courses who are nice to me. At Quicksand Golf Course in San Angelo, they gave me free playing privileges. I used to put my bag in a golf cart and drive out to the course without checking in at the shop. The owner told me I shouldn't do that. I would also hit range balls onto a random hill at the course. That wasn't good for the kids who had to pick up the balls. One day I felt guilty about it and gave a $5 tip to the poor kid who had to pick them all up.

I'd be the first to admit those were things I shouldn't have done. You know what? I've been a real pain in the ass at times. Constantly cutting corners and playing by your own rules is by definition a dishonest thing. But basically I've had a lot of co-conspirators in the process. They are the star-struck fans who let me off the hook when I didn't play by society's rules. There is a danger with celebrities, a temptation to start taking advantage in ways you shouldn't. There are all sorts of blurred lines. You start thinking you're exempt. We all have a certain phoniness. Mine is that I've had a reasonably good career; so, as a result, I've always felt entitled.

The basketball player Charles Barkley made a controversial statement years ago: "I am not your child's role model." That was right, he wasn't; but the real question is, should he have been? There's a lot of investment built up in star athletes. The people who should be policing their activities don't want to crack down too heavily on athletes' behavior. That's how they themselves make a living. It seems the baseball officials did a wink and a nod with the steroid scandals. In my opinion, they knew what was going on. Everybody did. Another factor is that athletes are all young, and teenagers just do stupid things. We handle star athletes with kid gloves because they're the bread ticket. You don't want to kill your stars off. It all gets back to the dollar.

There's also an intangible there that's not necessarily finance-driven. People need to have heroes. Once you become a role model in the eyes of the public, then they aren't going to want to have that torn down. Maybe that's what the O.J. Simpson trial was about, to some extent. Would he have gotten off if he had not been a famous football player? Nobody can answer that question. But it is a legitimate dilemma. How do you prosecute a sports icon? We don't want to prosecute heroes. Celebrities live by a different set of rules. There is definitely a double standard.

I don't think celebrities should be exempt from the law. I'm all for sanctions. If athletes take steroids or go against certain rules, they should be punished. Celebrities shouldn't be excused to the extent that they are.

On the other hand, there is sometimes greater accountability for—and scrutiny of—celebrities by virtue of the fact that they live in the public eye. The actress Christina Ricci was criticized once by animal rights activists for wearing fur. She issued a public apology. I was barred from playing in certain countries, some 20 of them (like Mozambique) because I had played in South Africa during apartheid. The way they saw it, I had basically benefited from a system that was guilty of human rights abuses. Of course it was my choice to do that. However, the tennis great Frew McMillan was also barred from playing in Mexico because he was a South African. That didn't seem fair—he couldn't help it that he was born there. He had no choice in the matter. So celebrities are often held to a higher standard, even if it isn't a fair one.

It used to bother me that I was being judged unfairly just because of who I was. But I've come to understand that maybe I'm gonna be placed under a microscope. I've come to terms with that. That's just part of the deal.

The question could be asked: did celebrity contribute to my depression? The celebrity thing is tough because you know you're being scrutinized more than others. If you mess up, folks are going to talk about it. They put you up on a pedestal.

People don't understand. One day a local college coach saw me out on the golf course. I must have been frowning. He said, "Come on, Cliff, it can't be that bad. Smile!" Well, yes, it can be that bad, partner, and furthermore, it's none of your damn business! That comment cut me pretty deep. Without all my successes, some of these conversations would never take place. They're jealous of my success. It's the little things like that.

People have been critical of me, especially in my home town.

In some cases, rightfully so. But the intensity of it has probably been stronger than it would have been without the celebrity factor. People in town know I have a high profile. I'm a scratch golfer. I don't work. So they think I must have a privileged life.

Overall, the caché of celebrity is a huge plus and not a negative. But withdrawing from society is a hallmark of depression. When you don't feel like being sociable, they think you're stuck up. If they only knew how much you were suffering. . . .

You have to ask the question: what does celebrity do to child actors or prodigies of any kind? What does all that do to a young kid? You really are taken outside the norm. You're constantly being told how good you are. You have trophies and press clippings to prove it. And then one day, suddenly, all of that's gone. Your 15 minutes of fame have passed.

I don't like to look at my scrapbooks. That phase of my life is over. You could count on one hand the times I've looked at those since Mom made them. I enjoyed those times and it brings back so many memories, but it gives me a funny feeling. I don't like doing it.

Sometimes I look at the trading card in my wallet and wonder whether I am the same person who did all those things. When I've been around famous musicians (like my good friends the Gatlin Brothers) and complimented them on their music, they just shrug their shoulders. They take their talent for granted. They've done it so long, it's in their DNA! People can't believe I don't play tennis any more. It's like that was my identity, and now it's all in the past.

There's sort of an unreal quality to some of the accomplishments I had. They started out as a dream in my mind. And, in some ways, they stayed that way. Success can be fleeting. It's hard to put your hand around it and really hold on to it. Some athletes say it's not as great as they thought it would be. I wouldn't say that. But parts of it are certainly surreal.

I don't think there is necessarily a correlation between depression and success. I'm sure there are a lot of depressed people who have never had any tangible successes in their life. In fact, maybe that's one of the reasons they're depressed! Many people have problems that I've never experienced. I would be the first to say that it doesn't even make sense for me to have major depression, looking at it from the outside. I've got one of the greatest lives I could ever imagine. I've got a life that's so perfect, it's spooky. A lot of my "triggers" are very self-centered. And yet my depression was just as bad as that of someone who had more of an apparent "reason" to be depressed. It's a real disease that can attack anybody, at any time. That's one of the mysteries of clinical depression.

Clinical depression does not match the celebrity image. It's so incongruous. And yet, the intersection of celebrity with depression is another argument in favor of its being recognized as a *bona fide* disease. It doesn't just happen to the down-and-out. It can happen to anybody! Even to people who are hugely successful.

In fact, celebrities in general may be more prone to depression. There might be a correlation between driven, workaholic perfectionists and depressives. They are extreme people anyway. Depressed people who are highly accomplished may not feel or experience their successes in the same way as others. They never allow themselves to enjoy their victories. Not many people go into a profession with our same degree of vim and vigor. It's no secret that within the celebrity world, we tend to call everyone else "civilians."

When Pete Sampras retired after winning more Grand Slam singles tournaments than any other man, he was quoted as saying, "Thank God I'm not on this merry-go-round any more." There are a lot of guys who were great tennis players but had some of the worst personal lives you could imagine. Pancho Gonzalez was one of the all-time tennis greats, but he was often a miserable son-of-a-bitch. He was married four different times. I remember once when John McEnroe quit a match. The umpire announced, "Mr. McEnroe has been forced to retire." Then he turned off the mike and looked at McEnroe, who was sitting on his chair on the side of the court with his head down under his towel. The umpire asked, "Mr. McEnroe, may I ask what is the nature of your injury?" He replied, "Brain damage!" Of course he wasn't serious, but that could be a metaphor for what the game did to all of us out there, sooner or later. It's like a meat grinder. It just chews you up and spits you out.

If there is a pattern here, then why hasn't it been talked about? Why isn't this thing better recognized? One reason is that the "symptoms" or stresses of celebrity life probably mask the symptoms of depression. Celebrities already lead an abnormal life. Life on the tour itself was enough to create a monster, what with all the parties and free booze.

Another celebrity pitfall is to start believing your press clippings. To start thinking you're invincible. I was good at tennis almost immediately. I was bringing home trophies already at age 12. In the juniors, I hardly knew what losses were.

On top of that, you have people telling you that you're special. Sporting goods companies are paying you to use their equipment. You're making commercials. It's all going your way.

That's one of the traps. You don't want anything to come into your life that's negative. When it does, it hits you doubly hard. You're used to being exempt. You don't know how to cope with loss. When you put it all together, celebrity sports was the perfect little petri dish to grow the disease of clinical depression.

I suspect a couple of tennis players I know are probably also prone to depression, but I've never talked to them about it. There was one other player of my generation who I think suffered from the same thing I have. I did a tennis outing with him after I went on an antidepressant in the late 1990s. We were talking about a mental health benefit golf tournament I had organized. Judging from his interest in Zoloft and my mental health activism, I felt like he had probably been on antidepressants himself, but he was afraid to come out with it. He is still making a living in the tennis world.

I don't blame him. I know how it is. I don't like the way it is, but I understand it. I don't blame the poor guy. He still has to inhabit that world. I don't. That's one of the things that has allowed me to come forward about my illness: it doesn't endanger my livelihood to do so. And it can potentially help lots of people. As a reporter for my local newspaper wrote, the decision to go public about my depression has constituted my biggest "ace."

Maybe there should be a sub-genre of depression or a specialized diagnosis concerning a form of the illness that occurs only in celebrity athletes. That idea is not as off-the-wall as it may seem. They say there might be 18 or more different classifications within clinical depression. Some day we will know a hell of a lot more about it than we know now. It has been proven that mind-altering drugs such as heroin or marijuana can alter your brain chemistry. I wouldn't be surprised if professional sports careers, with the high levels of cortisol and adrenaline involved, might provoke similar changes in your brain.

Some day depression may come to be recognized as part and parcel of the celebrity lifestyle. That lifestyle already fosters instability. You're beholden to the public. You're only as good as your last performance. Your whole life is lived in black and white. Guess what, guys? Celebrities are people too. We are not automatons. We still feel the pressure.

Celebrities are not robots, but sometimes we have to act as if we were. I remember back in 1969 in Las Vegas, we were in one of those old hotel casinos. We went to see a performance by comedian Alan King, who was a huge tennis fan. I said to him, "If I've had an argument with my wife, at least I feel like I can take it out on the tennis court. How do you go out there, if you've had a bad day, and still manage to be funny?" He said, "When you're a professional, you have this little button that you push. You just go out there and do it. The show must go on."

It takes a certain variety of person for me to really be friends with. My friends tend to be entertainers or athletes who have also led a lopsided life. Those guys who have faced that uncertainty every day of competition, that pressure of giving live performances on stage. We've been in that bunker together—in the trenches. I kid about being one of these guys who will die on the tour. We can't find the exit ramp. You either have to be a little bit sick already to live on the tour—or else, sooner or later, it will make you that way!

I'm as particular now about my environment as I am about my friends. I really don't like country club settings. I grew up in them as sort of an employee. I've met very few country clubbers who really knew what competition is all about. I know they're the normal ones. I realize I am the odd one out. But I don't even like resorts. That's where I work. I don't like the clientele that hang out there. I can't relate to most of them. They aren't my friends. It's kind of an ass-backwards existence. But you get spoiled when you're used to having all your trips paid for. I never go to sports events or resorts to be a spectator. I go to participate. I have to go by contract, whereas most people look forward to going there as the big event of their year. I'm more of a muni guy. I honestly prefer municipal golf courses.

I don't like the sterile environment of resorts and country clubs. I've led a very exciting life. What an education! But at the same time, it's difficult for me to enjoy what other people are dying to do. It's like, if I were to just go on vacation, where would I go? What would I do? I guess I could do a little touring. See the Sistine Chapel and what not. But eating out, sightseeing, a football game, a concert—I don't enjoy that stuff. I probably should want to do some of those things a little more. I know that I'm too set in my ways. But the exciting life I've led makes other stuff, frankly, start to seem a little dull.

The one thing I do value is success. I'm hung up on success the way a lot of people are hung up on being a member of a country club and having a lot of money. Success is my status symbol. Instead of being a jetsetter, I drive 25,000 miles a year. I enjoy it now because I never did that before. Most people work hard so they can afford to fly, not drive. I did exactly the reverse. I do enjoy going out to restaurants with friends or family some now. But after eating out every night on the tour for 30 years, it's just not that big of a thrill. My substitute for eating out is going to a WalMart Supercenter to buy cold cuts, cole slaw and a loaf of bread. I take that and sack out in front of the TV at a hotel.

With the depression I've had, some people would go to a fancy spa to recover. I go to a municipal golf course. Either one can be a tool for seclusion.

I've thought about volunteering to clean urinals just to totally remove ego and see what that feels like. I've had a fleeting fantasy of showing up at McDonald's and applying for a job. Perhaps volunteering with United Way for a year.

Maybe some day I'll do one of those things. But even if I don't, depression has been a humbling experience. I'll never again be in danger of getting too impressed with myself. As the confluence of depression with celebrity demonstrates: it ain't all autographs and sunglasses.

CHAPTER ELEVEN

Playing at High Altitudes

At 6,000-foot altitude, the ball reacts differently. The ball zips through the air at greater speed. So it's difficult to make shots with much precision. My strategy in that situation was to come to the net, which was not what the other guy was expecting. If my opponent had to make a passing shot over and over and over again, through the best of five sets, I figured: if I came to the net 150 times over the course of a match, I was going to win the majority of those points. The primary goal in that situation is to keep the pressure on.

We also used different balls at high altitudes. It's like the acoustics in different concert halls for musicians. These are factors in a tennis match that most people have never even thought about. But they are well-known within our industry. At high altitudes, you get out of breath more easily. A lot of players had a hard time adjusting to that. I found that you can adjust pretty well if you give yourself a few days. Some tennis players felt that no matter how long they practiced at high altitude, they would still be at a disadvantage. I was the opposite. I was somewhat prone to leg cramps in a long match. I could sweat out 12-14 pounds of liquid on a hot day. Another issue was that I tended to hyperventilate. That threw off the chemical content in my blood. Less oxygen at high altitude was actually good for me. It meant that I didn't cramp so badly.

Stress is like altitude. What's stress for one person is not necessarily a stress for another. Many players did not adjust well to altitude. I used it to my advantage. Try to do that with stress. Make the stress work for you. What are some adjustments you might have to make at high altitudes? What are some changes you can implement at times of greater stress? You have to react more quickly in thin air, just like you do emotionally at times of intense strain. The whole thing accelerates. You have to be ready.

To prepare for high altitude, you can use worn-out tennis balls with no fuzz left on them to practice. They act just like balls in thin air when you're up high. They "carry" another three or four feet further than you want them to. They end up going out a foot past the baseline. That same shot would be "in" at lower altitude. The other thing you can do is to string your racquet at a different tension so the ball comes off your racquet in a different way. String your racquets at a higher tension so the ball doesn't bounce off like a trampoline. These are some of the things you can do to improve high-altitude performance.

Johannesburg is one of the mile high cities, along with Denver and Mexico City. I won the South African Open there in 1972, one of the seven biggest tournaments in the world at that time. An article in *World Tennis* magazine proclaimed: "Cliff Richey finally wins one of the big events." I never did win a major (the U.S. Open, Wimbledon, the Australian, or the French). I got to the semifinals of the U.S. Open twice on my worst surface, grass. In 1970, I lost to Tony Roche there in the semis after winning five matches prior to that. I lost to Arthur Ashe in the 1972 U.S. Open semis. I also made it to the semifinals of the French in 1970.

But even during that golden year, 1970, my shine was starting to tarnish. That year I played in the Belgian Open, one of the larger pre-French Open tournaments, and lost easily to Ilie Nastase in the quarterfinals 6-2, 6-4, 6-1. They announced the draw for the

I won the South African Open in the mile-high city of Johannesburg in 1972, defeating Manuel Orantes in the final.

French Open a few days before the tournament started and he and I were seeded to play each other in the quarters. However, we each had to win four matches first. I called Dad up in Texas and asked him to fly over and help me develop a plan to use against Nastase. I knew I was going to need it. Dad's trip to Paris was a crutch for my confidence. The game plan he devised for Nastase—hit high to his forehand—helped me beat him to reach the semifinals. It was the first time I reached the semis at a major tournament. Although on paper 1970 was my best year, playwise, I was already starting to feel myself slip.

What began as a slight decline, undetectable by anyone but myself (or maybe Dad), soon developed into a full-fledged slump. In January of 1971, I started losing matches I wouldn't have lost only a few short months before. Part of the reason was that I was just tired. I was so fatigued after winning the World Point Title, that Japanese doctor thought I had hepatitis. It was stupid to go back on the tour right away after that. We didn't realize how much 1970 had taken out of me. I should have rested at least until April.

I was also starting to lose my backhand. My backhand had always been my strongest weapon, physically. I could do more damage with my backhand, hitting aggressive shots—especially passing shots, when someone came to the net on me—than I could any other way. It wasn't a huge shot like Arthur Ashe's serve, but it was my shot. It was actually a little unorthodox. My backhand had a small glitch in it which gave it a tendency to "pop" but it had worked fine for me up to that point.

When you're successful at something, you feel that it's built on a firm foundation. It's exactly like layers of a child's building blocks. If the bottom layer shifts, all the top layers start to crumble. It was like that with my backhand. Ground strokes (forehands and back-hands) are such foundational shots in tennis that losing either one of them is enough to destroy your tennis game. Of course, I never lost it entirely. It's not like I couldn't still win a lot of points on that side but it wasn't the reliable weapon I used to have in my arsenal. I didn't really know whether I could count on it or not.

Most athletes can go until their mid-30s without a natural aging process reducing their skill. The unorthodox nature of my backhand was what made it so powerful; but when I lost it, that also made it harder to fix. It's not like I could go to some manual and follow the directions for how to hit a backhand. I wanted it to feel like it used to, but suddenly, it was gone.

Depression is not hard to diagnose, but it can be a moving target. It's anything but a stable condition. Like the problems I was having with my backhand, it appears and then may seem to subside for no apparent reason. Depression is not a "once and for all" thing, and it doesn't come on with the same intensity all the time. Some episodes of clinical depression spontaneously subside. Ebb and flow. That's one of the things that's tricky about it, which may also make it difficult to detect.

At Ellis Park, where I played the South African Open, I had to compensate. I knew I did. Instead of winning matches with shot-making, like I used to, I was having to strategize even more. I started to chip and charge. I started forcing my opponent to show his hand early in the game. I started winning on court position. In the thin air of Johannesburg, I knew that with the high altitude, I should try to make my opponents come up with a passing shot early in the game. They wouldn't be able to do that in thin air. So even as my skills began to leave me, I started finding other ways to win.

I had to win lots of times, from 1971 through 1978, by strategy more than power or physical skill. In Austin, Texas, I won the CBS Tennis Classic in 1974, beating Rod Laver and Ilie Nastase along the way. My game had already deteriorated. I was playing on hard courts, which were not my best surface. But as my game grew worse, I was able to use the surface of the court to my advantage. On a super-fast surface like grass (and to a lesser extent on hard courts), you have to serve and volley. You can't stay back. That helped me in my later years because I was wanting to get to the net as quickly as possible anyway. I actually started to prefer the faster surfaces I had once disliked.

Before, in the best years of my career, I had been a baseline player. I had preferred slow surfaces like clay. U.S. clay was my best surface. The American balls were faster than European balls because ours were packed in pressurized cans. Our balls had less "nap" or fuzz on them, even when they were new. Likewise, European clay was a slower surface than American clay. Usually in northern Europe, the weather was also a little bit cooler, with the sky overcast. The weather is another factor that can make playing conditions slower because of atmospheric changes in air pressure which affect the travel speed of the balls.

From 1972-78, my game just got worse and worse. At the best of my game, I didn't make very many errors. I played long points. My strategy was to play until the other guy missed. When I had more physical prowess at my command, I could afford to be patient within each individual point. I could afford to play a defensive game. When I lost that, I had to get more aggressive. I had to end the points quickly. I had to assume superior court position earlier in the points. It's easier to do that on a surface where the ball bounces faster. It's the strategy we used to call "chip and charge." In that way, I could really use court position to my advantage. I liked that scenario. I could put the other guy on the defensive. The best shot to come up with in tennis is a 100-mile-an-hour bullet that hits close to a line—but that can be very hard to do. There are a lot of good things that can happen from assuming superior court position. Dare the other guy to pop off a winner, to get it past you. Then he'll feel pressured. The odds are in your favor that the more quickly you come to the net, your opponent won't be able to produce a winning shot.

In the last six or seven years of my career on the main tour, I won some good tournaments that way. Six years after I won the

South African Open, in the same location, I was 31 years old and won another event there, the Peugeot Open. I won that tournament with smoke and mirrors! I beat Colin Dowdswell in the final. I was glad he had beaten Guillermo Vilas in the semis as I didn't think I could beat Vilas. Any shot Dowdswell would hit, no matter what it was, I would always come to the net. Sometimes the older guys are not more fit than the younger ones—we're just smarter. We've been around longer and know all the tricks.

It was because of strategies like these that I came to believe my very best weapon on the court was my mind. So what happened when that started to disintegrate? In 1974, I beat John Alexander of Australia to win the 1974 CBS Tennis Classic in Austin. The day after the final, we were both in the same courtesy vehicle on our way to the airport. Even though I won the tournament, I must have been going through some depression, because I remember we were talking about my emotions. His theory was that my negative emotions had something to do with the fact that I sweat a lot. I didn't really buy that argument. Still, I didn't seek help.

I can honestly say that the depression was less tied to losing matches than to losing skills. It's not that losing matches didn't affect my depression in the mid- to late 1970s. Of course I didn't like to lose! Even beyond alcohol, my drug of choice was winning. I liked that feeling of alleviating my anxieties. I was always looking for a way to solve underconfidence. I was always needing to prove myself again. It became very difficult once I wasn't having as much success in the latter stages of my career. I wish I could have stayed at my peak longer, like maybe for 12 out of 15 years. Instead, for the last six years I played the regular tour, I knew I wasn't really at my best. The tournament losses just compounded the depression I was already feeling due to loss of skills.

Anything that is important to you, if you lose it, can result in at least some form of Post-Traumatic Stress Disorder. You re-enact the trauma of loss. Something most people don't understand is that you don't have to be a soldier in a war to come back from certain life experiences with PTSD.

If you operate on somebody's eye, that's more stressful than a match at Wimbledon. So you could say that I'm under less stress than most people. But the problem is, I don't assimilate stress in the same way. Stress can take many forms: moving residences, changing jobs, perhaps losing a girlfriend or a wife. People who have depression don't react normally to those things. I don't want people to think, "Oh, poor Cliff." I don't have a stressful life. I'm under less stress than many people I know. It's not the stress *per se*, but how you handle it that counts.

Also, you would think stress is stress, but it's not. What kind of stress are you talking about? I handle very well the stress of a tournament. But other people handle the everyday stresses better than I do. When you prepare to do battle that many times, and your cortisol levels get that high, the aftermath stays with you the rest of your life. Once that cortisol pumps through your system for the 900th match, it's like your shock absorbers just get worn out. You can hardly handle any stress at all.

I usually did handle tournament stress reasonably well. Of course, there are always some factors you can't control—like the crowd. The only time I felt like the people in the stands were a factor were those times in Davis Cup when the home crowd cheered my errors. That often happened in Mexico, Ecuador or Brazil. That was not kosher to do in tennis, ever. But they were more like soccer crowds than typical tennis crowds—unruly and rude. As much as you try to block out the crowd, you're still aware of it and know that the fans might become a factor.

In November of 1966, I won the South American Championship and the Argentine Championship combined (at that time they were one and the same tournament). Then I defended my South American Championship title in the fall of 1967. Once again, I was successful. Then a few weeks later I was playing in Porto Alegre on the center court. Something happened in that match. The crowd became a little upset. I heard some sarcastic comments in Portuguese coming from the stands right above and behind me. I said something derogatory under my breath, but evidently loud enough for people to hear it. When I got to the locker room, I was told by the tournament committee not to leave the building for a while because there were people out there who wanted to do me harm. So the crowd is definitely a "wild card" in all of this, a factor not necessarily within your control.

I never had nightmares about being in front of a crowd. Even when my career took a downturn and I became more tentative with the physical side of my game, I never feared playing in front of people. I never worried that I would go out and embarrass myself. You know you have to get up for it and try to do a good job. The crowd is just a part of the scene.

The exception to the rule is when somebody like Ilie Nastase, who can speak 11 languages, would seduce the crowd and turn them against you. Nastase used to mock me and really play to the crowds. He made fun of the grunting and groaning sounds I made when I hit a ball. He got the crowd to start laughing at me. The occasion I remember the most came when he taunted me in Paris at the Masters in December of 1971. He had the crowd on his side, outright laughing at me. He was mimicking the way I acted. He turned it into a complete sideshow.

When I got off the court, I went into the locker room. I asked Zeljko Franulovic, "When a guy pulls something like that, what are you supposed to do?" He said, "You should have jumped the net and attacked him." I was always known as a bit of a bad boy, but I never did anything like that!

In January of 1972, a few weeks later, we played a tournament at the Royal Albert Hall in London. Clark Graebner played Nastase in the semis and I played the other semifinal match against Lew Hoad. Graebner did not like the way Nastase was acting and actually crossed the net to get in Ilie's face in a threatening manner and said, "You will not treat me the way you treated Richey in Paris!" All of a sudden, Nastase defaulted the match. When reporters asked why, he said, "Graebner frightened me." In instances like that, yeah, man, you bet—you really do feel like you're being thrown to the lions.

Depression is like a tennis match. There are some factors you can control, and others that you can't. Depression is both genetic and acquired. I like to use the skin cancer analogy. You can be genetically predisposed to depression. It's like having fair skin. But then additionally, through life circumstances or interests, you come under a lot of stress. That's like being exposed to the sun. An investment banker with fair skin who works in a high-rise all day long probably won't develop skin cancer. But a roofer (of whatever complexion) probably will. It's a genetic predisposition. But anybody can develop it. It also has to do with nurture early on and life circumstances—whatever mix you happen to be dealt with all of those.

In tennis, you learn to limit the unpredictability of it all by concentrating on the factors you can control. I couldn't control my leg muscles' cramping. They would get so bad, so painful, that I literally would have a hard time walking. There were players who would use that as an excuse. I was never like that. Rather than use cramps as a cop-out, one of my incentives for training as hard as I did was to prevent them from happening. I used to run two or three miles a day in addition to tennis workouts. I did that for 25 years. The main thing I learned from Harry Hopman, the Aussie Davis Cup team captain, was that you need to be so fit physically that you can play as well in the fifth set as you did in the first. That, at least, is something you can control.

Likewise, you can show up early for a tournament to adjust to the climate, the altitude, and the court surface. One week you might play at high altitude. Then the very next tournament might be at sea level. In that case, you have to adapt in reverse. Everything feels slower and heavier. You feel like you're running through water. That's what happened to me right after I won the South African Open. The next tournament after that was on clay in Charlotte, North Carolina. You tend to have longer points on clay anyway. You stay at the baseline longer. You play longer rallies. Also, in that climate, there was more heat and humidity. So I had several conditions conspiring against me that week. I lost to Ken Rosewall in the final.

The other factor that week, of course, was psychological. I was coming down off a really big win. There's a certain manic high to that. Once again, there I was, flying pretty high. I was playing at high altitude, having a heady experience! After that it was time to go back to the U.S.—in essence, to come back down to earth.

There are some specific psychological pitfalls to which athletes are more prone. It's dangerous to get too high after a good performance or too low after a bad one. Any good coach will tell you: "Stay away from extreme emotions. They are a trap." Unfortunately, the sports world promotes that "extreme" type of thinking.

You would think that your self defenses or human instincts, some sort of internal guidance system, would steer you away from things that are particularly stressful. But it's just the opposite. It's like a magnet. Like how once you have been abused, you're attracted to abusive people. At some deep, subconscious level, I had to know that putting myself right back into the crucible of competition was bad for my fragile mental health. But once you've tasted the drug of winning, it's almost like gambling. Even when the odds of success are lower, you still want to try. It's very, very hard to give that up.

Losses hit me even worse because of the negativity of depression. Dick Savitt, one of the old-time tennis greats, won Wimbledon in 1952, but shortly after that, he told Dad that he found his losses were starting to hurt him too badly. He found himself sitting in the stands after a match, in a trance. He knew at that moment that it was time to get out of the game. He went into the oil business down in Houston. That was probably a very wise decision.

In contrast, Jimmy Connors is a pit fighter. He likes the action. He loves to get out there and knock heads. Losing doesn't seem to bother him much. I admire his attitude. He understands that you have to let go of that previous high.

Paradoxically, as a competitor, you almost want to feel a little more down to get back to that neediness of winning again. Provided I didn't get too low, I always felt more comfortable going into a tournament feeling agitated, anxious, or even melancholy. It scared me if I went into a tournament feeling manic and on top of the world. I didn't play as good that way. I played better from the valley perspective, not from the very top of the mountain. I needed to go through the process of climbing the hill. If you start off at the top, where the hell do you go from there? The only place you can go is to fall off.

My guess is that I've got some manic depression too. I would say I'm about 70 percent clinically depressed and perhaps 30 percent manic depressive. I haven't gone out and spent $100,000 in three days or tried to convince people I was the king of some new province in Texas. But sometimes I was very affectionate. Then, suddenly, I would go stone-cold.

Depression is not a disease that when it strikes, you are forever after not normal at all. It comes at you in waves. Other times, you actually feel pretty good. It goes in cycles. I think I have a little bipolar in me. I remember saying to my doctor that with the kind of career I had, I wasn't the best father in the world. That probably had something to do with the down periods of my depression. He said, "Yes, but look what you've accomplished during your upswings." So I don't have too many regrets.

The manic phases of my life were very creative. I would be riding the crest of this "up" mood. I remember one of those stretches, where I won 16 out of 17 matches. It was an incredible train of success. The downswing, provided it didn't get too far down, could act as a big motivator to win. But if I'm in a particularly good mood, I tend to be leery of that. I know it's likely that I'm going to crash.

Depression and mania are like horrible magnifications of what everyone feels. Those two extremes are exaggerated to such an extent that you're miserable (and everyone else around you is miserable, too!). It's like playing tennis at high altitude and then dropping back down to sea level. You're moving in slow motion. You're in the twilight zone.

There would come a point when I felt like I couldn't pull myself out of it. It was like I just couldn't speed back up again. My old strategies to compensate just didn't seem to work any more. I had not only lost my backhand, my No. 1 ranking, and my WCT contract. I knew I was starting to lose my mind.

CHAPTER TWELVE

Bull in a China Closet

Everyone on the tour had a nickname. Ken Rosewall's was "Muscles" since he didn't have any. Rod Laver was known as simply "The Rocket." Bob Carmichael used to be a carpenter, so we called him "Nail Bags" (Nails for short). Pancho Gonzalez became "Gorgo" after he won a title people thought he didn't deserve. So after that, he was the "Cheese Champion" (for Gorgonzola cheese).

My nickname on the tour was "Bull." Around 1966, Lew Gerard from New Zealand said kiddingly one day, "You play like the wild bull of the Pampas." It just kind of stuck. Frew McMillan at one point sent a letter to me. It was addressed to Mr. Cliff Richey, O.B.E. (Order of the Bull Empire). One time I called him up to do a mock telephone interview as a practical joke. When he caught on, he burst out, "Is this the bloody Bullock?"

The sports writers must have heard the name "Bull" and assumed it was short for something else. Howard Carr, writing for the *San Francisco Chronicle*, once described me as "a San Angelo, Texas native who looks like a husky Mickey Rooney and plays a little like an unchained bulldog." That was because I was usually wild-eyed, loud-voiced, and foaming at the mouth. There really was an awful lot of truth to that moniker. I was the bull tearing through the china closet of the genteel game of tennis.

When I was a kid, I broke some tennis racquets during my tantrums. I would get frustrated. I threw them across the court. There have been a lot of tennis players who, in their youth, have thrown racquets. Believe it or not, even Björn Borg once did! He learned his lesson when his parents told him he couldn't play any more. What finally taught me was that I ruined a few. Once those wooden racquets cracked, they couldn't be repaired. My dad's old pupil Tut Bartzen sold tennis racquets for Wilson. He was the one who got me my first free racquet. I was doing real good in the kids' division. (You really weren't supposed to accept free equipment to remain eligible for interscholastic tournaments, but everybody did it anyway.) Tut found out I had broken that racquet. He and Dad both said, "If you ever break another racquet, you won't get any more free ones." So I stopped breaking racquets because I wanted the freebies.

I used to yell and scream on the court. I shouted some curse words occasionally but I was never known as a vulgar person. I didn't use obscene hand gestures. I just tended to berate the linesmen. Often I would have some linesmen removed. If they made enough bad calls during a match, you could ask that they be replaced. Very rarely would I go after the guy I was playing against. That would have been too negative. I did stuff that just wore on my opponent, like taking time to argue a line call. I was like John McEnroe, or, more accurately, he was like me. In fact, we were compared to each other with some frequency. People used to say I sort of invented his whole routine. I was known (not so) affectionately as the "Original Bad Boy" of tennis.

If things weren't going my way, sometimes I would even yell at the whole crowd. One time I was playing Frank Froehling in a tournament final in Milwaukee. He started to loop big high shots up to throw off my tempo. We called them moon balls. He did that on every point! The crowd, which totaled about 3,000, starting laughing and carrying on. I yelled, "Shut up, goddammit!" And they knew I

I may look innocent in this Jantzen Sportswear promotional photo, but my wild-eyed, loud-voiced "bad boy" behavior helped earn me the nickname "The Bull."

was talking to them.

I've also been known to tear up the court. I performed some pretty bad antics. There was an incident in Washington, D.C. on a clay court when I ripped up a line. It was a public park. They had synthetic tape lines nailed down without the best maintenance in the world. When I was playing Andrés Gimeno from Spain, I slid on the clay into the shot. My foot caught on the tape, which wasn't secured properly. I could have twisted my ankle or hurt myself badly. I got so mad that I reached down and ripped up the line. I just tore it right off! There were nails flying everywhere. We had to stop playing. I felt kind of bad about it later. I had just done it instinctively. I didn't really think about what would happen. I offered to default the match. That would have been the fair thing to do. But Andrés said, "No, let's play." They called the repair guys. It took them 20 minutes to repair the line. Andrés ended up beating me anyway. After all that, I figured he deserved to win!

There was only one time when I actually went after my opponent. It was in January of 1970, in Ft. Lauderdale, Florida. We were at Chris Evert's dad's club, a public facility. Jimmy Evert had called me and asked if I would play. I was playing against Clark Graebner and, as I remember, I wanted some ball boys or umpires to move out of my line of vision. Clark thought that was an unreasonable request. He said something to me. I got so mad, I went after him with my tennis racquet! I told him, "If you want a piece of me, I'm right here." The local newspaper printed a picture of me "attacking" him the next day.

Another incident came at the Foro Italico in Rome at the Italian Championships. The Romans were known to be a pretty tough crowd, but they were also a funny crowd. I played one of their great old players, Beppe Merlo. He used to string his racquets real loose. You could hardly hear the ball coming off the strings. That's tough to play against, because you use sound in tennis to gauge how good a shot your opponent has just hit. That's why someone who grunts a lot on purpose is almost cheating. In the beginning of the match, it was nothing but "Bello, Beppe" and "Bravo, Merlo." He was kind of an unorthodox player. He had a very different style. I reached a stage in that match where I was two sets to love down. I was a little disgusted with the whole situation and actually "pulled a Nastase." I had no idea it would work. Beppe had a funny way of hitting his backhand which I started mimicking between points. The crowd loved it—they ate it up. They loved the theatre. Sure enough, I came back and won in five sets! I felt sort of bad about my behavior afterward. That was really a disrespectful thing to do, but all I cared about was winning. Beppe and I actually became friends later on.

Eventually, my antics caught up to me. I did suffer some negative consequences for my behavior. In 1964, I had a year that would have warranted me a top-10 American ranking. Instead, the USTA ranked me No. 11. Mary Hare, a former British player and a tennis insider, told Dad she had it on good authority that because I had gone over and raised hell in Rome that year, they had knocked me down a ranking. They did it as a punishment for poor behavior in Europe. I still think it would have been more fair to give me the ranking I deserved, but suspend me from playing for a month or two. I was successful, but they went out of their way to knock me down. I'm upset by some of that stuff to this day.

I can see where people thought I was a little over the top, though. Heck, I was well-nigh incorrigible! Another time when I played at the Spectrum in Philadelphia against Phil Dent from Australia, the crowd was getting on my case for complaining against some line calls. I was not the most pleasant person to play that day. I ended up winning the match. After I shook hands with Dent at the net, I put my racquet down and walked back out on the court. I then showed my rear end (not bare) to the crowd on all four sides of the court. It was a fully-clothed moon—to the north, south, east and west. I left my shorts on because I didn't want to get banned from the game permanently. I heard that there was a guy in the 1930s who got himself banned from the game forever for dropping his pants on court! The director of the WCT sent me a letter of reprimand for that.

It was well known among the players that you could get away with less bad behavior in England than in most other countries. England was just so strawberries-and-cream. Wimbledon is the epitome of all that genteel bullshit. But it's the same way throughout Britain. One year, I was playing Arthur Ashe in the semis of the event in Bristol and we split the first two sets. I hit a backhand volley that caught the net tape and bounced back into my court. Incredibly, the exact same thing happened again on the next point! I uttered some curse words right by the umpire's chair. He heard me. He gave me a reprimand. I repeated the same words and then some. He got down off the chair and said, "Mr. Richey, I am defaulting you." In other words, the match was now over.

Arthur just sat down at the back of the court and looked at me. He came into the locker room a few minutes later and said, "Come on, let's go out and finish the match." I said, "You don't understand, he defaulted me." I don't know if that had ever happened before! Back in those days, nobody ever got defaulted.

I showered and changed. Mickie was embarrassed. This tennis club had a bar area with slot machines. I went back to the bar so Mickie and I could have some privacy. I was sitting there, trying to explain to Mickie what had happened and the next thing I knew, there was a TV crew with cameras filming us through the window! They were in the back alley. I got up from the chair and ran outside. I grabbed one of the TV crew's cameras and was about to smash it to the ground. Luckily, Herbie Fitzgibbon happened to be standing there. He grabbed the camera, held me still, and said, "Bull, I wouldn't do that if I were you." It's probably a good thing he was there.

The next day, you would have thought I had killed somebody. It was on the front page of all the papers. England was a place where tennis was seen as this little gentleman's sport. Donald Dell, our Davis Cup captain at the time, happened to fly in from the States the next day. He contacted me and said he had already talked to everybody at the club. I told him my side of the story. In my defense, there were some other people who also thought the umpire had overreacted. That pretty much jived with what he had heard. He said, "I've told them it would be a good gesture, to diffuse this, if you would act as a linesman in the final match." I said, "I'd be happy to." That day I got a taste of my own medicine. I got to see how tough it can be to call some of those lines. You're out there calling 120-mile-per-hour shots. Serves are usually the most difficult to call. And it's harder to call lines on grass, because the painted lines bleed. But I did such a good job that neither of the players could find fault with any of my calls.

The next week at Wimbledon, I played against Dennis Ralston in the second round. It was eight all in the fifth set and the base linesman foot-faulted me. He said my foot was touching the line. Everybody thought that linesman had it in for me because of what had happened the week before. But I kept my cool completely and didn't even react. I had already worn out my welcome that year with the Brits!

Looking back on it now, I'll be my own critic. It was wrong to mouth off. Some of that stuff did not help me play better. I invited the negative repercussions that followed. The moral of that story is: if you do act the way I did, you're leaving yourself wide open to criticism.

My reputation on the tour was controversial. I was difficult to get along with for other players and officials. However, that was off-set by a general feeling that I would always give it everything I had. If I lost respect from some of the guys who thought I stepped over the ethical line at times, I gained respect on the other hand because I never, ever, ever, quit. Even my detractors respected me for that.

The tennis officials didn't all dislike me, either. There were people who secretly got a kick out of it every time I raised hell. They never knew what I would do next. It was like a wrestling match. People need some grit. The fans want to see that. They were put through an emotional roller coaster every time they watched me play. At least, those were the comments Mickie heard from the stands.

I will say one thing: it wasn't an act. It wasn't a rebellion against anything. I was just mad about getting a bad call. It was actually pretty honest. That's what people liked about watching me—the genuine emotion. What you see is what you get. Or so it appeared.

I remember one comment from when I was about 14. We were getting ready to move from San Angelo to Dallas. It was May or June of 1961. I was two years into my career already, but still only in the eighth grade in school. I had been playing some junior tennis in the San Angelo area. During those matches, to put it mildly, I let it all hang out—temper tantrums and what not. People in San Angelo knew that we were moving. We were going to Dallas so Dad could take a job at Brook Hollow. It wasn't the first time we had moved to a big city. But San Angelo thought so. Brook Hollow was a fancy country club. A person came up to me and said, "When you get to Dallas, try not to embarrass your parents like you have here in San Angelo."

What that person didn't realize was that, fortunately for me, Dad's sixth sense told him not to "tone me down" or beat the fight out of me. In fact, in a vicarious way, he used to enjoy it when I raised hell on the court. I was sticking it to the very people he wanted to rebel against. His tolerance in this area was in line with the rest of his coaching philosophy. Dad used to say he'd rather have a student with a temper because that meant he really cared whether he won or lost. He could work with that. What he couldn't do was generate a killer instinct that wasn't there. Because of my "fight," because of my temper, when a match was on the line or I was hopelessly down, from his perspective, I was actually better off.

You can use anger to get you where you need to go. Dad used to tease me. He always said, "You'd have been better off if I'd sent you to a military academy." He used to call me a ring-tail tooter. But he wasn't serious. If you take a bucking bronco to the rodeo, before you get there, you don't want to break it entirely. It's not such a bad thing to keep at least a touch of that natural fire.

I became known as the angry young Texan. I didn't try to present an angry image to the world, but I did want people to think that any time they played me, they were in for a battle—that they were going to have a tussle on their hands. Dad sort of trained me to carry myself in a certain manner. In any relationship, he felt, one person would naturally dominate. His philosophy was that you can control those roles from early on. In a match, we used to spin our racquets to see who would serve first. If it was a Wilson racquet, it would have a W on the end. We would call either W or M (for upside down W). It's the tennis equivalent of flipping a coin and calling heads or tails. I used to assume authority by taking charge of that situation. I'd walk out and say "Call the racquet." I wouldn't wait for the other guy to initiate that. I tried to project dominance and strength. You have to, really. You know it's going to be a cock fight out there.

In my defense, I wasn't always a sore loser or a bad sportsman. I suffered a bad loss in 1971 against Rosewall at Wimbledon in the quarters, after having a couple of match points. The match is considered one of the best ever at Wimbledon and is included in Steve Flink's book *The Greatest Tennis Matches of the Twentieth Century* as one of the 40 greatest tennis matches of all time. We were playing on Wimbledon's Centre Court in front of a standing-room-only crowd of 15,000 people in the stands. There was an electronic scoreboard outside the stadium with several hundred more people standing there and watching the score. After each point, the crowd would roar. Then, after a short delay when the score was changed on the outside scoreboard, there would be another loud reaction from the fans outside the stadium. It was almost like an echo. It felt very weird. After four and a half long hours, I lost 6-8, 5-7, 6-4, 9-7, 7-5. Even though it was a heartbreaker of a loss, I jumped the net to go shake Rosewall's hand. Usually you only do that if you win, but I wanted to be the first to acknowledge that we had just played a great match.

So my conduct was not always unsportsmanlike. That ought to mitigate my Bad Boy reputation somewhat. But as Dennis Ralston used to say (he was also labeled a Bad Boy): once that label sticks, you could carry roses onto the court for your opponent, but it wouldn't matter—you would still be called a Bad Boy.

Temperamentally, I'm a hyper A-type. I'm a highly competitive person by genes. And then on top of that, I had the environment of Richey, Inc. I just wanted to win so badly. In those days, I didn't spend a lot of time trying to figure out how I came across to other people. I didn't care. I only had one desire: to win as many tennis matches as possible. To prove to the world that I deserved to be on the tour, once I got there. If I got a bad line call, I complained about it. If the crowd turned against me, I'd let them know. If anything, I wanted more commotion. That was fun. It was like, "I dare you. You're going to hear from me. "

If you think about it, the tennis court was my office—except that I didn't have the luxury of transacting business behind closed doors. The tennis player is just trying not to get screwed out there. Sometimes he feels like the linesman is giving him bad calls. I didn't usually go after my opponent. It wasn't malicious. It just happened so quickly in the pure heat of the moment.

In all honesty, it also comes down to a question of strategy. I was known as fiery on the tennis court, but I was not a hothead, really. "Hothead" implies that you can lose your cool when it matters. I never did that. The toughest moments in a match were when I was calmest. I was very composed. I did not purposely try to break my opponent's concentration. I just complained about line calls to break

Ken Rosewall (left) and I walk off Centre Court at Wimbledon after he beat me in an epic quarterfinal match in 1971.

up the rhythm of a match—to create a different flow out there. To change the tempo. Maybe that was a little over the line.

A tennis match has a natural flow to it. It has a certain cadence. The match almost takes on a rhythm of its own. Instinctively, I would cause a distraction to break up that rhythm—to try to change the hue of that match. In junior tennis, you would always break after the second set. In men's tennis, it was after the third. You could go for 10-20 minutes to the locker room, change clothes, even take a shower if you wanted to. If one of the players wanted to go in and take that break, then both of them had to take it. Conversely, if both players wanted to continue, then they could keep on playing. The smart players would always try to use the breaks strategically.

The same principle was at work with trying to challenge a line call. Pancho Gonzalez used to advise intimidating the linesmen because if you challenge them on a call, even if you don't prevail in that specific instance, you might influence them later to judge in your favor. Basically you're out there playing a little mind game. At the latter stages of a match, I would often instinctively get into it with the umpire or start a discussion. It wasn't a plot. More like instinct. It probably wasn't the "good sportsman" thing to do.

To be fair, I also wasn't as bad as some of the other guys. I remember a good Italian player named Fausto Gardini was playing a match somewhere in Europe and was unhappy about everything. He went over to the side of the court, put his racquet in the racquet cover, went over and took the net down, shoved it under his arm and left the court! I never did anything like that.

The most notorious Bad Boy of us all was without question Ilie Nastase. His nickname was "Nasty" because of the dirty tricks he pulled. I remember one match where he wore a T-shirt under his regular collared shirt and when he got mad at the crowd, he lifted up the first shirt to reveal his T-shirt with a picture of the infamous middle finger. He was literally saying "F you" to the crowd! I really think Nastase enjoyed the carnival atmosphere more than anything else. I think that was his way of escaping the pressure. He would take a situation and make it into something he felt more comfortable with. That way he could pretend he was in control. He won the French Open and the U.S. Open that way. He was known as the Clown Prince of Tennis.

Nastase is still a good friend of mine, but there was a time when we didn't speak to each other for a full year. During one match we played, the base linesman called a foot fault on his serve. Nasty kicked his shoe off at the linesman. I was waiting for him. He pretended that he couldn't untie the knot to get his shoe back on.

I finally said to the umpire, a guy named Hague Twofink, "I'm not putting up with this. The rule says 'continuous play.' I'm claiming the match." I took all my stuff and went back to the locker room. I already started talking to reporters about claiming the match. My host that week, Bernie Koteen, came to get me and said, "You'd better go out there. They're about to default you." So I went back out on the court and told Twofink, "I'll play, but his foot fault stands. He only has one serve left. If he doesn't put the ball in play within 10 seconds, I'm leaving. I don't care who you give the match to." Twofink agreed. He announced that Nastase would have 10 seconds to serve. Nastase refused. The crowd started counting down: "10, 9, 8," etc. Nasty never put the serve in play and was defaulted.

One player who was emphatically not a Bad Boy was Arthur Ashe. In fact, he was the antithesis of all that. He was black, grew up in the late 1950s and early '60s, and played tennis, which was at that time a white man's game. His coach, a man named Walter Johnson, trained him to just sit back and take every bad call without saying a word about it. He told him not to be obtrusive, stick out like a sore thumb or become a "controversial" black man (whatever that is). Arthur always handled things really well. He was known as a gentleman on the court—and off the court too. But we all knew that if he had dared to rock the boat, he would have been destroyed by malicious racists who thought he didn't belong there in the first place. As my roommate, Arthur was always intrigued by me because I made so many waves. I could get away with stuff that he would never have been able to.

For our era, the stuff we pulled must have seemed pretty bad, but our antics would have been more accepted in a different sport. Tennis isn't like football or baseball. If you look at baseball—the classic American pastime—it's a well-established tradition to complain about umpires' calls. People would almost be disappointed if you didn't! Those baseball guys, they scratch their crotch. They chew tobacco. They stream vulgarities. They're covered with dirt.

But tennis—now, that's a different story. You're supposed to sip tea with your opponent after it's over. And don't you dare complain about a line call! That's not in the spirit of the game.

In fact, in baseball, hockey, and all the other big sports, there's not a year that goes by that fights don't break out between opponents—and occasionally even among teammates! In ice hockey, the saying goes, the fans came to see a fight—and oh, by the way, a hockey game broke out. In other sports, cursing is the standard. It's actually considered a part of the fabric of athletics. So taking all that into consideration, I ask: what did I ever do that was so bad? I wouldn't have been called a Bad Boy in any other sport. It was only because tennis was such an upper-crust game. When I first started, all the tennis players carried whitener with them in their bags. It was considered lack of decorum to walk out on the court if your tennis shoes were not perfectly white! I didn't like all this prim and proper bullshit. We were actually almost timid compared to other sports. I was always proud of the fact that I brought a little more manliness to the game.

Was my Bad Boy image, at least in part, a creation of the media? It's true, they loved to report all that crap. I was out there raising Cain, doing unusual things. I got unbelievable press coverage. I loved every minute of it. So in a sense you could say I courted the media, but I didn't really do it for that reason. I never debased myself by cozying up to them. One time I got mad at a reporter from the New York *Daily News*, Mike Lupica, who credited my win over Laver in 1972 at the U.S. Open to Laver having a bad back. I started out the next news conference by saying, "Where is that reporter? I want to talk to him!" So I wasn't out to make any friends, reporters included. I just got a lot of press coverage because of the way I was.

Looking back, it's also probably indicative of how much the game has changed. The code of conduct was instituted for tennis after my era. (Who knows? Maybe they had to institute one because of me!) Once the code came in, they started taking points off for prohibited actions. Profanity was one. Guys like Connors and McEnroe would still utter profanities, but they would cover their mouths to muffle it so no one could understand the words. It was actually quite humorous the two times I played McEnroe, considering that I was almost over the hill at that point, while he was still a young kid. The first time was in September of 1977 at the Cow Palace in San Francisco. It was one set all, and he began to pull his *shtick*: going after the linesman, challenging the call, the whole usual tirade. Amused, I just sat back for a while and watched. Finally I got tired of waiting. My muscles were getting cold. I shouted, "John, for Pete's sake, show some respect. You got nothing on me. I'm the Original Bad Boy! Let's just get on with the match." Suddenly he looked like a child who'd been chastened by an elder. He straightened up right away!

Three months later I played him again in the final of the Bahamas Open. Before the match I said, "Let's make a deal. I won't challenge the line calls if you won't." He agreed. We split the first two sets and got to 3-3 in the third. He got a call he didn't like. He jumped the net, stormed over to my side of the court, and was about to start challenging the call. I cuffed him and said: "Get back over there. We had a deal." Meekly, he put his tail between his legs and went right back over to his side of the court! Eventually I went on to win the match.

I love McEnroe. We see eye to eye on a lot of things. I may have beaten him on the court that day, but that didn't keep us from being soul mates through the years. That match was like "Original Bad Boy meets Junior Bad Boy," the tennis equivalent of "Madonna meets Britney Spears."

My bad behavior carried over into life off the court. I was hell for my Davis Cup teammates to be around. Herbie Fitzgibbon used to complain that I washed my mouth out by the side of the court and spit out the water on all the racquets with gut strings, thereby

145

ruining them. In fact, my teammates used to take turns rooming with me because I was such a pain. In every hotel room, I used up all the towels.

Speaking of towels, I destroyed a few of those too. Down in Perth, Australia in November of 1975, I did a several-week tour while hanging out with Dino Martin, Dean Martin's son. We went out to dinner one night in the hotel restaurant, but when we arrived, the host told me I had to have a neck tie on to enter the restaurant. Dino already had a tie on. He was smart enough to know better. Undeterred, I went back up to my room, took a pair of scissors, and cut up a hand towel from the bathroom. I went downstairs, wearing the towel as a neck tie! I smiled at the *maître de*. Technically, he had to let me in. We both knew he was stuck. He got me back, though. Several days later, when I checked out of the hotel, I was going over my bill. I saw this $7 "miscellaneous" charge. I asked at the front desk what that charge was for. They said "that's to pay for the towel you cut up." What could I say? I tucked my tail between my legs and paid the bill.

During those years, I was just pretty much a poster boy for bad behavior. There were times I had too much to drink, and someone would tell me later I had done something that I couldn't even remember. In Paris in the early 1970s, I got drunk one night and evidently borrowed the equivalent of $50 cash in French francs from Nail Bags Carmichael. He came up to me later and said, "Hey Bull, you owe me 50 bucks." I thought he was kidding. I was so drunk, I had no recollection of that! I ended up paying him, though. It certainly sounded plausible enough.

In 1975, I played a WCT tournament in Ft. Worth. The WCT guys had a trainer there named Bill Norris. I could never remember his name, so I started calling him Norton. I was in his room at the hotel, where we started tipping a few beers. I had lost in the tournament already and was due to fly back to San Angelo, so I carried on more than usual. At one point, I got up on one of the beds and started trying to pee into a beer bottle. Needless to say, I did not do a very good job so there was urine all over the floor. I fell asleep in his room that night and we both missed our flights the next morning. Poor Mickie didn't even know where I was. She put up with a lot of shit from me.

The next tournament was in Toronto. Norris looked at me and said, "By the way, you owe me $75." I asked, "Why is that?" He said, "Remember that night in Ft. Worth? One of us threw a lamp out the window. I don't remember if it was me, but they sent me a bill for $150. How about if I split it with you?" I couldn't remember who it was either, so I just paid him the money.

That wasn't the only hotel room I wrecked. In September of 1973, I played a very young Jimmy Connors in Boston at the Longwood Cricket Club. We both made it to the quarterfinals on Friday, but then both of our matches got rained out, so we had to double up on Saturday and play both the quarters and the semis. That way the tournament could still end on Sunday, as planned. He and I both won our first matches—his win was easy; mine was tough—so we were scheduled to play each other four hours later. I went back to the hotel to rest but when I opened the door to my room, all my stuff was gone! I went down to the front desk and asked what had happened. They explained apologetically that the hotel was oversold, so Jimmy and I would have to share a room that night. They had taken the liberty of moving all my belongings to his room! Not knowing what to do, I took the new key and let myself in. He wasn't there. I had been there not more than 10 minutes when I realized: this just wasn't going to work. We had to play each other four hours later. The last thing we needed to do was try to make small talk or have a chitty-chat. I went back to the front desk and asked them to move me to our road manager's room instead. They gave me his key, so I let myself into that room and sacked out on the bed. I was dehydrated from my first match, which had lasted three hours. I had been drinking some beer and some Gatorade (in no particular order). I guess that combination made my stomach a little upset. I felt like maybe I had to pass gas when suddenly, I found myself swimming in my own shit! I had just crapped all over the guy's bed! I was so tired, all I could manage to do was to clean myself off and go get in the other bed. By the time I woke up, I had forgotten all about it. I went out and lost to Jimmy, as we both had anticipated I would. In the locker room afterward, the road manager came up to me. "Hey, Cliff," he said, "I'm sorry you broke your hand." It had been a crazy day already. Now I thought I was hearing things! I asked, "What on earth do you mean?" He said, "I figured you had to have broken your hand since you couldn't pick up the phone to call the maid to come clean up that mess!"

Now, this many years later, I can see that my antics—both on and off the court—really were a reflection of emotional distress. I always lived a little on the edge with my nervous structure. I got a kick out of bringing some rough and tumble to the game. But the bottom line was, I played with a lot of emotion—and a lot of heart. That helped me play better because I cared about it so much. I channeled my temper into a weapon on the court.

I guess I got kind of lucky in the sense that my lack of social skills actually rewarded me in competition. I was totally oblivious to social norms. The less aware of yourself you can be in an important situation, the better you're gonna do. Fluidity, lack of self-consciousness, being in that creative bubble—it's that "zone" people talk about.

I was not self-aware. I didn't care what people thought. As Nastase used to say, I was an "Animal." Normal socialization I never had. It's like the guy who gets out of prison after 50 years. How's he gonna blend into society? He's never been there.

Ironically, I might have looked like I was in a fiery, angry mood when in fact I was just flat sad. I scare people. I'm aware of that. I always projected an air of toughness and combativeness. I gave off an aura of strength. Like, "You don't want to mess with me." And some of that came when I was at my weakest! What they didn't know was, it was purely self-defense.

It's kind of funny, because in the case of either my opponents or the crowds who used to watch me, if they had heard I was really running on abnormal fear, they would not have believed it. What they perceived as arrogance was really my response to being scared. What you see is not always what you get.

I think a lot of people thought that, since I had dropped out of school, I was just totally committed to tennis. They knew I spent many long hours on the practice court. There was this perception among the people I played against that I must have really been in love with the game. I did love the game of tennis, but the reality was also that I was never a very confident person. My motivation was, at times, too much a fear of loss. I wasn't out there on the court all the time doing drills because I loved it so much. I was just out there trying to get my game back!

Some people probably guessed that there was a little bit more going on behind the scenes than they were really very comfortable with. I was never a friendly opponent. I wanted the other guy to be afraid of me. I was happy if that took place. I wasn't interested in being nice to him, or being friends with him. I was only interested in going out there and beating his ass! Mickie used to say I looked like a rabid dog on the court. She said she would have been terrified to play against me. There were times people thought I might be a little unbalanced and somewhat unstable. I wasn't afraid of mixing it up with a competitive fight. They never knew what to expect. I might go into a skyrocket tirade. It's like running into somebody in a dark alley at three in the morning. You're already frightened, but if you know the guy is a little bit nuts, that makes it even more scary!

It might be thought that my antics were subconsciously an attempt to find an acceptably "male" outlet for my distress. But I don't think my court tantrums occured because I was in depression (yet). It was just raw emotional content. Short temper. Low patience. The height of agitation. Even in the years before I felt depressed, I was a very high/low, volatile kind of person. I had the classic personality to be a candidate for emotional disease.

I never did learn how to handle my volatile temperament. I didn't channel my temper off the court in a mature way either. I yelled and screamed at home. Being part Irish may have something to do with it. I don't suppose it helps to have a last name that ends in -ey. But they don't have anger management classes for nothing. That's part of rehabilitating yourself from depression. It's a multi-faceted recovery process. I can still work on improving in those areas.

I've been very deficient in handling what "civilian" life threw at me. I was adept at handling the fires of battle, but it was a lopsided existence. When you've got bad emotional content most of the time, you're going to come across as arrogant or insensitive or a sour puss. I looked like the Sour Dough Boy. It's all wrapped into a big ball of either being in good mental health or not. Nothing else was going on except my trying to fix myself. It wasn't so much arrogance as just plain feeling shitty. I'm not saying there wasn't any cockiness at all. When you become really good at something, you start having a pretty damn high opinion of yourself. But I always thought it was funny when people called me that. If anything, I felt underconfident. I was overcompensating for what I perceived to be a real lack.

If I had it to do over again, I would temper the way I came across to my fellow competitors. I never used to speak to them before I played. Now I realize it's even scarier to be nice before the match, and then hit them full force once you're out on the court.

I'm man enough to say that it probably got out of hand sometimes. I probably was too negative, but that was a weapon too: for them to know how badly I wanted to win. There were even some guys who tried to find excuses to avoid playing me. What they did not know—how could they, since I didn't even know it yet myself?—was that I was really out there on that tennis court, fighting for my frigging life.

CHAPTER THIRTEEN

Gut Strings

I can't believe Dad never taught me how to string my own racquets. That would have taken some of the load off him. He and Mom both knew how to string racquets. Maybe he always liked to be in control. Or maybe we just never asked! Neither Nancy nor I ever learned how to string a racquet. We were probably trying to get away with having somebody else who was willing to do it for us all the time.

But there were times I used to wish I knew how. If I had strung racquets myself, I would have had a better feel for what I wanted. I do know pretty much about it, just from watching Dad do it so often while I was growing up. To string a racquet, you put it in a vise. You use a weighted device to string the racquet to the tension you want. Forty-five pounds is extremely loose; 80 pounds is extremely tight. In the old days, there was no gauge. You went by feel. You could tell how tight it was by the sound. I remember Dad would pluck the strings one by one, just as if he were playing a guitar.

I usually wanted gut strings. The gut was made of lamb intestines. That's why it was so expensive. A set of gut strings cost $15-18, even back in those days. That would be more like $100 today. Most of the time, the racquet companies would give me strings for free. Now most people use synthetic gut. They had it back then too.

But it plays like a bad regular radio compared to a stereo system with speakers!

I would always use thicker, 16-gauge gut for a slower surface. The 17-gauge gut was thinner. I wanted that for a faster surface, like grass. The basic rule was, I wanted a thinner gauge gut and a tightly-strung racquet whenever I had to play on faster courts. But 17-gauge gut was harder to come by. All the top players would stock up on it. Basically, you would buy it immediately if you could ever find it some place.

If I was on the road and needed a racquet strung, and Dad wasn't there to do it for me, I would go into a pro shop and say, "I want my racquets strung at 60 pounds. Show me a racquet you've done at 60 pounds." So many times I'd get the reply: "My gauge is accurate. Why do you need a racquet to see?" They just didn't understand. I was also usually wanting a rush job. And then, when my racquet came back, I used to obsess over the shit job somebody just did for me! If I wasn't happy with the string job, I would just rip it out. And then there would be that dejected look on the guy's face. It broke his heart to watch me take a perfectly good set of gut strings, using a knife or pair of scissors, and cut it out.

A good string job would typically last a week to 10 days. Once a gut string started to fray, you knew it didn't have much life left. You could try to apply a lacquer to it called Gut Life. But then the gut strings felt like nylon strings. What was the point of having gut strings if they felt like synthetic?

A racquet could be restrung several times in the course of its short life. If you popped a string, sometimes you could try a patch job—but it really didn't work. The entire string job would be looser by seven or eight pounds. So then you'd have to restring the whole racquet.

With the move from wooden to graphite racquets in the 1980s, it became easier to get a good string job. Graphite is more consistent than wood because it's a man-made material. Wood can shrink

I was pretty damaged by the time I finally took myself off the tour after the 1978 season. By that point, I had a lot of frayed emotional strings. This tournament in Stowe, Vermont was one of the last events I played on the ATP circuit.

or expand in response to humidity. The other problem with wood was that the more you used a wood racquet, the head would fatigue. There would start to be more flexibility in that racquet head than you could tolerate. Eventually, if you used it long enough, the wooden head would start to crack.

The normal life span of a racquet was a couple of months. Then you'd have to retire it. You couldn't afford to keep playing with it for sentimental reasons. Once a racquet wasn't giving me good service any longer, I had to discard it.

I still have one racquet hanging on the wall that lasted longer than the rest. I won like seven tournaments with that thing! I carved a notch in the handle for each tournament win. It was a Bancroft Player's Special. I framed it. That racquet was a reliable weapon, that's for sure. It's my all-time favorite racquet. With it in my hand, I won the U.S. Indoors in 1968, two South American Championships, and that tournament in Tulsa the year I met Mickie. It was my lucky racquet. What a great feel that racquet had! It was like a Stradivarius violin for a musician.

Looking back, I would compare myself to that long-lasting racquet. It damn sure went for the long haul on stuff. It took a lot of abuse. There were a lot of string jobs done on that racquet, and a lot of strings that snapped! You can tell when your gut strings are starting to get frayed. You can always tell when they're about to snap.

When I finally retired that racquet, it had never cracked. Certain areas of the tennis racquet routinely take more stress than others. So certain places on a racquet are more likely to crack. You could always see on the racquet head where a crack was starting to form. A lot of heads crack! That is the case for both racquet heads and human heads. . .

When a racquet head cracked, you knew then it was time to take it out of service. It was damaged. You wouldn't try to string that racquet again. I was pretty damaged by the time I finally took myself off the tour. By that point, I had a lot of frayed emotional strings.

From 1971 to 1973, I was gradually seeping into depression. Depression is not just "Boom! You've got it. You're a lump of clay all day long. You can't do anything". If you have any other kind of chronic disease, usually that illness can get bad enough to stop you. Depression, in contrast, can just nag at you so that life is miserable, but you can still keep going.

In 1972, I signed a four-year, 104-week performance contract with Lamar Hunt of World Championship Tennis (WCT). It was for $100,000 a year. That was the largest contract of its kind that had ever been signed in tennis up to that point. Dad helped me negotiate the terms. The down side was that WCT could pretty much dictate my schedule. But we negotiated the deal in two different ways that made it impossible for me to turn down: 1) I had a personal contract with Lamar in case WCT, Inc. went bankrupt; and 2) if, even in the first week of the contract, I was permanently injured, WCT still had to pay me all $400,000.

In 1973, I was contracted to play so many tournaments, I hardly knew where I was when I woke up each morning. During one stretch, I played Hilton Head (South Carolina), Atlanta (Georgia), St. Louis (Missouri), Brussels (Belgium), Munich (Germany), Johannesburg (South Africa), and Göteborg (Sweden), one week after the next, with no breaks in between. All in a row! Three continents in seven weeks. That was the worst year of my career on the regular tour. I remember one time when I came back from Australia, I was so fatigued, I thought the door knobs were talking to me. It was like there was music coming out of them. That was from lack of sleep, exhaustion. That's an indication of just how tired I was.

Around about that time, we had started trying to have a baby. Mickie had her first miscarriage in May 1973. It was during that last tournament in Göteborg. She didn't even know she was pregnant. She just started bleeding in the bathtub. That night I was out drinking. I stayed out almost all night. I had just lost a very important match. We didn't know she was pregnant and certainly didn't know she was having a miscarriage. But I wasn't even there. She called one of the other pros, Bob Carmichael, to try to find me. To my shame, she never did succeed. . . .

The next day, I had one roaring hangover. I wouldn't even go to the drugstore to buy her some maxipads. I was AWOL. She didn't want to go to the hospital in a foreign country. She didn't even know how she was going to get on the plane. The bleeding eventually let up, but she still had to wear a wadded-up towel under her clothes during the entire flight home.

By that point, my mood had really started to take a nose dive. I wasn't upset about the miscarriage, although I probably should have been. There wasn't much, unfortunately, that could get to me back then. Nothing could penetrate. I don't think I had the ability to experience empathy. I was just in so much pain myself. That's one of the awful things about depression: you're in such hell, you can't really tune in to other people. You're finding it hard just to get up and motivate yourself to make it through the day.

From 1973-78, I was in a depressive phase of my life that was just horrendous. It was one long blur of constant play-prepare, play-prepare, play-prepare. During my four-year contract, come hell or high water, I had to play the tournaments on the WCT schedule. I withdrew from a few tournaments and blamed it on a fictitious injury. But during those years, I was what you might call a functional depressive. Rod Steiger, the actor, has said that he often hoped no one on the movie set realized how depressed he was. That's what it means to be a functional depressive. You feel shitty, but you just try to continue on with your daily routine.

During that time, I was playing roughly 24-26 weeks a year. That would often include at least three trips to Europe. Lots of jet lag. The stresses and strains of tour life. When I was contemplating going from one city to the next, it didn't give me a warm, fuzzy feeling that I got to go to all these neat places. It didn't help me escape my problems in any way. But it was probably worse being at home, due to the strangeness of our living arrangement. We were still living with my parents four or five months of the year. We had moved out in 1969 to an apartment for a while, but then we moved back because I didn't want to spend a lot of money. So in effect, we lived with them for the first six years of our married life.

There was no privacy. Whereas Mickie admired my family's work ethic—the trophies and pictures on the walls demonstrated our success—there was a price paid in terms of relationships. Nancy and Mickie had some similar interests, such as sewing. Mom and Dad were very kind to her. That was never a problem but it was strange and unnatural not to have a place of our own.

I was very moody. As I became less of a kid and more of a man, my father and I argued a lot. Pro didn't understand how anyone could talk about the love of his life (tennis) in that negative a way. Until the wee hours of the morning, we would have screaming matches about our divergent philosophies on competing. I was disrespectful to my father. There's not a lot of excuse for the things that went on. There's not a lot of white-washing I can do with some of that stuff. The behind-the-scenes dynamic isn't the way people think. There's not a lot I can say to defend myself.

Throughout the later 1970s, there was this constant, low-grade thing that never seemed to leave. It was debilitating. I had chronic anxiety, flaring in spurts into depression. There weren't that many times the stresses were off. I didn't win many tournaments during that period. I was out of sync with everything and everyone. I was just kind of existing and moving from place to place. I was certainly not feeling well-adjusted.

People around me at that stage were not aware I was depressed. I think some of them must have thought my behavior was strange. There were times when I drank too much, and the other guys on the tour knew that. But very rarely could a guy beat me because I got worn out. I was always in excellent shape physically. I imagine they must have wondered why I drank so much, when otherwise I was in such good physical condition. Also, I never wanted to practice early in the morning because I was having real problems sleeping. They might have wondered about that too. But nobody knew I was depressed, because I didn't even know it back then. I didn't know it or own it at that time.

Dad could detect some of my grandfather (Dadda) in me. He always thought I would turn out an alcoholic like his father because I was like him temperamentally. Dad thought alcoholism was a sign of weakness. He always thought his father could have quit if he had been strong enough. Dad was a textbook case of the child of an alcoholic.

I was aware of this theory of his, so I didn't want Mom and Dad to know that I drank too much. I hid that from them. I knew that inside the value system of Richey, Inc. that was a wrong thing to do. That may have been one of the reasons I finally moved out of their house. In 1973, the same year we moved out, my drinking really began to go full force. That's the time I would say it went from normal partying to self-medicating with alcohol. It was a gradual thing, but it got worse over the next six or seven years. I really looked forward to drowning my sorrows with booze. I was a mess. It was hellacious. I was in this black, gray fog I wouldn't wish on my worst enemy.

Like the strings on a racquet, my internal strings were stretched taut. We both reached a point where we began to get frayed. You might wear out gut strings faster on a clay court because the clay particles wear on the strings. But often there's no real reason why one set of strings lasts longer than another. Depression is like that. You're never sure exactly what causes the worst wear and tear or what it is precisely that causes you to snap.

At first on the tour, if somebody had foretold that I would have such problems with depression, I wouldn't have believed it. I was a darned good set of gut! But there were times, almost unpredictably, that I started to fray and break.

They say the average age of onset for unipolar depression is 27 years. Looking back, I was real close to that age. The beginning phases of my first battle happened at 24 or 25. But I did not go into *bona fide* clinical depression until 1973—the year I turned 26.

I had terrible problems with insomnia. On the tour, particularly during the indoor season, you might get off the court real late, as late as 1:30 AM. And the only time you could practice was before the next day's session started. I remember one night in Virginia when I did not sleep at all, period. I used to pace the halls of hotels at night sometimes when I couldn't sleep. One time I ran into Rod Laver doing the same thing in a hotel in Atlanta. I guess he couldn't sleep either that night.

Another time, in Ft. Worth, I was upset after losing a match and ended up driving around in the middle of the night in a brand new courtesy car from the tournament. It still had the dealer's license taped onto the back window. A cop stopped me after I ran six straight red lights. He then became suspicious because the car didn't have proper license plates. He was worried I might have stolen the car. I explained to him that I was a pro tennis player and that the courtesy car was on loan from the tournament. He shined a flash-light on my right hand to look for calluses. He asked whether I had ever really worked a day in my life. I replied, "I like to think so, within my profession." He looked disgusted, but he let me go. . . .

I started taking Valium to try to sleep. That is an awful drug. You can have hangover effects from Valium. It is frequently pre-scribed for anxiety. It was dangerous for me because it can feed depression. I found out later from my internist that chemically, it acts as a depressant. I remember being high on Valium, walking out to play a match in Atlanta in the mid-1970s. It was against this Australian, Allan Stone. I could hardly feel my feet. I had never lost to that guy. I was hoping he stayed true to form. I figured I could even beat him while I was high. I guarantee you, I wasn't fit to drive a car! But I was still out there, playing a pro tennis match. Not only that, but I won 6-2, 6-1!

In my situation, a lot of guys would have quit around about 1975 or 1976. But I stuck it out. I was a fighter. I was a profession-al. That's how I was raised. Never for a moment did I think, "I'm going to make a wholesale change here." One night when I was sitting in John Newcombe's hotel room, he asked me, "Why are you still playing? You're obviously not enjoying it. You're miserable. It's painful to watch." I knew he was right, but tennis was the only thing I had ever done. Even with the sick morass I was in, quitting was unthinkable. For one thing, those last years on the main tour gave me a small ATP pension. I figured I might need that in the years ahead.

In January 1974, to give me a dose of "medicine," I won one of the biggest tournaments on the WCT Tour. It was called the CBS Classic, held in Austin, Texas—practically in my own back yard. I was on Cloud Nine. They filmed the whole thing for TV. I had my own little TV series on network television. I was able to feel, at least for that week, that I deserved the contract I had received.

When my first daughter Hilaire was born that June, I was happy. There was a big picture in the paper with the caption: "Another Richey Net Star?" I didn't know what to make of the idea that I was a father, though. I had to leave immediately after the birth. I turned around and got right back on an airplane. It wasn't until I was in Cleveland the next month that I finally got to be around the baby. Mickie brought her up there to visit some relatives of mine. That was when I first started to figure out what it felt like to be together as a family.

Like with winning a big tournament or witnessing the birth of my first child, during this period, I'd have some good events that would make me feel emotionally better. But in hindsight it was a crazy and, in many ways, sick roller coaster ride. How long did each high last? Winning only gave me an excuse to go out and celebrate. And then, of course, I would drink some more beer. . . . I was self-medicating, no question. At least for a couple of hours each evening, I had found a way to get out of some of that horrible pain. It was an overall nightmare for six years, but not a continual nightmare. There were some respites, some reprieves. But most of the time, I was the most miserable son-of-a-bitch who walked the

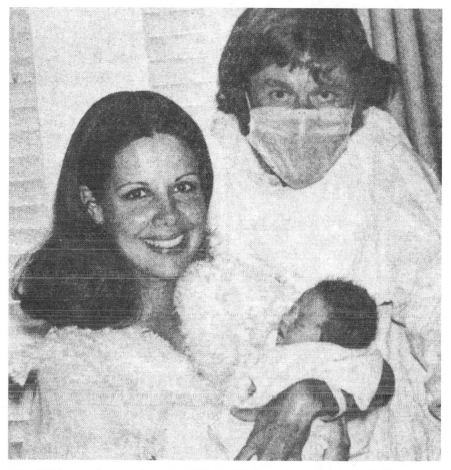

After Hilaire was born on June 13, 1974, I had to leave immediately to play in another tournament.

face of the earth.

    That summer, I injured a rib muscle while playing World Team Tennis. In the fall of that year I went to Hawaii, Tokyo, Sydney, and Christchurch (New Zealand). All of those events fell back-to-back. The fall tennis season, for me, was usually better than the spring. I see now that part of my depression was cyclical. It was like the reverse of seasonal affective disorder. I've noticed that for my whole life, I have tended to get more depressed in spring time. Each year as spring is breaking, I find myself in a low mood. I think that's the reverse of the normal pattern. For me, spring time meant the start of the tennis season. I always had some apprehensions about the new season approaching.

My apprehension and nervousness translated into negative motivation for winning. When I was a child, there was more positive motivation than negative. By and large, tennis was a fun thing. I won trophies and got some recognition. At the beginning, my motivation for playing tennis was probably 70 percent positive, 30 percent negative. Later the negatives took over to such an extent that I started playing in a negative way.

My contract with WCT expired in May of 1976. Three months later, our second daughter Amy was born. Mickie had been having a little bit of a problem with that pregnancy. Probably a week beforehand, I was playing a tournament in North Conway, New Hampshire. I remember talking with the family on the phone—hearing that there were problems with the pregnancy.

When Amy was born, the doctors said she might not make it. She couldn't breathe. It was scary. One of the nurses baptized her at the hospital because we were convinced that she was going to die. I stayed around long enough to know the baby would be able to pull through. It was kind of like there was a crisis period, but then once that was over, the prognosis looked pretty good. I went off to play the U.S. Open, and then, after losing in the third round to Jan Kodes, I went off to Bermuda, where I actually won the title—my ninth of 10 career ATP tournament wins. So I left pretty quickly again. That fall, as usual, I played in Europe. The upshot was, I was there for the actual birth of our second child but not much of anything immediately before or after.

That autumn of 1976, it was still in flux whether Wilson was going to renew my racquet contract. I had been with them since

March of 1969, but I was still waiting to hear whether they were going to renew me. On the first business day of 1977, I called and asked if they were dropping me. They said, "Oh, by the way, we're not renewing you." They didn't even have the courtesy to let me know in advance so I could line up another contract! It just really bothered me that I could be with a company that long and still be treated that way. I even had an autographed racquet line which they still had on the market! Talk about feeling like just a piece of meat. I called the president of Wilson Sporting Goods, who personally extended me six months to give me a chance to find another company. That's when I signed on to endorse Yonex.

About that time, I remember going for one of our annual visits to Houston for Mickie to see her family at her father's house. They had a bottle of vodka or gin in their cabinet and in a matter of a few days, I damn near drained it. My father-in-law came up to me and asked, "Is there anything you think I can help you with?" He had noticed how much I'd been drinking. He might have suspected I had some depression. I didn't talk to him long enough to find out.

With the old wooden racquets, we used to "bore them out" when they were still brand new. First we'd take old pieces of gut string (from other racquets we had slashed with a knife). We would thread the old gut through the new holes and pull it in and out a few times in order to make grooves and runways for the new gut. That way the rough edges of those new racquets wouldn't fray the gut string as much. That was how we prepared a racquet to be strung. We called it boring the racquet out.

If there were any imperfections in that wood, the tighter you strang it, the rough spots would rub harder. Depression is like an imperfection in a wooden racquet head. It's a genetic defect that makes the racquet—or in this case, the person—several times more susceptible to damage.

But racquets don't only crack because of innate defects or flaws. They also crack whenever they are strung too tightly. The tighter you string a racquet, pound-wise, the greater the chance that during the stringing process, the string will suddenly snap. Or, even worse, that it will fail you right when you're in the middle of a match.

If you know you have depression, don't string your emotional racquet too tightly. Don't add additional stress, like the pounds on that stringing machine. You might not be able to control the innate flaw in the wood. But you do have control over some of the other variables. When it comes to mental health, please, don't be afraid to use it.

I've gotten to where I don't mind going to the dentist or the skin doctor any more. They stick needles in me, cut off skin cancers, just pretty much whatever. The actual amount of pain involved isn't really that much. It's almost better than the rest of what I'm going through!

Athletes are conditioned to play through pain, but that training came back to bite me in the butt. I had been taught to see pain as just one more thing to compete against, to the extent that I did not even see what was staring me right in the face. Terry Bradshaw, another depressed athlete, has said he didn't know what was wrong with him. Where does sadness cross the line into not being normal?

CHAPTER FOURTEEN

In the Zone

In sports, when an athlete is in an extraordinarily good spot in terms of their playing abilities, we say that they are "in the zone." It's kind of like being on automatic pilot. There's no thought, really. Everything is flowing. An athlete's concentration doesn't waver. It can last for a match, a whole tournament, or even go on for several weeks.

Part of the "zone" is just not being aware of self at all. You are totally uninhibited. You lose all concept of time. You're so completely absorbed in what you're doing. You think to yourself, "If people could feel this, they'd understand why I love it so much." I have always liked that feeling—the feeling that you are so into something that you literally merge with it. It becomes who you are. You are tennis. Tennis is you. It's your identity. It's a feeling that's sort of hard to describe. It's showtime, folks. The spotlight's on you. Take a deep breath. You're in performance mode.

Being "in the zone" also means feeling detached from yourself, observing yourself from up high or from a distance. The classic example of that for me was the last time I beat Rod Laver. It was the semifinal of the senior tour championship (which I went on to win). For me that was really coming full circle, since I had played my first pro tennis match ever against him at Madison Square Garden

15 years earlier in 1969. This time, it was starting to look like he had me hopelessly beat. But all of a sudden, I started playing well. I started hitting some winners. It all started flowing. Pretty soon, I had turned the match around. I was on auto-pilot. No conscious thought. It was almost like I was observing myself out there. I was watching just like one of the spectators. . . .

I've had the same sensation a little bit with depression. It's the same thing, but in reverse. They call it disassociation. There are times when your healthy self is observing your sick self. Maybe the people who commit suicide don't have a part of themselves left to grab onto. But short of that, whatever little sliver of healthy self you have left realizes just how sick the rest of you is. You feel apart and separate from the rest of the world. Alienated. Like you're a spectator of life.

It's not like a coma or amnesia. You wish you could remember your healthy self a little better. But the bad thing is actually that you do remember your healthy self so well. Eventually, the contrast becomes unbearable.

I remember one time I felt like I was observing myself from a distance. It was on an airplane. My healthy self was standing there in the middle of the aisle, looking at my sick, pitiful self in the seat. Wondering why the hell he was flying off to go play yet another tournament. My depression seemed to be getting worse by the minute. I was in a real depressive fog.

In show business there's a saying: "I'm fighting my personal demons." I would say that was true of me at the end of my tennis career. It would have to be demons, plural, because there wasn't only one demon I was fighting. I was fighting the depression demon, the anxiety demon, the one of Dad not understanding why tennis was no longer fun. I was also fighting the demon of not being as good as I used to be. I knew how good I used to be when I was at my best and I was trying desperately to get back to that place. It was damned difficult. Yet I knew I had to compete against that too.

It was hard to play somebody younger and know that at the age of 23, I would have beaten that guy's ass into the ground.

The real wear and tear was the constant keeping in shape. I was tired of staying in tip-top physical condition. I was tired of going to the tennis court each morning and putting in that two to three hours, five days a week. I just didn't want to do it any more. That was one of the demons tapping on my shoulder. It was saying, "Guess what, Cliffy? It's time to go to the tennis court." It was so irritating. To top things off, I had to play practice matches against much younger players. For months on end I had drilled their asses off and now I had to play practice matches against them and pretend it was a real tournament?! I never had to wonder who would win.

When I would come home from a tournament—sometimes I had a week off, sometimes a month or six weeks—I would take three or four days to rest. I would play some golf but then, I would have to start practicing again every day. I would do drills for 10 days. Then "pretend" tournament play—whole sets and matches. The week before a tournament, I would always simulate the mind-set of what it felt like to play before a crowd. Try to simulate the tournament conditions. But I could only fool myself so much. I'm not a robot. I would try to set a "par" against a given guy. I'd always beat him, but I would set a goal for how badly: 6-2, 6-2 might be under par. That's how I would gauge my degree of preparation for a tournament. I would have 10 or 12 weeks of real tournaments each year, then another 10 or 15 weeks of simulated play to prepare for those. The rest of the year, I did drills. I remember playing five practice sets in 30-degree weather through dry snow flurries. It was hard-ass tennis.

In January of 1979, I quit the regular tour. The only tournament I played that year was in the Bahamas in December. They invited me back as a former champion of that event. Mickie and I went with little Hilaire. It was almost a hit and a giggle for me. At that point, I was picking up a racquet maybe once every 10 days. I remember it was a struggle even to scrape together enough racquets to take with me. I didn't even care what kind of racquets they were. I used some cheap aluminum Yonex things. I didn't give a damn. That was kind of ironic, for someone who used to care as much about the racquet specifications as I did!

The only tennis I continued to play during that time period, really, was the occasional exhibition match—usually to benefit some charity. At one point, Herb Fitzgibbon called me up to play in a little tournament in Cervia, Italy. It was basically an international team competition. They paid expenses, but no prize money. He was the captain of the American team. I had sort of injured a muscle before I left and realized once I got there that it was worse than I had thought. I had to pull out. I was stuck there for several more days with nothing to do. I heard that down the street, near the hotel, there was a topless beach. Pretty soon I found myself hopping on one leg down that street! I had to laugh. I thought: "Is this how a great tennis career ends? Have I degenerated to this point?" But I kept right on hopping. . . .

When I quit the regular tour, I made the conscious decision to throw my big boy toys away. I did nothing but decompress for 19 months. I enjoyed just staying in one place for the first time. During those two years, I would say I didn't feel too much depression. It was more like oblivion. I was in escape mode. No tennis. I just totally bummed out with golf and unsavory friends. I remember taking a golf trip to New Mexico with one of my good golfing buddies. He was much older than I. We were in the middle of a round of golf. All of a sudden he looked up and stared at me, real intently. He asked, "Now what are you going to do?" That really got to me. At my relatively young age, I had already amassed a sizeable net worth. But people still asked, "Well, now what are you going to do?" What if I didn't feel like doing anything for a while? Already I had this long résumé. But somehow, all that just wasn't enough.

For those two years, 1979-80, I didn't do anything but play golf.

I just enjoyed going out and trying to lower my score each day. That was the first time in my life I had ever made any friends. We played the Barbecue Tour, which consisted of small two-day golf events in West Texas. We played in towns like Sonora, Del Rio and Midland. There would be a barbecue one night, and then we'd play all through the next day.

I started chewing tobacco around that time, right after I took up playing golf. It made me nauseous and dizzy. It made me sick the first time I did it, but I did it again—now how dumb is that? In part, I guess, it was a social thing. It was something the guys did out on the golf course. Those two years of just kind of bumming out probably resembled what some kids do in college. I partied hard. That felt good, since I never really got to have that experience.

Meanwhile, my personal habits were really starting to slide. I gained weight. I became a total slob. I left beer cans in the bedroom, along with rotting apple cores on the floor. I drove an old beat-up Suburban with no air conditioning and several doors that wouldn't even open. In the back, I kept my fishing rods and several large barrels of fish bait. About the only kind of fish that could survive in Lake Nasworthy (Lake Nasty Water, we used to call it) was catfish. The bait we used for catfish was rotten, fermenting grain. It made that car stink so bad, you could smell it from a hundred yards away!

I was told 25 years later that during that time, Mickie had another miscarriage. She never even told me about that one. She didn't go to the doctor or have a D&C. Instead she just kept it to herself. I guess I was so unsupportive with the first one, she figured I wouldn't be much help anyway.

It's indicative of my lifestyle during that time period that one of my most vivid memories was from a bar. One of the coaches for the Houston Oilers, King Hill, was in town. He had taught me how to swim when he was a Rice University student years before and had been a quarterback for the Rice Owls. We met up at the Red Rooster to shoot some pool and have a few beers. Meanwhile, my mother called our house, looking for me. Mickie said I was at the Red Rooster, drinking. That was all my mother needed to hear. She got all dressed up in a white suit and marched into that dark, rowdy, smoke-filled bar. I looked up and saw my mother staring at me, hands on her hips, with narrowed eyes. If it had been God or Jesus, I couldn't have been more surprised! In that white suit, she almost looked like an angel. She treated me like a six-year-old. I deserved it. She took me to a corner, gave me a good talking-to, and then left. So did I. She certainly broke my party spirit that night! I had degenerated to such a sorry state.

That's not the only time my mother tried to put me back on the straight and narrow. I normally kept a pack of cigarettes in the glove compartment. Every day, I'd get through practicing tennis at the court behind my parents' house. I'd be rushing off to the golf course. I would smoke one cigarette on the way to the country club. I kept the cigarettes well hidden—inside the car manual! I reached to get a cigarette one day and found a note from Mom. It said simply: "Holy Moly knows." I thought, "Man, I've been violated!" That's how she got her nickname of Holy Moly (Molus, for short). She was the spiritual guru of Richey, Inc.

My drinking became so reckless and irresponsible that I actually put my family's life in jeopardy, at least once. Usually I didn't drink and drive, but this time we were in Bellville, Texas visiting Mickie's sister Susie. There had been some beer drinking going on, both in the car and out, on that particular evening. I don't know if I would have qualified as drunk on a breathalyzer test, but on our way to Susie's, right after we picked up some fried chicken, there was this fork in the road. I was driving too fast on a road paved with gravel. Suddenly I saw this telephone pole. I was headed straight for it. I threw the brake on, but not fast enough. The car skidded into the pole. Somebody called Susie's husband Mark, who got to the scene first. There was fried chicken strewn all over the car. We had to call the police because of insurance and Mark was quick to pick up all the beer cans so I wouldn't get in trouble.

We went to a little emergency room there in Bellville. Mickie had broken her nose. I got lucky because I had a golf cap on, which gave me added protection when I hit my head. Hilaire just rolled around on the floorboard of the backseat, where she was asleep (kids didn't have to use car seats back then). I don't remember where Amy was. But then, I don't remember a lot about those years. . . . It was an alcoholic haze. You can still see the bump on Mickie's nose where it broke that night.

By that time, I think you could safely say our marriage was on the skids. We actually separated for a few weeks at that point. In March of 1981, I was at a senior tour event in the Woodlands, near Houston, and Mickie and I had a discussion about her father. I can't remember the genesis of the discussion but I said some things which were very critical of him that she didn't want to hear. But I felt like I was saying some things that she really, in her heart, agreed with too. To my ears, she was defending him in a way that didn't even ring true. We got into a big argument in front of our two little girls. At one stage, I left the condominium where we were staying. When I came back, the door was locked. I knocked on it to get back in, but Mickie didn't want to cooperate. She refused to open the door, so I beat it down with my foot. She called the security guard and once he arrived, he was physically standing between us. I said, "OK, I'm out of here. You have all our money. Give me some cash to get home." She gave me $200. I went to the airport and left town. She drove our family car to Houston to stay with her father for a couple of weeks. He told her, "You've given him the best 15 years of your life. Divorce him." I'm not going to defend my actions, but she and I were both critical of that throw-away approach to relationships.

We did get back together, but even then, we were both treading water. We had a totally codependent relationship. She remembers that around that time, she went to a Bible study. There she heard something she could really hang on to: "A human being is a human

171

being. All have fallen short of the grace of God. Don't become too dependent on any mortal person. Depend only on God." She could really hold on to that. That's what got her through.

It wasn't just my wife who suffered the consequences of my oblivion. It was possibly even worse for my kids. I had an absolute pattern of abusing my kids through lack of attention. I didn't go to my daughters' dance recitals. Performances of that kind were so minor compared to what I had been involved in. That's a pathetic excuse. It was like I did not have the normal instincts that a father should have for his children. I don't really know why. In some ways, that bothers me now. I didn't feel that guilty about it at the time, though. I was too busy just trying to lose myself.

In all honesty, from the bottom of my heart, I know that I wanted to be a father. Mickie and I had planned not to have kids the first few years we were married, and we didn't. But when Hilaire was born, we were very much trying to have a baby. I was surprised at how hands-off a father I ended up being. I was surprised that I didn't cotton to it like I should have. It's a mystery to me, too, in a way. I did provide my kids with private schools, country club membership, dance and piano lessons, a beautiful home. But I didn't provide them with good fatherhood. That's more important than all of that other shit!

Every night I used to eat dinner alone, from a tray I took to the recliner in my bedroom. I ate in front of the TV. I felt hassled at the end of the day. Dehydrated and worn out. I liked to have quiet and just "veg" out. Often when I came home, my oldest daughter would greet me at the door. She would have a happy, expectant look on her face. I didn't give her a chance to say anything before I snapped, "Don't even think about asking if we can all have dinner together!" Then I went to the kitchen, grabbed four beers, took them to the bedroom and slammed the door.

One time I remember I was just sitting there, drinking coffee in the kitchen. Hilaire was a little girl, maybe eight years old. She was

After Hilaire, photographed here with Mickie, was born, I was surprised how hands-off a father I ended up being.

doing something at the sink. She had the water running. I wasn't in a very good mood. She looked over at me. I don't think I said anything. But I know I looked at her in a mean and disgusted way. She got this hurt look on her face. Her eyes said: "Why, Daddy? What have I done?" It dawned on me that she didn't deserve that. As bad as I felt then, it still registered that I shouldn't be treating her that way. I felt guilty about it. There was no excuse for me to act that way toward my little girl.

Of the two kids, Amy had more of a volatile personality, especially as she approached her teenage years. When we rubbed each other the wrong way, we let each other know it. Amy irritated me. If I was in a foul mood (which was most of the time), she was the one who was likely to get confrontational. Then again, I didn't need any help in that department! One time I slapped Amy when she came up close and started yelling. With an open hand, I remember slapping her sassy face. My Dad said, "Don't hit a little girl who's going to bruise and have to go to school like that. You were wrong." Even with my skewed thinking, I could see his point. I resorted to other measures to punish her, like grounding her instead. I had things way out of proportion. Once when she was a teenager, I actually tried to ground her for a whole year! I remember being scolded for doing that—by the town drunk, no less. I guess the word had gotten out. Now that was really bad—a guy you have no respect for, telling you you're a lousy father. But what could I possibly say in my defense?

You don't assimilate certain stresses like a normal person does when you are in clinical depression. I would come home a basket case. I just wanted to decompress. But all of that is abuse if you have a family. You just become so self-absorbed.

Why do you abuse the ones you love the most? Well, you're around them all the time, for one thing. You're beating up on yourself all the time too. You don't have any patience with yourself. You're irritable. You have anxieties. It's not a mystery why you act the way you do.

You're not really trying to take it out on other people. That's just how you are at that point in time. It's your state of being. You're a sick cowboy, man. "Taking it out on people" makes it sound like you have a choice—or as if it were an isolated event. But it's an equal-opportunity deal. You're not trying to make everybody else miserable. You're just totally miserable yourself. The great tennis player Roy Emerson's favorite line was "Hey, miserable." Then he'd laugh at you if you turned around. Most of the time during those two years, I could have answered honestly to that greeting.

We used to eat together as a family when I was growing up. That was something I rebelled against later when it came to the formalities of family life. I was fed up with the suffocating closeness of Richey, Inc. But it wasn't just my wife and kids who got the short end of the stick. Still every day, even when I was well into my 30s, I would go over to eat lunch at my parents' house. Mom would ask me a simple question, such as "What do you want for lunch?" or "When is your tee time?" I would basically just bite her head off, saying "Don't bother me. I don't want to deal with that right now." Mom would say, "You don't have to act that way! There's just no excuse for your being that irritable."

My mother would do anything for me. She's one of the kindest, sweetest, gentlest souls that ever lived. When someone that gentle is making comments like that, then you know you must be off-base. But you don't know how to fix it. I felt like my brain was in a storm. She didn't understand. I didn't really, either. All I knew was: it felt like I was focused on major things, and she was busy asking me all these minor questions. That sparked my anger.

After each of these incidents, you go back into your own little world. The frozen popsicle is still frozen. It still hasn't thawed out. It's frustrating because, in many ways, you're two different people. On the one hand, you can be this confident, gregarious, affectionate guy. On the other hand, you're a miserable wretch.

By the time I got home, during my kids' childhood, the negative self had won out. I went along, sopping up four beers every night and taking Valium to sleep. Both of those things are depressants. They're bad for your nervous system. All the while, I was compounding the problem without even knowing it.

When you're in a down period, it's frustrating because you don't just forget how fun life can be. You've got a memory of that other person in your mind, but it's like you can't get that other person to come out. You can't find that other person. You wonder: where did he go?

Hope is a wonderful thing. Hope makes you believe you can get things done. You might get a job promotion. Rise up the ranks. It means you have a healthy idea of what your abilities are. With depression, you don't have any of that. You're just sitting there, lucky to breathe. Your whole concept of self, of what your life is, of what your career is, gets totally twisted. Your thinking is skewed. You feel terribly frightened and insecure. You don't really feel responsible for things you would normally feel responsible for. The only thing you can think about is your pain.

When you are depressed, you are still in control of your actions. But there are certain things you just can't do. Don't ask me to attend a social function. I'm not going to do it. I can't do it. You don't lose your brain, your senses. But you are definitely not getting much sleep. You're like a zombie. You don't have any joy. Somehow you are existing on the bare fringes of life.

To put it simply, you're in the zone. Except this time, it's the twilight zone. Instead of that mythical mental place where athletes flourish and sports magic happens, all of a sudden, you wake up and realize: you're starting to choke.

CHAPTER FIFTEEN

Starting to Choke

"C hoke" is the word we use to describe what happens when a player is not performing well at a crucial moment in competition. We all have choked on some matches. There are certain areas of a match where a player is more likely to choke, like when he is serving for the match. When I started getting into the choke area of a match, I started getting defensive with my shots. By contrast, when Arthur Ashe choked, he got too aggressive. So everyone chokes in his own different way.

There's a battle going on out there between two minds. I could sense when someone was starting to break down mentally. In the crunch time, it's easy to get nervous and choke from wanting to win it too badly. One of the most difficult areas of a match mentally is right at the time you feel like you've got it done. You need to close the deal. That's the clincher. Seal it in the envelope and put it in the mail.

I had a way of playing that wasn't the easiest when it came time to close out a match. It's easier to win at big moments with weapons like a huge serve. I didn't have a serve powerful enough to knock anybody off the court, so I had to find alternative ways to win.

I never worried if other players thought I had a tendency to choke in a tough spot. Fred Stolle predicted I would choke in 1970 when I led the American team to victory in Davis Cup. But I didn't. Nor did I choke in the famous "Sudden Death" match that decided the No. 1 U.S. ranking that year against Stan Smith. So in the choking area, I disproved my critics at least as many times as I proved them right.

The first time I remember starting to choke in a big match was the summer of 1962. I was 15 years old and playing in the USTA National Boys' 16s Championships. I grabbed Dad and said, "Hey, I need to talk to you." We went into the dorm room alone. I told him that I was feeling apprehensive. He grinned and said, "You're feeling pressure. You're blanking out on us here." By following his advice on how to cope with the pressure, I was able to go out and win the tournament.

The same thing happened when I won the U.S. Clay Court Championships in Indianapolis in 1970. I was playing against Stan Smith in the final with Dad there watching the match. He was glaring at me from the stands. I won the first two sets 6-2, 10-8, but lost the third set 6-3. Back in those days, we always took a break after the third set of a five-set match. During the break, Dad came into the locker room and started reading me the riot act on how I should go out and play. I had to win one more set somehow. He basically just grabbed me by the shoulders and told me I had gotten too cautious. I went out and won 6-1 in the fourth.

At the time, his words sounded harsh, but he wasn't trying to hurt my feelings. He was just being brutally honest. He was right on the money. That's why coaches are so valuable. I didn't realize that I had gotten too cautious and was trying to just wish victory instead of making it happen.

Those are some examples of times when I felt myself starting to choke. However, the all-time tough one was when I lost to Zeljko Franulovic in the semifinals of the French Open in 1970. Mom and Dad flew over to Paris to watch me play. On the court that day, I would be the first one in the world to say that I choked. It was a

Mickie and the rest of the family had to endure my choking, where I was not performing well at crucial moments of my life.

choke job. I got more nervous than I should have. At one point in the match, I questioned a line call. I still think I was right, but I shouldn't have done it. It turned the crowd against me. French crowds are very excitable. I had three different match points. During the last one in particular, I really choked as I hit the ball off the wood frame. Zeljko was so far away, he was over there in East Paris someplace and all I had to do was hit it into the open court. But I choked. I got upset when the crowd turned on me. I lost 7-5 in the fifth.

I had that match on my racquet and in my hand. All I had to do was stick it in my pocket! It was my tournament to win or lose and I handed it back. . . . I would have played a guy in the final, Jan Kodes, to whom I had literally never lost. Kodes and I had breakfast together four years later at the CBS Tennis Classic and he told me, "Cliff, you know I could not have beaten you." The French Open was mine to lose.

After that match, I was as mad and upset as I've ever been for losing a tennis match. I was beside myself. I always carried a tournament bag. I remember taking the tournament duffle bag that I always carried with me and heaving it across the player lounge. I was devastated. I just wigged out. If someone asked me, "Were you momentarily insane?" I would have to say, yeah, I was goofy nuts. I mentally and emotionally snapped. It wasn't like I snapped out on the court. I never lost my temper once while I was on the court that day. But afterward, in the player lounge, I took my racquet and started beating it against the backs of chairs. I was really scaring Mom. She kept saying, "Cliff, just calm down!"

In all ways, that's the worst loss I ever had. To this day, it bothers me. That's the loss that affected me the most—the one that really got to me. The next day, Nancy and Mickie wanted to do some sightseeing in Paris. I guess I decided to go with them because I didn't want to be alone at the hotel. I was still too upset. It was an awful day.

Tennis and golf are two of the premier individual sports in the world. For individual sports in particular, you'd better watch out, because there's no one there to take the blow of a loss except you. There's no team surrounding you. Individual sports are peculiarly conducive to depression. On top of that, I had the underlying predisposition.

During my first real bout with clinical depression, I did not have any clear idea of what was happening to me. It came in fits and spurts. It's so easy to write it off and chalk it up to the fact that you're in this super-competitive career. Thirty of my first 40 years were filled with competitive tennis. You blame it on the sport

180

instead of looking for other causes.

Usually the people who have bad depression for the first time in their lives don't have it for three years initially. Neither did I. But each episode can make you more prone to have another one. It's called the kindling effect. It sets you up for falling into depression more easily and for the bouts to last longer. My first real onslaught lasted several months.

In the fall of 1989, I had a four-month, horrific siege of depression. My heart started beating irregularly. It had given me some problems before, off and on, but never as bad as this. I was so worried about it that I went to the Cooper Clinic in Dallas—one of the best medical facilities around—to get it checked out. Dr. Kenneth Cooper wrote the book *Aerobics*, emphasizing physical fitness and its effects on your heart. When you go in there, it's like an assembly line. They give you all these tests during the day. I had everything checked: hearing, eyesight, blood test, etc. At the end of the day, the doctor sits down with you to discuss the results. At that time, it cost about a grand.

I was diagnosed with premature ventricular contractions, PVCs. It's a benign heart condition. My dad had heart problems, namely atrial fibrillation. Atrial fibrillation can cause the heart to throw off blood clots, causing a stroke. By itself, it's not lethal, but it's more dangerous than PVCs. I worried that my PVCs might turn into that. PVCs can become dangerous if you then develop heart disease on top of them. I thought my problem might be a precursor for something worse.

After doing an electrocardiogram, a stress test (running up and down the stairs in an office building), and wearing a Holter monitor for a 24-hour period, I was told not to worry—my PVCs were perfectly benign. But I'm still glad they did all those tests as two things emerged from them: I have an enlarged heart from so much athletic training and the amounts of adrenaline pumping through it have created a sensitivity to stimulation. The doctor described it as like having a pace maker in my chest. So while the PVCs might feel scary, they aren't going to do me any harm.

The other thing that could have emerged from the testing (but didn't) was that there was a psychiatric component to the exam. On their report, the doctors noted that I had a very negative outlook; but curiously, they did not recommend treatment for depression.

Some warning signs of depression are extraordinary anger and frustration. You don't crash all at once. You feel yourself tacking in a different direction, like a sailboat being buffeted by the wind. Try as you might to stay up, you can't. You go under for a while. When I feel like my thinking is getting balky, cranky and critical, or when I stop enjoying the company of good friends, that's a warning sign. Waning mood is another important indicator.

A bout of depression will often occur in response to specific triggers. For men, one of these can be financial distress. As Bill Styron said in his book *Darkness Visible*, the spark point for depression is a sense of loss. The man thinks it's his job to provide. There is a real urgency there.

With me, financial security was perhaps even more important than for a lot of guys. Like most athletes, I had a very short window to make money. I come from a long line of fiscal worriers anyway. We're the ultimate squirrels who store up for a rainy day. When I felt that I was falling down on that job, pretty soon I became deeply depressed. It affected me more than it might have a different person.

By the fall of 1989, I had already played senior tennis for eight years. I had gone back to play the senior tour after a two-year hiatus. But at the age of 42, some of my senior tennis opportunities were declining. I was getting older and worried about maintaining my fitness level. But then a freak accident happened which really plunged me to the depths.

I was getting ready to go to the senior invitational event for the U.S. Open at Flushing Meadow. Right before my trip, I was with Amy in our den, horsing around with her. She was a little upset with me and sort of pulled away. When I reached out to give her a hug, my hand hit her arm by mistake. I sprained my right thumb. I went out to play golf the next day, but my thumb was too sore. I tried to play tennis and noticed that that, also, was difficult. By the next day, it had swollen to the point that I couldn't use it for anything.

Needless to say, I was very disappointed. I had already prepared to play that tournament. Additionally, I didn't know just how badly I might be injured. That was a big concern. I had injured that same thumb back in Paris in 1965 (the DMSO episode). I still had a scar from running into that metal fence. I went to see a hand specialist, who said I had a syndrome called Game Keepers' Thumb. If the condition gets bad enough, eventually, you have to have surgery. It worried the hell out of me. Plus the fact that I couldn't go up there and earn some money—I had really been counting on that.

I never played for the money except at the end of my career. My prime earning days were fast running out. I had started playing the senior tour in 1981. My heyday in the senior game was 1983-86. I won five senior tour events in all, but once I turned 40 years old on December 31, 1986, I started getting more injuries. I was still serious about tennis, but in my heart, I think I knew that I also needed to hang in there for the money.

With this injury, I panicked. I was afraid I might never play sports again. More importantly, I was worried that I might never be able to earn a living that way. I wasn't fit to do anything else. In fact, I had no other training whatsoever!

I went into reactionary mode. I decided we would have to cut back on expenses and try to conserve. We had a ledger where we kept a record of the family's cash flow. I took that over to Nancy's, and we sat down together to figure out ways we could save more money. My goal was to cut our annual expenses by one third.

Once we had identified categories where we might be spending too much, I called a family meeting to announce my plan. It was known simply as "The Budget." It affected everything from luxuries to groceries. We put our house on the market. I was preparing for the worst-case scenario.

Mickie and I started arguing. She thought I was going overboard. We were in great shape financially, according to most people's standards, but I was trying to control the future by micromanaging the present. I didn't want to leave anything to chance.

Some of "The Budget" was the depression talking. I'm an extremist anyway, but depression, by its very nature, is negative and extremely skewed. When I told Mickie's father we were selling the house, he told Mickie I needed to take an aptitude test. To go out and get a job—until I told him our net worth! Then he must have thought I had gone completely nuts.

When depression is descending, there's usually a little bit of panic. It is unspecified fear. Things are closing in on you. Like, "Oh no, here we go again." You've felt it before. You know all too well what's coming next.

I overreacted with "The Budget." That's what you do when you're in depression. First a crisis situation, then combine that with the disease. It acts as a multiplier. Your reaction will always be extreme.

One of the horrible things about depression—in addition to the foul, odorous, sick, deathly mood you're in—is that you're now spending so much of your time, almost all of it, just trying to fix yourself. You're consumed by, "How can I fix this horrible thing?" You don't have time for people or anything else. It's very hard to concentrate. It hard to sit down and read a book, or go to the bank, or get a haircut. Whatever. Forget about it—everything looks difficult.

During the next three months, I was so depressed, I stopped even getting out of the house much. The stresses that hit me that fall would probably not have affected someone without clinical depression in the same way. I got so frustrated one day on the golf course, I took a putter and beat it against the side of a tree. I felt parched emotionally and spiritually, just like the West Texas landscape. I

Mickie, with Hilaire, Amy and our "third set" Sarah, photographed here In 1983, had to endure my alcoholism and irrational fears.

was going through what had to be about my sixth burnout. I was salving my wounds with tobacco and beer.

I started drinking fairly heavily. I had won a Pinch Scotch Whiskey trophy full of booze. I drained that baby. I was wanting to get my hands on more alcohol, and it just happened to be sitting there. Before that I would get drunk maybe five or six times a year. The nights I really wanted to tie one on, I would keep drinking past four beers. But I didn't drink only beer. I didn't discriminate. I drank wine, gin and tonic—whatever. I never saw it as "hard" or "soft" liquor. It's all alcohol.

As part of "The Budget" we started eating rice with red beans. That was our staple meal. We ate the same thing several nights a week. About once a week we would have chicken. Only once a month did we buy beef. I instructed Mickie only to buy the vegetables that were on sale.

During this time I still wouldn't eat with my family, but I had other ways of making my presence felt. I used to label the good stuff in the fridge (like my favorite Blue Bell ice cream) with masking tape that said: "Property of Cliff—Do Not Touch." That should have been a warning sign that I was sick! But at the time, such behavior seemed perfectly logical to me.

The rest of the family, taking their cue from my actions, started to follow my selfish example. The items considered "prime" foodstuffs started popping up in the most unexpected places. First Mickie started hiding Snickers bars. Then the girls stashed away cans of Campbell's cream of broccoli soup. They hid them under the bathroom sink!

Meanwhile, we had been unable to sell our house, which was located in the nicest neighborhood in town. It needed a few repairs. The roof was leaking. We only ran the heater when it was absolutely necessary. We would sit there shivering in our woolen sweaters. The whole situation was dysfunctional and out of control.

Like our chilly house in winter, the agitated form of depression feels extremely cold. You're wanting to get up and move around. It's like trying to stay warm.

I was never devoid of feeling. I just had overwhelming negative feelings. Big-time sadness. Irrational fears. A certain kind of free-floating anger. The anger produces a sort of compounding effect. In addition to the losses that triggered the depression, you are also angry about being in that state.

I've never really felt insane, but that depends on what your definition of "insane" is. You don't always feel like you're losing your mind, necessarily, but you definitely feel sick from the Adam's Apple up.

When I'm in a black mood, it's like Jekyll and Hyde. You feel this thing come over you. You don't want to talk to anybody. You're impaired. You're afraid you might not sound like the same person. But even more than that, you don't want to expend any emotional energy. You're rationing it out. You're constantly check-ing your gas tank and running on empty.

The fall of 1989 was a lot like losing the semis of the French. I had three match points where I should have won the thing. But once I started choking, I could never turn it around.

With depression, I had several chances where I should have been able to get help. The doctors at the Cooper Clinic might have picked up on the fact that my heart condition was psychosomatic. Even my thumb doctor, if he had been trained to recognize my symptoms, might have intervened. But no one did. Like that elusive French Open victory, the prize of mental wellness was not to be had. At least not by me. Not yet. Not until I came to recognize my opponent.

I didn't know it at the time, but this match was more important than the semifinal round of a major. The stakes could not have been any higher. This time, instead of a tennis title, I was fighting for my soul.

CHAPTER SIXTEEN

Black Bags

I played my last competitive tennis of any kind in December of 1992 in Coral Springs, Florida. I was 46 years old. I had injured the same calf muscle multiple times. I just kept re-injuring it. There was so much accumulated scar tissue that I had no flexibility left in that muscle at all. Scar tissue is not as resilient as normal tissue. I just reached a point with this chronic injury when I knew I couldn't play tennis any more.

It may not be scientifically demonstrable, but you can also build up scar tissue in your brain. Not the physical kind of scar tissue resulting from a sports injury, but the emotional kind that comes from sustaining repeated depressive episodes. Depression leaves you with scar tissue that stays with you forever.

As devastating as it was, the depression I suffered in 1989 was only a warm-up for what came later. It was only a frigging dress rehearsal! Somehow, at the end of that three or four months, I was able to pull myself out of it. I was able to put myself back together again. That was the same thing I had done after countless shorter periods of depression in the past.

But this time, my psyche reacted just like my leg. It had no more flexibility left. I sensed that this time, I wasn't going to be able to snap out of it. This time, I couldn't recover without help.

On July 26, 1994, I was feeling queasy and nauseous. I had had a real bad stomach for the past several months. I had gone in for a thorough medical examination. Nothing was ever diagnosed. It was probably gastritis, or inflammation of the stomach lining. All I know is, I wasn't feeling very well.

That day, Mom called me at the country club, where I was playing golf, and asked me to stop by her house. She wanted me to pick up a book she had found for me. She said, "I think I know why you're sick." The book said four drinks a day, which was the level of my alcohol consumption, would lead eventually to some type of disease. Mom said, "I want you to promise me that you'll quit drinking beer and chewing tobacco."

I didn't want to hear it, but I knew she was right. I said, "I don't wake up every day for the sole purpose of drinking and chewing." But I had no defense for those two habits. I wasn't about to try to defend something for which I knew there was no defense.

I decided to quit, cold turkey. I probably slept no more than one hour that night. The pangs of withdrawal were immediate and intense. I had been drinking beer for 23 years and chewing tobacco for 16. Medically, if you take either one of those two habits away —even for someone who's not prone to mental illness—it could be enough to send that person into depression.

A couple days later, I was down at the tennis court. I was still hitting tennis balls four days a week, even though I didn't play professionally any more. I remember looking up to see Dad standing in the entrance to the court. I was in tears. I told him I had never felt worse emotionally in my life. There was this feeling of catastrophic loss. Like it couldn't get any worse, except maybe if somebody close to me died. To this day, I'm completely convinced he had no idea what I was feeling. My parents hated those habits of mine so badly. They couldn't imagine why I wasn't blissfully happy to have given them up.

They say changes and losses are the big things you have to

watch for if you are predisposed to clinical depression. That was a period of enormous upheaval in our family. Mickie and I had just sold the house. It took us five years to sell it. At that precise moment, we were in the process of moving into a little patio home. We decided to downsize rather drastically. After that scare with my thumb injury which, among other things, precipitated "The Budget," I was in fact able to play senior tennis for several more years. So by that point our finances were not as strained. But now that I had laid down my racquet for good, we had decided to buy a home which was only half the size of our former one. I didn't even want Mickie to hang my tennis pictures up on the walls. They mocked me, like the trophies did. Neither one of us realized then that the photos would stay packed in their boxes for the next 10 years.

By mid-August, I was a complete basket case. I flew up to Cape Cod to play a golf tournament. I got there and played 18 holes— one practice round. Then suddenly the paralysis struck. I had to quit. I drove back to the clubhouse and found transportation to the hotel. I called Dad and said: "I can't go on." I pulled out of the event. I turned right around and flew home. I made up some lame excuse about a bad wrist. I would have told the tournament people it was emotional distress if I had thought that they would understand.

That was the beginning of three horrific years. To put it in boxing terms, I was down for the count. I don't know what it feels like to be in a diabetic coma, but I imagine it's a little more than just feeling lightheaded. The diabetic coma is equivalent to clinical depression. It's more than just a little bad mood.

Your sense of time is warped in depression. It just drags on and on. You're in misery. You feel like you've been rendered useless, without hope. You're a frigging protozoan sitting there. You don't want to do anything. You're bored to the max because suddenly nothing is important anymore.

Part of depression is a futile spinning of your wheels. Like may-

190

be God is taking you out of the action for a while. It's an enforced rest. But it's not even as good as spinning your wheels or treading water. That would imply you're holding steady. Instead, depression is forcing you under with a strong current. The next thing you know, you're fixing to drown.

As was often (but not always) the case, on the sports end of my life, my mental anguish mirrored a perceived loss of skill. I had just reached such a pathetic point. Tennis had become too painful. Golf, up to that time, had been refreshing. I took to it naturally. I never really had many lessons. I was a born athlete who could always count on good hand/eye coordination. The calf muscle couldn't bother me too much in a sport where, essentially, you play standing still. Pretty soon I went from playing the Barbecue Tour to entering some big-time competitive events. Unexpectedly, my golf had suddenly become a way I could replace some of the income I had lost when I quit tennis.

But right around that time, my golf skills started to erode. Try as I might, I couldn't recapture my swing. I became obsessive/compulsive, as I had been with tennis, only more so. I hit so many practice balls on the driving range that I busted two ribs. I would get more and more frustrated with each ball I hit. My thinking was becoming increasingly neurotic. The same thought would come back over and over, bouncing off the four sides of my brain. It was like hearing loud music playing in a small room. I was plagued by repetitive thoughts.

There finally came a point when I had to forcibly make myself quit doing it. I had to limit myself to hitting 50 balls a day. I was like somebody trying to quit smoking by rationing cigarettes. No matter how badly I wanted to hit more, I wouldn't let myself continue.

When my golf swing went south on me, it was hard to get help because I had taught myself to play in such an unorthodox way. It was doubly traumatic because my golf was one of the few things in my life I felt like I owned. My tennis game always sort of felt like

191

Dad's creation, or at very least, a product of Richey, Inc. My golf game was self-taught. I was proud of being a scratch golfer, but I was even more proud because I was the one who had discovered it. When my skills began to deteriorate a second time, in a second sport, it was almost more than I could handle. It felt just like losing my backhand in tennis. I was re-enacting the trauma of loss.

That's the closest I ever came to quitting anything. I put my golf clubs away for a few weeks. At the age of 50, I announced that I had decided to quit all competition. I said I would just go grocery shopping with Mickie and live a life of no stress. With characteristic wisdom, Mickie said, "Let's make that decision when you feel better." She knew that wasn't the real me. That was the depression talking. A classic symptom of clinical depression is to convince yourself that things which are important to you really aren't.

It's worst upon waking up. It hits you like a ton of bricks. You're blanked out, pretty much. You start reaching pain levels you didn't think were there. It's pretty flat shitty. Your whole being is in pain. On top of that, you're afraid. You're fearful that you're gonna stay the way you are now. It's an awful trance. Heaviness descending over you. It sits on you. Your normal emotions are slowly being snuffed out.

In January of 1996, I started going to counseling. I found a Christian counselor with a Ph.D. in psychology who ran a ministry for burned-out pastors. I thought at the time that's what I had. The official reason I was going to counseling sessions was to get some help with clinical burnout.

I told the counselor, "I can't face my next golf tournament." As one of the tournament regulations, we were obligated to walk the golf course. We were not allowed to ride in a cart. We were also required to have a caddy. That presented a unique problem for me.

In my state of mind, I couldn't stand the thought of walking to play 18 holes with a caddy who would be a total stranger by my side. The very idea of making conversation with someone I didn't know just totally freaked me out. I told my counselor that the way I was feeling emotionally, I couldn't do it. He gently said, "I think you should try to play this event if you possibly can because God would want you to err on the side of being bold."

I went home and told Mickie my dilemma. Her response was: "Well then, I'll caddy for you." This slender, petite little woman was offering to carry my heavy golf clubs! She had to take some of them out of the bag to hold in her other hand because if it was full, the bag would be too heavy. Now, that's sacrificial love. She ended up getting fibromyalgia later. I realize now it may have been from carrying too much weight. She sacrificed her body for my sake. There's no greater love than that.

I really was not fit to live with anyone for a long while at this stage in my life. I guess in some kind of Greek-tragedy way, if it's any solace to those who were around me at the time, I was definitely more miserable than they were. I was trying to fix myself all day long. That's one of the reasons depressed people are so impatient with conversations, etc. They're constantly obsessed with trying to fix themselves.

Mickie didn't know what else to do but be supportive. She walked around on egg shells. She just tried to make things as perfect as she could on her end. Not to upset me or get in my way. Actually, as a result, her behavior became sick too! She had told me years ago that she thought something was kind of wrong with me. But she became an enabler. The counselor even said that: sick behavior begets more sick behavior. She adapted to abnormal circumstances through being a kind-hearted person. But that, in the end, made her behavior sick too. She realizes that now. She was trying to handle every possible thing: the house, the finances, anything that needed repair—all so I could be free to deal with my illness. I was suffering so much, she wanted to take as much of the load off me as she could.

She had felt the same way most of her life in relation to her mother. She had been put in the same position ever since she was 12. She was the oldest of six. She was not a sister to her siblings. Instead, she functioned more like a second mother to them. She tried to do everything expected of her as perfectly as she could in the hope that it would make her mother better or she might somehow get well. That's how it is when you're caring for someone who is mentally ill. It's an illusion. But that's all that's left for you to hold on to.

Clinical depression can destroy a marriage. It all comes down to three words: not getting well. I wasn't the only one dealing with symptoms of Post-Traumatic Stress Disorder. In caring for me, Mickie was reliving her childhood nightmare.

Nothing about clinical depression is normal. It's just such a cunning disease. It's telling you 24 hours a day that you're worthless. You don't want to do any of the things you once did. You don't want to change clothes, shower, shave, get a haircut. Everything is an effort. You don't want to be around people. You certainly don't want to be around gregariousness or joy. You can't believe anyone could be that happy when you're feeling as bad as you are. You know in your heart that they're the normal ones. It's just a minute-by-minute reminder of how sick you've become.

Traveling to that golf tournament in Fort Lauderdale in February of 1996, I had to grit my teeth and force myself to step onto the plane. It required a supreme effort of concentration just to put one foot in front of the next. The fear was so great, so overwhelming. I stayed in a dark hotel room with the shades drawn until it was finally time to go out and play golf. I would sort of cry. Even so, I finished seventh out of 70 guys.

It's remarkable how, just short of being grounded with severe clinical depression, you can still remain somewhat functional. But then all of sudden, your ability to do anything grinds to a screeching halt. That's the next stage in the progression of the disease.

I was "grounded" in January of the following year. I remember that because Christmas of 1996 was when I lost all pretense of normalcy. We were planning a small family get-together at our house. Mom and Dad kept calling to see what time they and Nancy should come over. Mickie had to tell them, "I don't know. We might not even have Christmas today." They didn't understand yet how bad off I was.

When they came over that evening, I was sitting in a chair facing the front door. They knew something was wrong. I just started crying. I got up and went into the bedroom. They knew the evening was over before it had really begun. I didn't do it on purpose. I was one sick cowboy. It was this flood I felt like I couldn't control. My family knew then, if they didn't before, that I was in pretty bad shape.

I can't imagine anybody feeling worse than I did. The only thing that would have been worse is if I had blown my brains out. I was a perfect candidate to check myself into a mental institution.

Clinical depression is a lie. Don't believe it, even when it's screaming at you. The disease of depression will yell at you 24/7 that you have no hope. That you should give up, because it's not worth it. Your emotional reserves are depleted. Your normal zest for life is gone. All your negatives are highlighted. It's the depth of negativity. You don't have normal instincts: hopes, pleasures, desires. You can't feel proud of any accomplishment. You loathe yourself. You're totally underconfident. You just wallow in this intense psychological pain.

I got rid of our country club membership. I wasn't going out there to play any more. Occasionally, I would go to an isolated park to hit a few balls at a time of day when I thought no one else would be around. Most of the time I wasn't able to drive a car. Since I had gotten almost no sleep, I just didn't feel like doing it. Nor did I think it was a very good idea. I sensed that I shouldn't be driving at a point when I was so ill. Normally in our marriage, I used to do all the driving. So that was a big change for me. I'd just sit there in the passenger seat, feeling like a lump of shit.

One day I went in the car with Mickie to pick up our daughter Sarah at junior high. I remember just sitting in the car, crying. I didn't want to be alone. My wife was such a comforter in every way. I also felt like I needed someone with me all the time. I didn't want to stay behind in an empty house.

My constant presence got to be suffocating for Mickie. One time she went and hunted some rocks in the back easement, just to get away. Irrationally, I became fearful that something would happen to her. I stood up on the edge of the bathtub to peer out the window so I could see where she was. I didn't want her out of my sight. I couldn't stand the thought of her not coming back.

As the clock would edge toward bed time, it was scary. I knew I wouldn't be able to sleep. I would wake Mickie up out of a sound sleep to talk in the middle of the night. She and I would pray together. She would hold my hand while I cried. She would sit there for hours by the side of the bed. Weeks would go by where I would sleep little or none at all. I truly had this fear that I might die from lack of sleep.

I put black trash bags over the windows. I sealed the edges with tape. I was beside myself. I didn't want to know whether it was day or night. I wanted a room that simulated night all the time, like a tomb. I couldn't see any daylight in my life.

My mind became dark; and then darker; and then darker still. The darkness of the room appealed to me. It was comforting, somehow. When it's sunny and bright and everyone is awake, it only serves to remind you how sick you really are. I was dark on the inside. I wanted everything else to be that way too.

After several months, the trash bags had cracked all the glass in the windows. They had absorbed too much heat from the West Texas sun. White surfaces reflect light, while black surfaces absorb it. The black trash bags served to intensify the normal effects of the sun.

My genetic predisposition to depression was like those black bags. It only served to magnify the heat of competition. For some-one else without that propensity, the stress could maybe have bounced off a little easier. For me, though, it proved to be a deadly combination.

I lost all sense of time. I wasn't on God's time clock any more. Instead, it felt like I was inhabiting some alien universe. Or maybe floating around in outer space. It's black there, too. I had this sensa-tion of free-fall.

The windows were not the only thing that cracked in the utter blackness of that room. Softly, alone in the darkness, my mind had cracked, as well.

• CHAPTER SEVENTEEN •

Change a Losing Game

Back in 1968, I pulled off the tennis tour for four months to do nothing but work on my serve. Going into the fall season, I knew my serve was not good enough to get where I needed to go. It had to become technically more sound. I was dead serious. It wasn't just a passing thought. That was the first year of open tennis. I needed to be ready.

I told Donald Dell, our non-playing Davis Cup captain, that I was pulling off the team. We were standing on the back porch of the Longwood Cricket Club outside of Boston. He was not happy to hear my announcement. He threatened to use his influence with the USTA to keep me from playing Buenos Aires that year. In those days, to play overseas, we had to get permission from our national tennis federations. I had won that tournament for the last two years. I was the defending champion. Sure enough, he kept me from playing that tournament. But rather than disheartening me, that only made me want to try harder. I knew what my game needed better than anyone else.

At that time there was still a pro tour that traveled the country. Some of the great names in tennis were involved: Pancho Gonzalez, Rod Laver, Roy Emerson—real legends of the tennis world. It just so happened that one of their stops that year was in Midland,

Texas. They played an eight-man tournament over there which Dad and I drove to go watch. We took an 8-mm video camera and showed up to film every one of those players' serves.

Dad had his own ideas about what I needed to do to improve, but it helped both of us to study those guys because, as with most mechanical movements in sports, there are across-the-board elements that create soundness in a particular motion. On the other hand, there are also idiosyncratic aspects that only pertain to that one person. Those are things you probably should not attempt to copy.

What we tried to do was to look at every one of their service motions and figure out what the common thread was. When the hitting arm and racquet were coming to the ball, what was the right shoulder doing? In all the serves we looked at of those great players, the right shoulder was acting like a piston going toward the target. Then we filmed my serve and compared. My right shoulder was stopping in the action too quickly. We tried to figure out why. We looked at the motion right before that. My right elbow wasn't doing what it was supposed to on the backswing. That, in turn, was causing my right shoulder to stop moving too soon.

That's all we did for four months. And it worked: I improved. One of the first tournaments I played internationally the next year was in Johannesburg, South Africa. One day I was out there playing and afterward, a player from Australia named Barry Phillips-Moore, a pretty good player who later ended up being a top coach, came up to me in the locker room and said, "I can't believe how much better your serve looks since I last saw you."

Any little change that you make in sports just feels huge. I was already 21 and had been playing for a long time. I already had a groove with the old way I hit my serve. You can imagine the thousands of times I had swung and ingrained those old habits! But I spent four months taking a long, hard look at myself. When I hit one I liked, I would use a hand signal to tell myself later on the video to copy that one.

I could have filmed more of the rest of my game, but I wasn't interested in that. We were after improvement in just that one area—and the focus wasn't only on me. We were flipping back to the other guys we filmed to make a good comparison.

It was neat to know, after we spent those months doing what we did, that it was a successful project. I never did have a great serve, but I improved it to the point that it wasn't as big a liability as it used to be. We did get tangible proof of that reward. There was one match two years later in the fall of 1970 when I beat Ken Rosewall in one of the tournaments leading up to winning the Grand Prix. It was a semifinal match at Wembley in London. Fast carpet indoors wasn't even my best surface, but I felt like I served him off the court that night with a high number of aces. He was one of the best returners of serve in the game, but that night, he couldn't return all of mine. I almost think I won the World Point Title because I had taken the time out to improve my serve.

Don't be afraid to "pull off the tour" for a while to take a hard look at one particular area of your life. The results and the benefits can be long-term. When I made that decision, I was even threatened with negative consequences professionally. I even missed the very first U.S. Open in 1968! But I wasn't afraid to take myself out of the action long enough to shore up my game. That was the decision I made. I voluntarily pulled off and went into a four-month seclusion. I tried to rework it. Studying my serve on video, compared to other people's, for weeks and even months gave me a chance to look at myself objectively.

In depression, you are forced into seclusion. It's involuntary. But in both cases, you are taking a hard look at yourself, at some things that need to be retooled. You're standing outside yourself and taking a look at how your actions might be affecting other people. In doing so, you gain a perspective you had not seen before.

Fast forward to 1996, when I was in a different kind of "losing game." I decided to discontinue the counseling sessions. I had done it for a year—about 30 to 35 meetings. I could tell the counselor was running out of ammo. He sensed that I really, beyond a certain point, wasn't getting any better. He also thought I should give up all competition in my life. Needless to say, I got a little upset with that.

My big break came shortly thereafter, when I went to my dermatologist to have some skin cancers removed. During his residency, this doctor had spent a year in a psych ward. He didn't say anything to me during my appointment, but later, he said to Mickie (he had been a long-time friend of the family): "I think Cliff is suffering from clinical depression. He's trying to lick it on his own. He won't be able to." He recommended that I go on antidepressant medication.

When Mickie told me, I remembered my counselor once had mentioned the possibility that I might have clinical depression. Strangely, it had only come up one time in the course of an entire year of counseling. I figured I had nothing to lose. It wouldn't hurt to try something new. When you're overboard and you're drowning, you're sure as heck going to grab a lifeline when it's thrown to you!

I called him and said, "My dad always told me to change a losing game. Call in the prescription." I asked him how he came up with his tentative diagnosis. He said, "I can read it in your face." I literally have creases at the corners of my mouth which make it look like I wear a permanent frown. From his experience in the psych ward, he was trained to recognize those warning signs.

There's a difference between thinking you might have depression and knowing that you have it. You finally become convinced you have a problem. The day that happened, it didn't scare me. I accepted his diagnosis. In fact, I felt stupid for not realizing it before. I was convinced he was right and that very minute, I tried to get help.

That doctor was surprised to get a phone call from me asking for a prescription. He had thought I might be too bullheaded for that. But I wasn't. In tennis, I was willing to adapt to changing conditions. To shore up deteriorating strokes. I was always willing

201

to change a losing game.

Be willing to adapt. Don't be stubborn or egotistical or macho in a bad way. Don't be too busy to listen. Don't be afraid to admit you have a problem.

As with any tennis match, there are times in life to change your strategy. Why go down with a sinking ship? Tennis players have been known to "tank" a set just to rest. Not expend energy. Save it for the final set. That's not giving up. It's just being smart.

When you're in the middle of a tough match, there's no time for niceties. No time for bullshit. No time for worrying about hurting anybody's feelings. No time for anything other than trying to figure out what you've got to do—which is the same thing you do when you go to war.

I'm such a competitive person, I want to feel like I can do it all. Like I can handle everything. But it's OK to eliminate unnecessary stress. Don't be so macho about thinking you can do everything all at once.

It's like the bills you have at the end of the month. Some of the bills, you can't do anything about. Those are built-in, fixed expenses. It's the same with stresses. There are certain stresses that are built in. One of the keys is to figure out which stresses in your life might be optional. Which ones you can eliminate. Which ones are not necessary.

I've made a life of trying to figure out what my strengths and weaknesses are—both as a player and as a person. Capitalize on the strengths and minimize the weaknesses. In tennis, I knew what my weaknesses were. It paid to know what they were. It's OK to be "weak"—it's what you do with that knowledge that counts.

One correlation between competitive tennis and depression is that you'd better not delude yourself as to how badly you're playing at a given time. You've got to know when you need to improve your serve or some other shot so that at least it's not a liability. Be as objective as you can. Don't overestimate or underestimate your opponent either. Own your advantages as well as your vulnerabilities.

At that point, I was desperate. I didn't care if the road ahead was tough. I just wanted to find something that worked. If someone had told me the solution was to get a rocket ship and blast off to the moon, I would have started looking around for a launching pad! The tragedy, as I see it, is with people who have so much to give, but are stopped either temporarily or—in the case of suicide—forever. Never be afraid to change a losing game.

Even before I knew what the problem was, I was trying to fight it and use my competitive skills against it. I certainly viewed it as an opponent, lurking there in the shadows. When it was unmasked, I saw it staring at me from across the net.

I'm surprised I didn't catch on quicker. It's crazy. I don't have an explanation. In hindsight, I can see what a stupe I was. Before blaming anyone else, whether it be my counselor or my family, I would have to point a finger at myself.

I remember hearing my father-in-law, Dr. Girard, talk about different kinds of mental illness shortly after we got married. I remember thinking, "I wonder what that feels like?" Years ago, I never thought I would need a hip replaced either. But now I have an artificial hip that squeaks. You never think it can happen to you.

Circumstances conspired against my getting help sooner. You think depression is something you just read about. You think, "This is just the way I react to life." As a competitor, you're also trained to believe that you're strong enough not to succumb to it. It's viewed as weakness, your parents didn't raise you properly, or you have too much sin in your life. Your ego is wrapped up in it. You never really believe you have it until you're already insane.

The way people sometimes view mental illness is that you're either nuts or you're not. You either have it or you don't. As if it were that cut and dried! It can be a very fluctuating thing. The slippery, tricky part is that some people will have one episode but then never have it again. Other people have multiple depressions; in that case, each one can make you more susceptible to experiencing another bout. It's also a progressive disease. So people who are diagnosed early may only need a very low dosage of medicine at the beginning. Then they might have to raise it later on.

Once I understood what I was dealing with, then a lot of the 30 years prior to that suddenly made sense both to Mickie and to me. One remarkable thing is that Mickie was a psychology major at the University of Texas for almost three years, but she never diagnosed me. She encouraged me when I finally did seek help. She had long suspected something was wrong with me, but she didn't ever look at me and say, "I think you have clinical depression." That's the degree of our powers of disassociation! That just shows how you can be blind to something that's totally staring you in the face. No amount of education can ever truly prepare you for the realities of mental illness.

I actually think my training as an athlete worked against me in this respect. Whenever I used to feel inordinately tired or draggy, Dad would say, "You're not disciplined enough." Stick-to-it-iveness can be both a positive and a negative. As a champion, you're used to playing with cramps or a fever or with only five hours' sleep in a time zone change. So you go down the same path longer than you should. I honestly think I was in denial because of sports conditioning. A misplaced notion of "toughness" kept me from getting help much, much sooner.

Don't let your ego say, "But Plan A should work." Just waiting it out will not help you improve. Don't be afraid to switch to Plan B. The most manly thing you can do, at times, is to admit you have a problem. To re-organize. You can't make it through sheer determination. When it comes to depression, sports discipline can actually be counterproductive.

There are certain warning signs that a person might be depressed. You can see stress in people's eyes if you know what to look for. A turned-down mouth. Slouchy posture. Lowered head.

Negative talk. Loss of appetite. Sighing out of nowhere. Running around unshaven. Suddenly not enjoying something you've always enjoyed. That's a big warning sign, right there. Or alternatively, one of the first things I ask anybody is: how much sleep are you getting? When do you wake up? Any significant changes in your routine? That can be another bright red flag.

When you look at a medical chart (there is no blood test for it yet), there are probably 10 to 12 classic symptoms of clinical depression. In a major episode, a person will probably experience at least half of those. If you have any of those symptoms for two to three weeks or longer, or particularly all of them together, then boy, you'd better watch out! It's a fairly easy disease to diagnose, with a knowledgeable doctor and a receptive patient (that is, of course, provided he's being honest).

I hope scientists doing research on brain chemistry will some day be able to answer more of our questions. Like in the area of using genetics as a marker. If people have certain predispositions in their chromosomes, then perhaps they could get diagnosed earlier. A positive diagnosis that is beyond conjecture can be helpful when trying to convince an employer or skeptical relatives.

Are we ever going to have a vaccine for depression? Or maybe a pre-emptive pill or injection in youth so it never gets very bad? More information would go a long way toward combating the skeptics (primarily insurance companies) who don't want to offer full coverage for mental disease. We need tests that are as reliable and respected as a diabetes test, for instance. Diabetic comas are taken seriously. Unfortunately, at least in our society, depressive stupors are not.

There was a real process for me of finding and adjusting the dosage on the right antidepressant medication. Everyone's body is going to react in a different way. That's a personal thing. I had to start with crumbs of medicine as small as granulated sugar. Thankfully, when I sink my teeth into something, I don't let go real easy.

I'm tenacious. A sports writer once wrote an article on me called "One Tenacious Texan."

First, I went on Elavil. That's an old-line antidepressant. My dermatologist was an older doctor and felt more comfortable with it. But I couldn't tolerate it. It made me feel like somebody had plugged my butt into an electrical outlet. I've always been pretty wired anyway. That medicine sent me through the ceiling!

That failed experiment with the first antidepressant was a real setback. Like being a break down in a match. Elavil is a dirtier drug because it takes a scatter-shot approach. It hits more systems in your body than necessary. I talked to another MD who was also a family friend. He was a heart doctor and an internist. He recommended that I try Zoloft. It's a drug that is more targeted, more specific. He had prescribed it for his own father once. He agreed to prescribe it for me, but he also wanted me to consult with a licensed psychologist.

I tried to take the lowest therapeutic dose, 50mg, which I couldn't tolerate. It gave me nausea. The psychologist recommended that I cut the pill in half. I started out with 15-20mg, like about a third of a 50-mg pill. I still had nausea and other side effects, but I was convinced that this was a drug I needed to stay with, at least to try it for a little while.

I kept a daily log of how much I was taking. After a week to 10 days, I would raise the dosage by 10mg. After a full month, I got it up to 50mg, which is the minimal therapeutic dose. After three months, I got it up to 75mg. Finally, I started to feel some relief.

My psychologist actually became impatient with waiting before I did. The day before I started to feel better, he advised trying a different drug, Paxil. I even got the prescription filled. But I decided to wait one more day before switching. I knew that even once you can finally get the therapeutic dose in you, it usually takes another two to three weeks before you feel anything. That's because your serotonin levels have to rise. At that point, about 70 to 75 percent of the people who try SSRIs (selective serotonin reuptake inhibitors) report that they do feel some relief.

I became convinced that Zoloft was the drug for me. But it was bloody sure the equivalent of a 30-minute first game in a tennis match! I invested four months in that drug without feeling much better. I couldn't tolerate it well enough to really get the drug flowing through my system. There at the end, I stood in my mother's kitchen and said, "I'm going to give it one more day." I just felt like I had invested too much in that process not to stick it out for the long haul.

Did I feel better the next day just from wanting it so badly? I don't know. But I guarantee you if I had still felt lousy the next week, I would have switched to Paxil. I even talked with my pharmacist, Marty Daniel, who helped me figure out what the therapeutic dosage was. He was a big part of my recovery. He would patiently spend a lot of time with me on the phone. He realized the value of making me feel comfortable with the medicine. He never once lost patience with me.

Looking back on it now, I waited out that son-of-a-bitch medicine for four and a half long months! When you're as depressed as I was, and you're on your knees asking God to kick the Zoloft up your ass and make it start working, even three hours can feel like a long time. Try four and a half months! I just kept hanging on to the fact that three out of four people who take SSRIs are helped by them. I was determined to give the drug a fair chance.

Right now I'm on a relatively high dose, 200mg. For most of the past ten years I've taken 100-200mg a day. Occasionally I've upped it to 300mg. I adjusted the dosage in consultation with my psychologist. When I called him, he asked, "How do you feel with this amount?" At one stage, I lowered the dosage too quickly. He told me that if I had to, I could go as high as 300-350mg. Thankfully, at least so far, I've never had to go that high.

Zoloft is also an anti-anxiety drug, not just an antidepressant, so I've had to learn how to compete while feeling good. There's not that uncomfortable drive, but you definitely get a lifting of mood—kind of like what I used to feel with two or three beers. It's just a little bit of serenity, a little heightening of spirit. Not a drugged feeling, but more of a natural thing. It's funny, but I don't feel zoned or drugged out.

I like to say that Zoloft "raises the floor" beyond which you can fall. That's a very complicated thing, really. That "floor" is not absolute. The other five percent of the time, you can still fall into depression.

It also doesn't elevate your mood past that of a normal person. It just levels the playing field. It gives you a window of opportunity to use your coping skills and prevent certain episodes that might degenerate real far, real quick. It definitely isn't a cure-all. But in my mind, my entire life is divided into pre- and post-1997 (the year I went on antidepressants).

I would even go so far as to say that antidepressant medication has been the single greatest factor in my recovery. But it's not the only one. The role of cognitive therapy cannot be over-emphasized. If you injure a muscle, you have to go through physical therapy. Cognitive therapy is like rehab for your brain.

In tennis, before a match, I always tried to study my opponent. For example, when I first played the world tour, I played Mike Belkin in Florida. He beat me. He was a really good clay court player. I thought I had to be aggressive against him and beat him with power. The next tournament was in Houston, at River Oaks. I was telling Dad about the match I had played the week before and said, "I just don't think I can beat this guy." He said I was being too negative. He said there was always a way. But he didn't have a plan. So I thought about it and realized I had been giving Belkin a target by coming in to the net. I decided to try not coming to the net at all and just be patient. Extract a few errors from him. Win by letting him make the mistakes. Break him down mentally. Before, I had been playing right into his hands. I went out that day and beat him in straight sets.

In any sport, there are game plans and strategies. I knew the kind of character and staying power each of my opponents had. A sports writer wrote once that I was actually one of the best strategists of the game.

Depression is like an opponent in tennis. It has a character. A given flavor. It has a certain way it likes to come at you, particularly after losses, or at times of extreme stress.

Try to figure out the personality of your particular kind of depression. Get to know it. Study it like an opponent. Learn all you can about it to help you strategize and, eventually, to win. You've got to devise a game plan to get your ass out of this crack. It's a hell of a lot bigger contest than a tennis match!

Psychotherapy can take many forms. It might mean talking to a friend. It's vital to have somebody who is willing to listen. If you're fortunate enough to have loved ones who will do nothing more than just listen as you pour your heart out, that might do you more good than a formal counseling session.

I'm convinced that "counseling" does not have to happen in an office. Counseling means gaining knowledge. Sometimes you can do that in a bookstore as well as on the psychotherapist's couch.

I realize I may be taking money out of psychiatrists' pockets by saying that. But I don't care. If going to the shrink's office helps you, great. But the vast majority of depressed people probably can't afford psychotherapy.

For those who can, I've seen some people rely too heavily on their shrink. If you're looking to a therapist to direct your life entirely, there's something wrong. A psychotherapist is like a coach. Coaches can be invaluable. But your coach can't go out and play your match for you.

Another real pitfall of psychotherapy, as I see it, is that the goal is to delve deeper for some incident of orgin. And if there isn't one, the doctor makes more out of some little thing than he should. It's fine to look at the game films but if the quarterback is having a bad day, it's probably not because his father was late one morning, dropping him off at kindergarten. It's probably just that his throwing mechanism is off! In sports, we often say: "Don't over-analyze it." Athletes have this great ability to keep it real. We may be dumb jocks but sometimes it's better to underthink something than to overthink it. In the sports world, it's called the KISS Method: "Keep It Simple, Stupid."

Medical people say cognitive therapy alone is the worst option. The next best is medication only. The best choice is probably some combination of the two. If you are going to see a therapist, then think of that person as your athletic coach. In other words, stick with one good one. Don't keep changing all the time. If you've decided to try to learn about it on your own, then go to the library. The bookstore. The internet. If you're depressed, it may take you three hours to read 50 pages, where it only used to take you 30 minutes to read that same amount. But just keep telling yourself: you can do it. You will get through this time.

When the great golfer Ben Hogan was asked about the secret of improving in golf, he used to say: "It's in the dirt." What he meant was that you have to learn it yourself. You have to go out and pound balls until you figure it out. One advantage to that approach is that when you do learn something that way, forever afterward, you will really feel like it is something you own.

It may seem obvious, but the next step is: apply what you've learned. I would sometimes work out a detailed game plan when I went out there to compete. When I played the U.S. Indoors in 1968, I taped a piece of masking tape to the side of my racquet with instructions for myself. It was the fastest surface we ever played on. Nobody thought I could win.

The first point of each game I served, my strategy was to get the first serve in play. For the second point, get the first serve in play again. For the third point, I might go for a big first serve and try for an ace. If I was ahead, I could risk not getting the first serve in the court. For the fourth point, if I was way ahead, I would go for a big first serve again. If not, then I would adjust. I stayed with that game plan about 95 percent of the time.

I wrote those instructions on the masking tape so that in the heat of battle, I wouldn't forget. I kept that piece of tape on the side of my racquet during the whole tournament. And I won. It takes discipline, patience, and attention to detail to implement your game plan well. But it's worth it. Do whatever it takes to remind yourself of the strategies you've devised.

Depression is a great time to have the buzzer go off—to make you wake up to some things in your life you might need to re-organize. I used to go over to Dad's when I had been crying for days. I had been reading books on codependency and parents who live vicariously through their children. I wanted to talk to him about it. I was one sick puppy dog. He would sometimes get defensive and not want to talk about things. I would say, "Dad, Dad, this isn't about you! This is about me getting well. I'm not trying to blame you for what happened. This is to help me so I can get better."

When you get to the root of codependency, it's like peeling back layers of an onion. If I tried to discuss with Dad the influence that his parents had on him, it became clear that that was a difficult subject. He always claimed, "It made me tougher." But I was seeing some dysfunction. Those conversations were very difficult. We argued a lot. Then I would come home and cry. That was all part of the process of getting through my codependency with my father.

In general, though, the reactions from family members to my announcement that I had clinical depression were almost uniformly supportive. They never proffered the opinion that I shouldn't be going on antidepressant meds. They were just tickled pink that I was finally getting some relief. There weren't any big denials or rancorous talks. They didn't always understand; but even at those times, I

211

knew they still loved me.

Thank God I got help when I did. Prior to that, I had actually thought about checking myself into a hospital. Mickie and I discussed it when I reached the point that I could not sleep. She didn't say, "You've got to check yourself in. You're beyond what I can cope with." It was more like, "If this goes on much longer, we might need to check you in." I think if I had agreed to it at one stage, we might have done it. I did not reject the idea. I probably should have gone, in some ways. It was definitely considered. Neither one of us wanted to do that, so we just held on as long as we could. Ultimately, we did get through. As beaten down as I was, I still had a reservoir of persistence left. Not to bull my way through, but to keep trying to adjust to the Zoloft—to get enough of it into my system. I had been through a year of counseling. We were doing a lot of reading. In other words, we were taking positive steps. We were not just sitting there, waiting for things to improve.

The flip side to the motto of "change a losing game" would be: "don't change a winning one." Don't go off the medicine just because you start feeling good. In the late 1960s, Wilson Sporting Goods started manufacturing racquets of the aluminum-metal variety. Before that, you never saw anything but wood. Wilson had just come out with a metal racquet, the T-2000. That racquet was revolutionary. Instead of holes, they used loops to string the racquet. It was like a trampoline! With less effort, you got a stronger hit. Jimmy Connors used that racquet for most of his career.

I tried to use those racquets, but on about the fifth hit, I'd get a "flyer." The ball would fly four more feet than I was expecting it to! That can be scary. You don't know when it's coming. At the beginning, Wilson was really trying to promote its new racquet. They were offering people double the money if they would use the T-2000. I used it in practice for a few months in 1969. But before leaving for Europe, I packed four wooden racquets just in case. When I got there, I went out and practiced with Cliff Drysdale from

South Africa. I knew on that very first day there would be no way I could use those racquets in competition. They were offering me a bunch more money, but it didn't matter. I needed to stick with what I knew.

Sometimes you need to fall back on your old weapons and not follow the lure of the latest new-fangled thing. If someone offered me a brand-new antidepressant, I wouldn't trade in the Zoloft. And I know that I'll be on antidepressant medication literally for the rest of my life. I've made my peace with that. If you've had at least three major episodes and you're over the age of 50, like I am, most doctors recommend that you stay medicated for the duration. Always change a losing game. But don't change what's working.

CHAPTER EIGHTEEN

Comeback Kid

Y ou really can get a second wind sometimes in a tennis match. In matches I played, there were times I felt that happen. It's the reverse of having the noon-time meal and all of a sudden feeling drowsy. All at once, you resuscitate. You come back to life again.

One of the toughest things about coming back is: not only are you down mentally, but also, you're physically exhausted. You always feel more tired in a match if you're behind! But you've been trained to marshal your resources. Maybe your game plan isn't working. You might have a secondary game plan. Your third game plan might be flying by the seat of your pants! You just need to bust the momentum. Throw something at him that he ain't expecting. Try to turn a losing situation around.

I could be way, way down in tennis matches when it had been predicted that I would choke. But my training was such that when it got tough, I rallied. My opponents never felt like they could get me so far down that I would then just give them the rest of it. They knew it would be a dog fight to the end. I had a good record of coming back from being in a real tight spot. On the tour, I was also known as the Comeback Kid.

You see, in a best-of-five-sets match, if I'm two sets to love down, I have an attitude at that point. I have nowhere to go but up. I've got nothing to lose. Close to victory, my opponent is probably going to experience a little bit of a letdown. And I'm gonna pounce on that. Even with a two-minute break in his concentration, that's still enough for me to gain a foothold.

There are times I would instinctively take longer between points, before I served, just in order to change the momentum. Then once I'd broken that cycle, the dynamic instantly started spinning back in my favor. A few minutes later, I would have won the next set. And then all of a sudden, I'd be right back in the match! Pretty soon, I'd be leading. By that point, it had been a long time since the other guy had had anything good happen.

When you're way down in a tennis match, it's easy to get discouraged—to give up hope. You don't feel like marshalling your resources. But somehow you have to pull it out of your guts in time to come all the way back and win the match.

It's the same with depression. Depression feels like an extremely foggy morning. Without medication, you can't even drive out of it. You're just sitting there, waiting for it to dissipate—for the sun to come out and burn off the fog.

With the help of antidepressants, you may be able to drive a little way out. But you don't come out of it immediately. You're still in the zone. You don't just miraculously get your life back all at once.

Whatever that monster is that's been on your shoulder for three years, now it's off. But you're still jumpy. You are wondering how much stress you can handle. You feel leery and shell-shocked. You don't see how you could ever return.

When that happened to me, my competitive instincts took over from my tennis days. On the court, I was known for my stubborn determination—for never giving up. That quality came to my aid in the fight against depression.

I asked a Christian counselor once how long it usually takes for clinically depressed people to get better. There is no magic formula.

It's like ripples in a pond. It can take a long time. But if you're will-ing to work hard enough, you can get there. There's no quick fix. Then again, that's like anything in life. We used to laugh at these kids who took five tennis lessons and then thought they could go play tournaments. It took me a long time to become a good tennis player. You have to give the antidepressant medicine a long, thorough try. It may take four weeks or longer before you feel much relief.

The basic rule is: how long it takes to come out of a deep de-pression depends in part on how long you've been in. I would relate it to the skills I've developed in tennis. If I have my tennis game in good shape, and I lay off for three days—meaning I don't pick up a racquet, don't even go for a run—I know from experience that it will take two or three days before I will really feel like I'm back in shape. If I lay off for three weeks or a month, likewise, it will take at least a couple of weeks.

The longer you're in depression, the longer it takes to come out. It will probably be 10 days to two weeks before I really feel bet-ter after a four- or five-week bout. It's a gradual process. It's not a "boom, you're out of it" sort of a deal. You slowly begin to feel like you can handle a little bit more. It's like having a fever. You start to feel that it's lessening a bit. You fear it's just a temporary elevated mood, but slowly you begin to ease your way back into feeling like you can handle life again.

After my three-year episode, I finally started to recover in April of 1997. Six months after that, I looked at Mickie and said that I felt better still. Then a year later, I had another incremental im-provement. I can look back and see that it was a process of starting to adjust to life again on a gradual basis.

Guys always want to know about the effects of depression on your sex life. Fortunately for me, until I went on the antidepressant, it didn't slow me down. But I'm going to be honest with you. The antidepressant does. It's known to diminish your libido. I prob-ably went from the normal once or twice a week to once every couple of weeks. You're fully functional while having sex. There's no erectile dysfunction, but I'd say the desire is roughly cut in half. Mickie joked once after I gave her a sexy little nuzzle that she was concerned that I had forgotten to take my medicine! As far as I'm concerned, though, you could take all the sex away, and it would still be worth the relief from depression.

There were a lot of other side effects in the beginning, including dry mouth and upset stomach. I had severely chapped lips at one time. I still use special toothpaste and mouthwash to prevent gum disease and provide lubrication. The kind I use only just recently became available. I guess it took a while for the toothpaste industry to catch up with the psychiatric one!

After I went on antidepressants and everyone could see I was doing a lot better, Dad did not understand the need for me to stay on them. He asked if there was a way I could wean myself off the medicine. He never liked medicine of any kind. In the end, he left it up to me. But we did have those conversations.

To be fair to him, I had good support with it, really. The only time I had to tell him he was off-base was when he wanted me to get off the drugs. He was worried about the side effects. I told him those were much less worrisome than the known side effects of depression—everything from heart disease to suicide!

There's a big difference between being down in a tennis match and quitting tennis altogether. But in either situation, to make a comeback, some of the same principles apply. It's tougher to come back from being flat-ass down than to rise if you've never had a slump. But it is possible. It takes will, determination, discipline and sacrifice. My training inside Richey, Inc. gave me all of those things.

Before I really went into recovery, I thought if I could ever feel halfway good again, it would be worthwhile. I never dreamed I could feel this energetic. Like with tennis, the comeback from depression may be even sweeter than my original accomplishments.

Looking back, in the fall of 1980, I remember thinking I needed to make more money. For the first time in my life, that was an incentive. It was for the security of my family. I didn't really start playing tennis again for that reason. I just got the bug to play again and to be more productive. After two years of being lazy, I needed to get off my butt! I didn't want to teach. I knew I wasn't temperamentally suited for that. I tried coaching a player on the main tour for a while, but that was abortive. I didn't have the right personality, like Dad did, to make a very good coach.

So at age 33, I decided to try to make a comeback into the game. I called Jim McManus at the ATP and told him I wanted to play again. I asked him for contacts to go play a satellite tour. I had lost my world ranking from being out for so long. I was getting very old to try to play the regular tour. He said "Well, Cliff, with your work ethic, if anybody can make a comeback, it will be you."

When I told my San Angelo golfing buddies, who were all much older than I was, that I had decided to play the tennis tour again, they were happy for me. They thought I would do well. I was much younger than they were. I said, "Yeah, but I'm gonna have to learn how to compete again. I have to dive back into that competitive pit." I had been out for two years. At the age of 33 or 34, there was a possibility physically that I could do it. But the big question mark was whether I could recapture that competitive fire. I sensed that I was a different person now. If I was thrown back into that crucible, would my outer layers be able to handle the heat? Although in this case, it was my inner layers that I really needed to worry about. . . .

I went down to South Africa to play a minor tour. Not a senior tour. It was actually a fairly young crowd. It was a satellite tour for up-and-coming players—99 percent of the guys were young bucks. I was coming at it from the other side. It was ass-backwards really. They were just trying to break into the game. But we had something in common because even at my advanced age, I was attempting to stage my re-entry.

I was welcomed onto that tour because I was a South African

Open champion. The tournament directors saw the value in having a more established name on their tour. They gave me a small guarantee to cover my expenses. The event that kicked off the tour was held in Windhoek, Namibia followed by stops in Johannesburg, Bloemfontein, Durban, and East London.

I was an old fart. I felt like a fish out of water. I would go out and practice with these young guys. I remember this young Belgian. Somehow he found out my age. He had thought I was much older than 33, maybe because I had started playing tennis so early. Or maybe because depression had taken its toll. He had heard my name for so many years. He was probably only 12 or 13 when I got to the semis of the French.

My game was very rusty. I had developed a real bad corn between my toes. I had had one in the same place in 1976. That time it got infected. I could hardly walk. There was a hole almost down to the bone. It wasn't that bad this time, but it was painful. It was getting to the point where I could hardly play at all.

I reached the stage where I said, "You know, this isn't working." I was homesick. I had been traveling alone for six weeks, literally halfway around the world. I had this spooky feeling that I was not only in South Africa—that somehow, I was on an entirely different planet! I was playing in these backwater towns. One day while practicing in East London I saw a Monitor lizard the size of a dog by the court. I swear that thing was like two feet long! Being there was such a culture shock. It felt like floating in the twilight zone.

I started getting claustrophobic. I had to take a 20-hour flight just to get home. I knew the only way home was this long metal tube (the airplane). That frigging 747. I started fearing it. I was almost fearful I wouldn't be able to get home. That's the only time in all my travels I ever felt that way. It was like I was out on a space walk with nothing but that tether between myself and the mother ship.

I went home. I told them I couldn't finish the tour. I had played the majority of the events. My foot was killing me. Datsun Motors, the sponsor, owed me some money. They didn't want to pay me. I called and called. Told them I had made a good faith effort. They finally paid up.

I had thrown the game away completely two years before. I was out of shape physically. I needed to lose some weight. My body had changed. At that time Fred Stolle, the Aussie great, was on the senior tour. He and I went back to 1962, when I was just a kid. All of my aggressiveness and bluster, he took with a grain of salt. He got a kick out of watching me play. In 1981, after I had played a few events, he said, "Hey, Bull, you've been training pretty hard, haven't you? I can tell because your thighs are thinner." It took me a full year to get back in good shape.

It helped that I had a clean slate to work with: the comeback slate. I wasn't as hard on myself. I was more accepting of my faults. I had never had a big weapon in my arsenal, like a big serve. I was more of a finesse player. In my heart of hearts, I knew I would have needed a big weapon to make a serious comeback on the regular tour.

After returning from South Africa, I went to Amarillo to play the Texas Open. Dad went with me to try to help. I didn't do very well there either. Dad and I had a discussion in the motel room in Amarillo. I said to him, "I still want to play, but I don't know where I can play." We both thought of the senior tour. I said, "Yeah, but those tournaments are run by management firms. Those might be impossible to get into." Part of Richey, Inc. philosophy was never to use managers or agents. We wanted to be totally self-sufficient. All the senior events were produced by major management firms and that was going to present a problem.

Characteristically, Dad didn't want me to give up so easily. He encouraged me to call the International Management Group (IMG) in Cleveland. IMG was the first of the huge sports agencies. The firm's founder, Mark McCormack, was the one who took sports management to a whole new level.

From 1981-83, the senior tennis tour for players 35 years old and over was called (fittingly) the Legends of Tennis. IMG basically ran the tour for its clients. Rod Laver, Ken Rosewall, Fred Stolle, John Newcombe, Roy Emerson and Ilie Nastase were some of the guys who played it. The criteria to play the senior tennis tour made it a very elite thing. You had to meet at least one of three standards: you had to have won a Grand Slam event, to have won Davis Cup, or to have been ranked No. 1 in your country. I had never won a Grand Slam; but by the other two criteria, I was well qualified.

The guy in charge of the IMG tour was named Alan Morrell. I had done an exhibition for him in 1978 with Ilie Nastase in Hershey, Pennsylvania. I called him up on the phone and told him I wanted to play the senior tour. He gave me a polite no—the courteous brush-off. My dad said, "Call Rod Laver." I had beaten him in the first money match I ever played at Madison Square Garden. To this day, I consider him to be the greatest player who's ever played the game. He was one of IMG's main clients.

I called him. I had only returned to the game, even practicing, within the previous five to six months, but I called him and said I'd really like to play some IMG events. He said, "We need guys like you on our tour. You always stay in good shape physically and compete hard." He didn't even mean that to be a compliment necessarily but it was exactly the encouragement I needed. The other huge source of encouragement at that time was Dad. If it hadn't been for Dad's persistence, his refusal to take "no" for an answer, I might never have played the senior tour.

I played my first senior pro event on the Legends Tour in March of 1981, in Miami, Florida. I lost to Laver in the final but earned $6,375. Not bad for my first senior tournament! Due in large part to his intervention, I played every event that year, from March of 1981 to the middle part of 1982. I wrote him a letter thanking him for helping me get on the tour. In my opinion the "Rocket" is not only the greatest tennis player of all time, but also one of the most

If it hadn't been for Dad's persistence—as well as some help from Rod Laver—I might never have played the senior tennis tour.

humble and genuinely nice guys you'll ever meet.

I played close to 100 senior tour events over the course of the next 10 years. On average, I played 10-12 a year. I earned about $3,500 a week, plus endorsements. I also did some corporate outings. A corporate outing is like a big party for a company's top employees involving a tennis clinic and round-robin doubles. You have to go to dinner with corporate executives and schmooze, then give an after-dinner speech and hand out the prizes. These corporate outings typically paid about $2,500-3,000 each.

One of the events I'm most proud of winning was the Legends Championship at the L.A. Forum. It was our senior tour finale. I had already been on the road for three weeks in a row. I was 36 years old and not getting any younger. I played on three different surfaces in three weeks: hard courts in Tulsa; clay courts in Stratton, Vermont; and now indoor carpet in L.A. At the first event in Tulsa, I was cramping so badly after I lost the final match, they had to put IVs in my arm. After beating Laver in the semis in L.A., I still had to play doubles that same evening and didn't get off the court until midnight. I was totally running on fumes.

It would have been so easy to say: "I've had a good run." I had already beaten Laver in the semis. I was set to play Mark Cox of Great Britain in the final. Even if I just simply quit at that point, I would still go home having been the runner-up in three straight tournaments. But my training was never to use anything as an excuse. I told myself, "Your job is not finished yet." Time zone changes, surface changes, all different conditions. A pro knows you have to go out there and give it your best, regardless. It's you, baby. You own this deal. You want to be the best you can be? This is your chance. There's no one else to take the lead. You are in charge.

I won the tournament. I won! I beat Cox 7-6, 6-3. I won more money in that match than I had ever earned in any single tournament on the main tour—$15,375—my largest prize money check ever. I had it blown up to hang on the wall. But even more important than the money was the fact that it was my first tournament win in five and a half years. Never before in my career had a victory felt so sweet.

I picked up a pay phone at the Los Angeles airport and called Mom. I had left the regular tour on a sour note. I guess I never went off the radar screen completely; but in my head, at least, my career was finished. I was a has-been. I told Mom, "I can put my racquet down now and feel like it's a closed chapter." I flew back to Texas that Sunday evening. It was late at night, and the last commuter plane to San Angelo had already left. I spent the night at a hotel near the Dallas/Fort Worth airport. I woke up in the middle of the night, wondering whether it had all been a dream. Had I really just won that tournament? I got out of bed, went over to the dresser and took the $15,000 check out of my wallet. I was holding in my hands the tangible proof: I had truly made it all the way back.

Coming out of depression, it's the reverse order of what it's like going in. Your stressors flip over. If your triggers stop firing, and you have a good run with everything, the anxiety starts lessening. You feel more capable, more patient. Suddenly you're having good days. Not feeling so stressed out.

Coming out of depression means relief. The pressure's off. The sun's coming up. You look forward to the day instead of dreading it all. You start feeling like you're among the living again.

It's been in stages, as far as feeling better. I knew I was beginning to recover once I started feeling a little more peace. By May of 1997, I played my first golf tournament since that worst depressive episode struck. It has been a progression since then.

There for a while, I had several episodes a year that were very tough. I have about one a year now. The ebb and flow of my moods is not that different from normal people's, except that the downs are not normal downs. They are sick downs.

It's still hard to predict how long a depressive episode will last. In a way, each one of them is a learning experience. What I tell myself when I'm in depression is: "You know the other ones have always passed."

For normal reversals, you sense that life circumstances will probably turn back around for you. That it's nothing serious enough to send you into a three-year bout. Instead, it might last anywhere from one week to two weeks or even perhaps as long as six.

Intellectually, you know this: the antidepressants will keep you from falling too far. Even with short-term reversals, you process them differently if you're depressed. You don't deal with them in a healthy way. You know they aren't that big of a deal, but you over-dramatize them anyhow. They don't feel like just a temporary blip on the radar screen.

There will always be permanent residues. You will never get to the point where you have completely conquered depression. There's a damaged, diseased part of myself that's still there, that I don't ever completely escape from or get rid of. I realize that my damaged side may only improve up to a point. I think the rest of me can improve more. That's the healthy side. I hope I can use my healthy side to override my damaged side. You learn to compensate. To tack a little bit more northeast than you used to, perhaps. Eventually you learn how to shift your sails.

You do have some control over the length of your bouts. With wise choices and good decisions, you'll probably shorten the episodes. I'm 63 years old, but I feel healthier and stronger than I ever have in my life. I try to exercise about 200 days a year, meaning that I go for a brisk walk. I feel absolutely wonderful. I feel great. Recently I have felt better more days of the year, on a more consistent basis, than I have at any other point in time.

I know what Zoloft gave me. It's not just my imagination. I had spent three years in hell. The medicine created a serenity in my brain. My family can see the difference. It gave me back my personality. The medication makes me more—not less—creative because I can see things rationally instead of irrationally.

I worried that it would take away my competitive edge. I thought I had to be mean to compete, but if anything, I'm able to be even more competitive now. Last year I played 10 or 12 sports events in a 14-week period. I still have the "want-to's." I still have the squeamishness, but not the anxiety. It's actually easier now for me to concentrate.

I will always have to face the very real danger of relapse, but I'd have to say I'm on a positive trajectory at this point. The bottom line is a plus sign, not a minus. I think my story will have a happy ending. Hopefully, that's a long way off, but in relative terms, it's getting closer. If it were over at this moment, the ending would be good. My recovery means more to me than any trophy I've got.

All in all, I've made one hell of a comeback.

CHAPTER NINETEEN

Real Men Do Cry

It's hard for me to believe our culture still has a stigma against men crying. Maybe in the last few years that taboo has been broken somewhat. But then again, I probably wouldn't know as I never have gone too much with the "herd" mentality. I guess it all gets back to self-image. My manliness has been wrapped up in going out and competing. I didn't always do it in a positive way. Maybe there was an underlying sense of inadequacy. I always felt like I was a fairly macho guy. Crying has nothing to do with whether you can stand up to a fight.

You see the same attitudes toward crying in the sports world, only magnified. Jocks are supposed to be too tough to cry. But I don't know—I don't think that ever would have kept me from crying. Neither publicly nor in private. There are probably lots of macho guys in the sports world who would say they think that's wimpy.

Real men do cry. Absolutely. There are too many men who cry for it to be an anomaly. I cry over certain things. I cry pretty easy. I can cry over sad things, over joyous things, sentimental things, just my feeling for somebody. There's a whole wide range of things I can cry over. I never used to cry after I lost. I would get mad as hell, but it didn't convert into crying. But I could cry over a lot of other emotions. It's certainly not something that, as a man, I've ever felt embarrassed about. If Dad saw me crying, he would always say, "Go ahead and get it out. Crying is good for you."

I remember seeing Dad cry when I was 11 years old. That was very healthy for him to let me see that. It was also very unusual for his generation. Maybe that's the reason I've never felt there was a stigma to shedding a few tears.

Dad would never say, "Oh, just be a man about it." Instead he would say, "You're feeling some pressure right now. Let's talk about that." I give a lot of credit to him. In Kalamazoo, Michigan in 1962, I was feeling weak-kneed. He let me talk. He wanted me to talk. He listened to me. And then he identified my problem. He was very receptive to my pouring my heart out—without kicking me in the ass two minutes later. He allowed me to talk about my foibles. He always encouraged me to get those out on the table, do something about them, and then move on.

Golf is a real macho game. One of the big deals in golf is how far you can hit your driver. It's one of the few sports that your macho business man can still play. Most good golfers would not play with my clubs. They're ratty-looking clubs. They look like they came out of a grab bag or a pawn shop. Mine are mostly utility clubs, not many irons. I have a mismatched set that is awful to look at. Everyone laughs at me. But my own golf clubs are the only ones I can play with. I'd be lost without those clubs. They are the most valuable thing in the world to me. I'm always worried about having them stolen. Rudy Gatlin asks me, "But who would want to steal that shitty set of clubs?" You can take my Rolex watch, man, but you'd better watch out if you touch my golf clubs!

The set I use, by most standards, is a "wimpy" set. But I don't care, as long as they get the job done. In fact, I'm quite a picture, out there on the golf course. I have a funny swing and use a set of girly clubs! But as the guys who really know me always say: "Cliffy sure knows how to make those things talk."

In golf, as in several other things like open tennis, perhaps I was just a little ahead of my time. Now utility clubs are considered to be not so wimpy any more. It's sort of like crying. People think it's wimpy for a grown man to cry, but I don't care. The way I see it, as long as I win, I can use whatever damn set of golf clubs I choose! And I also figure: with my track record as a champion, I think I've earned a license to cry. Maybe someday our culture will catch up with that.

According to a recent AARP magazine, only 30 percent of depressed men over age 50 seek help. What's that all about?! That's an unbelievable statistic, if you calculate: ten million men over the age of 50 are depressed, but only three million will admit it. Of those, around 90 percent find relief. That's why I want to get the word out about this disease!

It's a two-pronged problem. It's the way we as a society treat depressed people, but also the way depressed men see themselves. Maybe some men perceive clinical depression to be a "feminine" disease. Women are expected to be more emotional, to have greater mood swings. Men are supposed to be stoic. To hide their emotions. Come on now, guys: 'fess up. I know I'm not only the sixth man in the history of the world who's ever come down with clinical depression. There have to be tens of millions of us! I would even go so far as to say that the depressed male is the silent tragedy in our culture today.

You're starting to see ads in magazines and on TV about depression and antidepressants. But ten years ago? You never saw any advertising about it at all. It was just swept under the carpet. It was totally hush-hush. Thomas Eagleton in 1972 ran for Vice President of the United States with George McGovern. When it came out that he had been treated for depression, he had to bow out of the race. The military is also very intolerant of mental illness. They are afraid even to say that word. Their wives usually refuse to talk about it. I had a military wife confide in me once and say that I'm the first person she's ever told about her depression. She poured her heart out to me. Right before we talked, she had just started taking Prozac. I encouraged her to keep taking it. Then she asked me to call and talk to her friend about the same thing.

In defense of the military, they've started to incorporate mental health awareness into their training. I can understand why that disability might affect the military personnel's primary mission of defending our country. Maybe that's fair but in general, it's still very no-no to talk about and that attitude needs to change. We would be better served by military commanders on Prozac, if they need it, than for them to deny they have a problem and not get help before it's too late.

Perhaps new legislation would help stem the tide of this national epidemic. I talk to the director of Mental Health/Mental Retardation (MHMR) locally in Texas. They are constantly fighting budget concerns. The MHMR is almost entirely publicly funded. They've been cut back drastically in terms of state funding. Another good resource is NAMI, the National Alliance on Mental Illness. They say mental health patients are discriminated against in terms of health insurance coverage. It's easy to put depression on the back burner, since nobody wants to talk about it!

I think people who have depression and their families are the first line of defense. We have an obligation to get help. By seeking treatment, we are actually doing our employers and the rest of society a favor. There's health available. Take advantage of it, even if it means picking up the yellow pages and calling someone. A public health official. Those public health guys are good people. They can steer you in the right direction.

Did you know that you can go get medical help and keep that confidential? A lot of psychiatric offices have private entrances. Of people who have sought help, if you take a survey, most of them say they wish they had gotten help earlier.

We can break the code of silence. We all have to do our part. Start with the little things, like just talking and getting it out there.

The cultural landscape is changing somewhat. You've got the Larry Kings and the Oprah Winfreys. At long last, it's beginning to open up some.

The sad part is that depression is not a difficult thing to diagnose. The symptoms of clinical depression are easy to recognize. It's not the big mystery that it once was. It's no longer a deep, dark secret. It's the easiest mental/emotional illness to treat. An antidepressant for someone with clinical depression is like insulin for a diabetic. It's not just a "feel-good" medication.

I have no problem with people calling my clinical depression a mental illness. I am not in any way ashamed of my disease. And I certainly don't care who finds out about it. I don't have endorsements to lose any more!

I guess another thing which helps me to talk about my depression is the fact that I never really cared what people thought anyway. I know so many people have it. It's such a common thing. I have always enjoyed going against the grain. But I'm mad at our system that forces people underground. There is still such a taboo, still such a stigma. A lot of people don't believe that clinical depression even exists. When I hear that, I enjoy coming along and showing it up their nose. My sports success gives me a license to speak. I like to use whatever celebrity I do have for a good cause. I see myself as a cheerleader for the mentally ill.

I've made it to the top of my profession, so my life shows that depression can happen to anybody. It's not just the "losers" who end up depressed. In fact, perhaps it's the "winners" who more often do. As former football player and actor Ed Marinaro told me, "You've got the successful man's disease." Remember that just because you're successful doesn't mean you're a winner in every area of your life. Don't overestimate your strengths or underestimate your weaknesses. It might be even more difficult for a successful person to admit that he or she needs an overhaul. You're used to being successful at everything you attempt. And now you have this big perceived failure in your life.

If you're an athlete, maybe you have a tendency to handle problems on your own, particularly if you play an individual sport. But trust me: this is a disease that's beyond your control. You can't just "take the bull by the horns." It is a *bona fide* medical illness. It is biologically based. There's stuff going on in your body that your mind cannot overcome. If the human being were made of Teflon from the Adam's Apple up, then all of this would be a different proposition. But from the Adam's Apple up, you're still made of chemicals. And like anything else, those chemicals can go wrong.

You can't just talk yourself out of diabetes. Depression is like heart disease or high blood pressure. There's something wrong which your brain can't "will" to make right. It might go into remission on its own. So does cancer. But it's still in your best interest to seek help. The longer it goes untreated, the worse it is for your brain.

Some people think they are weak if they need to take a pill. To me, it's a sign of strength to admit you need help. I don't feel like less of a man because I rely on medication. It's not a crutch. It's something I need. I'm thankful that the drug exists.

Statistically, women are more prone to depression than men. But men commit suicide more often than women. What that tells me is: men don't know how to ask for help. It's like when you're driving and you get lost. Men don't ever ask for directions!

I will always be in recovery. At an Alcoholics Anonymous meeting, you introduce yourself by saying, "Hi, I'm Cliff Richey. I'm an alcoholic." In almost any context, at this point, if it's appropriate, I'm willing to say: "Hi, I'm Cliff Richey. I'm a depressive."

Professional athletes can't afford to lie to themselves. That's one of the differences between the professional and the amateur. Depression is part of my résumé. I can't just wish it away. I don't want to cozy up to the sickness. I don't want to give in to that. But maybe there's something significant about my habit of referring to it as "MY depression." When you're in recovery, it's important to own it.

Across the board, honesty is such a huge feature of the recovery process. It's like being honest about your career. I've never considered myself a great tennis player. The word "great" is overused. I was a darn good tennis player. I think I manage to keep that in perspective.

We all fool ourselves in some ways. But real men own up to failure. In tennis as in life, I didn't attain everything I wanted to. I would have wanted to win a major tournament. You've got to win one of the four Grand Slam events to be a superstar. Realistically, I would say I had a really good career. I won enough money to keep me off the street. I would have to say I reached most of my goals.

You have to bite your ego and make an honest assessment. You also have to be realistic about the possibility of loss. Every time I went out to play a tennis match, losing was a part of the equation. Now, a perfectionist might think that if you prepare enough, you can always win. But that just shows how far you can get off track. There is never any insurance. In my last years on the regular tour, I made the mistake of thinking: "I've worked so hard, I shouldn't lose." Show me somebody who's ever gotten perfect at anything! That's unhealthy. You're trying to do something that can't be done. You're falling short and beating yourself up. Excellent can be the enemy of good.

In 1983, when I made a comeback on the senior tour, I changed my thinking. I said, "Bring it on. I'm man enough to lose." I was just glad to be given a chance to play again. Put some reality back into the equation. Perfectionism is not reality. I had gotten off into an unreal area. It freed me up, to realize: "Hey, I'm a big boy now. I'm man enough to take a bad result."

Losing can be manly. Crying can be manly. There was nothing about losing that I ever enjoyed. But it can be masculine to accept a loss. Own up to the fact that that's what can happen. "Hit me on the chin, I'll come back next week." To be a real champion, you've got to be man enough to absorb the losses too.

There was a study done in the 1960s about why people watch sporting events. It was to see the outcome, of course! Reruns don't have a large viewing audience. One of the great thrills in life is to watch it unfold without ever knowing in advance what will happen. If the spectators enjoy that, so should the competitors.

I saw Jimmy Connors hooked up to IVs in the locker room after one of his epic matches during his run to the semifinals of the U.S. Open in 1991 at age 39. Mike Lupica of the New York *Daily News* came up to me and asked: "What makes Jimmy still want to do this at the age of 39?" I said, "He's a pit fighter. He loves the battle. Even when he loses, he's almost sorry it's over." It's the battle that should turn you on, not the victory. If there was a down side to Richey, Inc., that would be it: we tried to control the outcome too much.

Muhammad Ali had a move in boxing he used to call "rope-a-dope." He would lay himself against the ropes and cover himself up. He would let the other guy tire himself out, just pounding on him. It wasn't really hurting him, and the other guy wasn't scoring any points. All he was really doing was resting!

I tell myself to play rope-a-dope sometimes. Whatever weird dynamic I start to feel happening, I just let it play itself out. Let it pound on you for a while so you can rest. And then you'll come back. When you do, you'll be strong enough to beat the shit out of your opponent!

Why should I put myself in the line of fire on purpose just to prove that I can? There's a time you should pick your battles. Hunker down in your bunker and start dodging the bullets. You don't have to take them full bore. Live to fight another day. Back off your schedule. Cancel some appointments. Default a match when you're injured—don't keep playing until you injure yourself even worse! The principle is this: choose to lose the battle, so that you can still win the war.

There are times now when I'll be sitting there in my golf cart. I can feel my triggers start to go off. Whenever that happens, I pick up a pen and start writing in my journal:

"Default this day."
"Don't take this day to heart."
"I surrender. Wave the white flag. Just go back home and let the day win."
"Start over tomorrow."

At times like this when I'm really feeling triggered, for the next two or three weeks, my primary objective becomes to stay out of depression. Remember: there is a time and a place to pull back for a while. Accept lesser goals. The only time this disease is fatal is if you do yourself in.

After a celebrity golf tournament we organized, we held a reception at MHMR. Hall of Famer baseball star Johnny Bench was there. He asked me, "Hey, before we leave, can you show me your room?" He was like, "You're so nuts, you must live here!" We laughed. I didn't mind that at all. That's just good old-fashioned locker room humor.

I can laugh about my depression. I like to joke sometimes about popping an extra Zoloft pill in the morning to feel happy. Or about going to the pharmacy each month to get my personality renewed. In the sports world, we like to joke and kid about things. Just poke fun at it. At least that gets it out there in the open.

If the people around you know you take antidepressants, you might try poking fun at yourself. That can be one way to diffuse any tension. If we as a culture can get to a point where we joke about this, then maybe we can start to have more of a dialogue.

Real men do cry. And real men get depressed. In both of those areas, in our society, someone needs to break the ice. I'm willing to go first. I'll be the guinea pig. Maybe it's time for our culture to redefine what counts as "masculinity." Let's change the way we talk about depression.

• CHAPTER TWENTY •

Mulligans

A "mulligan" in golf is a second chance. You can buy a mulligan in a golf game so you can take another shot on a given hole. But unlike in a golf game, you can't buy a mulligan in real life. It has to be given to you by God.

I have been given so many second chances in my life. I started taking Zoloft on my 50th birthday, New Year's Eve of 1996. That was the first of many rebirths. The beautiful thing is that in recovery, almost everything in your life becomes a second chance. Hope is the foundation of our great country of America. Hope is such a driver of the normal human condition. The sum total of my awful disease was "loss of hope." That's the truly awesome thing about recovery: once you come back, your whole life after that feels like a second chance.

I first took up golf in July of 1977. I quit the regular tennis tour in 1979. I had no idea then that I would ever get serious about golf. It's not another career for me to the degree that tennis was. But in July of 1991, I was watching golf on TV and saw the Celebrity Golf Championship at Lake Tahoe. I saw flitting across the screen a logo for the Celebrity Golf Association, the CGA. I immediately thought, "They might be on to something here." The event was broadcast on NBC Sports with the main announcer for that tournament being Charlie Jones, a gray-haired guy with a great TV voice. I knew Charlie from childhood since he had interviewed me in the past. They mentioned in the course of the broadcast that Caesar's Palace Tahoe was the host hotel for the event. I figured that was where Charlie had to be staying, so I called the hotel and left him a message. When he called me back, I asked if he could give me info on whom to contact about the CGA. He said, "Send me your résumé and I will give it to the right people." He did that, but by autumn, I still had not heard from anyone. I knew I needed to call the tour director just to see what was going on. I called him and asked to be given a chance. I knew they had some huge names, and I would not claim to put myself in that category, but I had noticed that there weren't many tennis players represented. He said they didn't really divide it by fields, but just tried to get the best celebrities around. We talked for about 45 minutes and at the end of our conversation, he said, "I'm going to put you in the tournament." He was one leg of a tripod which supported that event in Lake Tahoe, along with NBC Sports and a management firm. Those three entities met later to determine what the field of players for the next year's event was going to be. John Miller of NBC said at the meeting that he had ball-boyed for me in Washington, D.C. in 1970. So I knew a couple of key players in that political scene.

By the start of 1992, I knew I was going to play my first celebrity golf tournament. They were offering a $400,000 total purse, with $75,000 as the first prize. I recalled that the year before, a score of five over par had won the event. I told my local club pro about the tournament and asked him if I should give up my amateur standing. He asked me if I thought I could play five over par for 54 holes. I said I thought I could. He told me to go for it—to play for the money and not worry about losing my amateur status. I knew there would be pressure on me with TV cameras and big galleries and such. To prepare, I went and played in five mini-tour events in the Texas area in the senior division, 45-and-over. I knew I had to get used to making those three-footers when it actually meant something, for a change.

At my very first celebrity event there in Tahoe, I shot five over par and came in sixth. I managed to hit the number right on the nose of what had won it the previous year. I won $10,000. Coming down to the last few holes, I was only three shots out of the lead. I was right there in the hunt to win the tournament! There were all these great celebrities playing such as Michael Jordan and former Vice President Dan Quayle. I already knew some of them. One of the players in that tournament, Maury Povich, had interviewed me in 1971 in Washington, D.C. for his TV show, *Panorama*. I saw Maury in the elevator. He said, "I hear you're a ringer" (meaning that I could really play golf), so that was even more pressure! Some of the celebrities were nice to me at first; others weren't. Some gave me the polite brush-off. When it became evident that I wasn't going to win the tournament, my goal became instead just to beat Jack Wagner, the actor, because he had thought I was a fan and brushed me off earlier in the week. And I did! He didn't even know who I was.

Coral Springs, Florida was the last real tennis tournament I played, in December of that very same year. It only happened one time that I packed my suitcases to play both a golf tournament and then a tennis tournament the next week. That was the only time I had to take both golf clubs and tennis racquets on the plane. It was a seamless transition from one sport into the next. Right as my tennis career was ending, all of a sudden this golf opportunity sprang up. Since then, I've won two events and earned an average of $3,000 for each celebrity golf tournament I've played. When the CGA dissolved, I became one of the founding members of the Celebrity Players' Tour which arose to take its place. It was almost miraculous! I'm not a fatalist, but it was such perfect timing. For reasons I don't understand, God has blessed me beyond belief.

I give God the credit for the timing, but I was also ready when it came along. I developed the talent He had given me. I don't consider my golf an absolute second career. I don't feel the same drive for golf that I did for tennis but precisely because of that, golf has given me the chance—in what's still a competitive situation—to undo some of the dysfunction that happened in those years.

You see, in golf you don't ever lose; you just finish. You'll never read a headline that says, "Tiger Woods upset." Golf is a better sport to play if you're depressed because you rarely, if ever, suffer an absolute loss. Anybody who makes the cut has a "finish." You just finish in a certain position. Nobody "loses." In tennis, when you're shaking hands at the end of the match, it means you've either won, or else he's beaten your lousy ass. Golf does not produce such a harsh psychological blow.

The great thing is, I'm out on the golf course and enjoying being there. On the tennis tour, I was in pain. One of the sad things I don't like from my tennis scrapbooks is: it would have been almost impossible to enjoy that phase of my life. In that tennis arena, I never thought, "Boy, people paid money to watch me play today." You're not enjoying it the way you wish you could, or even the way most people think you do. All you see is an opponent and a court. You just want to get the job done. You're never "here." You're always living in the future, "over there." That's why I don't like to look at the albums. What an unbelievable fairy tale life, not to have enjoyed it! Every time I think about it, it makes me sad.

The up side is, without the tennis, I would never have been given the chance to play celebrity golf. On the Celebrity Players' Tour, we entertain corporate America. It's a very specialized job. They have your résumé posted on the golf cart. You tell stories. You train yourself to remember CEOs' names and to get involved in their world. You come back to the same tournament the next year and see the same people. Our pro tournaments usually take four hours. The pro/am days (when the pros play with the amateurs) tend to be a little longer and more grueling. That part can take up to six hours or more because, naturally, the amateurs are slower. You know that they've paid thousands of dollars to play with you. Sometimes I'll give them my player card or an autographed racquet.

At an age when most people are just getting a chance to settle down, I am now traveling more than ever before. I still enjoy life on the road. In many ways, ironically, I am retracing my steps from my tennis career—going to some of the same cities, the same resorts. What a different experience, though! I actually have friends on the tour now! Inside Richey, Inc., we didn't have time for friendships. We didn't have time for anything else. Now I am returning to some of the same places, but enjoying it more than the first time around.

Golf probably saved me. I reached a point where I could not play tennis any more. It's too physical of a game. Golf gives me a healthy reason to wake up every morning. Even though it was a cause, to a degree, of my last major episode of clinical depression, it still has been a huge part of my recovery. Rod Steiger, the actor, also had bad clinical depression. He used to have a license plate that said: "Keep Moving." Golf helps me do that, to keep moving. Golf means I still have something I can be creative in. It's with different toys, and it's not as physical a game, but I'm trying to enjoy the ride this time.

I have been a burden to a lot of people in life. It was too one-sided. I went over the edge too many times. The next 30 years, I don't want to be a burden on my family. I don't want to be this sick case who cratered and now everyone has to tiptoe around. Depression shed a light on my selfishness and made me feel guilty about things I needed to see. Even at my darkest point, as I was losing my mind day by day, I still knew deep down that I wanted to be healthy.

My relationship with my daughters has improved significantly. We can laugh about things now. Come to think of it, the very existence of our third daughter constitutes another second chance in my life. Sarah Jane was an afterthought, an accident, a surprise delivery, whatever you want to call it—but a wonderful one. Mickie and I went out and played a third "set" so to speak! Being so much

Golf gives me a healthy reason to wake up every morning and was a major factor in my recovery.

younger, Sarah lived through the worst of my depression after the older two were already up and gone. Yeah, little Sarah Jane hung in there too. It couldn't have been easy for her to get out of class in junior high and be picked up in a car with me crying in the passenger seat. But that's the same Sarah who later teased me about the autographs and sunglasses, the one I call "Sarah Hollywood." With a lot of love, and healthy doses of humor, somehow I guess we muddled through.

Another area of my life where I've been offered a second chance is with friendships. Golf was the first time I ever called buddies to do anything, except maybe for the Scorpion Gang! There is a grave danger with total self-absorption: you lose out on a lot of good, healthy interaction. Late in life, I would say even after age 55, I began to see that relationships are important to me. Since my last major depressive episode 12 years ago, I've developed three or four close friendships that I value very highly. It makes you more prone to clinical depression when all you care about is your own selfish "gettings." Friendships can be a buffer in life.

I haven't lost any friends due to depression. If anything, I've gained friends in the process. Depression goes a long way toward defining for you what kinds of people you want to have as friends. I know now that I need to be around soothing, peaceful people who are not going to be as hyper as I am. I also stay away from critical people. My biggest fault is being too judgmental. Being around other people who are like that just enhances my own negative tendencies.

There are always going to be those people in life who, basically, you don't give a rat's ass what they think. As long as you don't have hateful feelings toward them, that's OK. Just mentally throw them in a basket and forget it. Write them off. Don't waste too much energy building fences around those people, because you need it to build bridges to the good guys. There are cactus plants in the world in addition to fir trees. The key difference is: they're more prickly. Avoid the codependence mentality, where your glitzy résumé buys you friends and then you spend too much time caring about what they think. Now, instead of worrying so much about needing friends, I've tried to learn what it really means to be a friend. How can I be a good friend to the people I care about?

In the last seven years or so, I've also used volunteer work as an antidote to depression. I've poured my heart and soul into it with no remuneration. It's a really neat feeling. It's a win-win in an unselfish way. You get recognition also, but it isn't a career deal. I helped organize a celebrity golf tournament to benefit the local branch of MHMR. Because of my situation, because I've had a good career

Me and my pal Ralph Terry, former World Series-winning pitcher for the New York Yankees, at our local celebrity golf tournament, which benefits mental health in Texas.

and know a lot of celebrities, I have the resources now to put this kind of thing together. Mine has been, in the past, a very selfish existence. It's been nice to try to help other people for a change.

As part of our mental health awareness agenda for the tournament, we provided a way for participants to be tested anonymously for depression. I found in the process of digging up sponsors that many businessmen wanted to get involved because they themselves or a loved one had suffered from the disease. It's amazing how widespread it is! The local newspaper launched a media blitz to get the word out about what we were doing. Raising awareness of mental health issues has become a passion for me.

Lynn Rutland, executive director of our local chapter of MHMR, told me there was a measurable drop-off in suicides in San Angelo for three years after the event. I don't know whether we can take any credit for that. But the year before the tournament, my home town's suicide rate had been at an all-time high.

That tournament was also nice for me personally because I finally had the chance to give something back to my community. For all practical purposes, I don't really live there any more. I maintain a residence there, but one of the things I learned in counseling was to seek out new environments. Not stay around old haunts that bring back my worst days. I knew early on that that would be crucial for my recovery.

Phoenix is now my home for about six or seven months out of the year. One of the reasons I began going to Phoenix was to start with a clean slate. I tried to look at mistakes I had made with people in San Angelo and not make those same mistakes over again. There were people in San Angelo who didn't want to see me come around. I had not been a blessing in their life.

When I started going to Phoenix, it would have been easy just to change locale without also changing the way I treated people. That's fool's gold. That would only have shown that nothing fundamental had changed. If I really wanted to start over, my attitude could not be: "I hope I don't run into the same kind of people I ran into in San Angelo." Instead, it had to be: "I hope the people in Phoenix meet a different kind of guy from the one who rubbed people the wrong way out in West Texas."

When I think about the symbolism of Phoenix, it's almost eerie. The name means Place of Rebirth. And there I was, just like that mythical bird, coming up again from the ashes. It would be no exaggeration to say that it was like a resurrection.

Depression basically forced me out of West Texas. It's like being forced out of your house due to foreclosure, which happens after you've defaulted on a mortgage. I have a lot of friends in San Angelo to this day. I'm not trying to avoid them. My reasons are not personal. I've just tried to escape that oppressive atmosphere and to put behind me forever the horror of those three years.

I may never again feel that my old environs in West Texas are comfortable. It's OK to isolate yourself. As the years go by and things continue to change, perhaps one day my emotions will allow me to be in San Angelo again without having flashbacks to the worst period of my life. But until that happens, I'm not going to push it. I'm damaged goods. I know that. There are some battles I'm just not willing to fight.

It helps me when I'm in a depressive episode to try consciously to be thankful for all the little things: the car I drive, the sheets on the bed. In contrast, I imagine the flies on the faces of kids in Somalia. I take the time now to savor moments that I never even noticed before. Little things. Just the act of opening my trunk and getting out my balls and golf clubs. I try to go into thankful mode instead of bitchy mode. Sometimes I'll walk the dog on the streets of a little town and hunt coins. Or maybe enjoy eating a big greasy cheeseburger with curly fries. For the first time in my life, I enjoy just looking out the window at the trees. There's this tranquility. I've found a peacefulness I never had. I love my morning paper. The smell of coffee. Going into a good bookstore. Watching the sunset. Since I've been in recovery, it's like I've been given a new lease on life.

I've learned many things from depression. It's actually been a blessing. That's how I truly feel. It hasn't been a waste of time. It has strengthened my character. It has shown me what true love can be. It's made me appreciate my accomplishments more. It's led me to form lasting friendships. It has shown me what is really important in life.

I do not wish that depression had not happened to me. It's taught me more than anything else. It helps me to realize when I'm becoming too critical. Now, whenever I see people do something weird, I figure they might have a good reason for that. Who knows? They might even be suffering from depression, too! Depression has taught me compassion. It humbles me. I'm less arrogant now. With enough pain, a lot of things can change.

John McEnroe has a saying about taking a negative and turning it into a positive. God has a way of doing that which is beyond belief. People ask if it makes me angry that depression has robbed me of so many pleasures. I really, truly, have never looked at it that way. In all honesty, it's the reverse. It's not a stretch for me to say that. My blessings far outweigh anything depression has taken from me.

I have a big heart, both literally and figuratively. The doctors at the Cooper Clinic told me that when I went up there to check out the PVCs. Many athletes do. Your heart is a muscle. Like other muscles, it grows larger with exertion and overuse. Sports has given me a big heart, literally. And depression has given me a big heart on the emotional level. When you've suffered as much as I have, you can really commiserate with someone else's suffering.

When you add them all up, that's quite a few mulligans. However, you don't get a second chance at everything. I know I lost the growing-up years with my kids. I regret that. I don't think I'd be a human being if I didn't have some regrets. I do wonder how my kids would have turned out if I had been a more normal, attentive father. In Hilaire's case, I think some of her excellence may have been fueled by that very dysfunction. (I know from my own childhood that that was the case for me.) So there's a sliding scale of justice, I suppose . . . I'm glad to see my competitive fire passed down to the next generation.

I've lost some years to depression. I do lament the time that was taken from me. One thing I do sometimes is to write down numbers representing the years of my life. I start with the year I'm in, to remind myself of the good years I have left. That's reassuring to me, somehow. With my new outlook, I know for certain that the best is yet to come.

If I could be any animal, I'd pick a turtle. Some kinds of turtles live 250 years. They can go for months without water or food. They can almost shut their heart down and restart it again. The turtle even predates the dinosaur. It is known as the most adaptable animal. You've got to admire the turtle. With my type-A personality, I've come to appreciate its slow, plodding ways. I wish I had more of a hard outer shell. You must not be able to hear much of anything in there! You could carry your protection around with you. It would still be there, 24 hours a day.

At last sighting, this old turtle was spotted in the Arizona desert. Very, very slowly, he turned himself around. He was last seen deliberately walking away from the chaos . . . that is, whenever he isn't just basking in the sun.

CHAPTER TWENTY ONE

"Never Give Up"

It's talking to me again. That piece-of-shit bastard is back. It's trying to get my attention. It's whispering in my ear: "Don't try to fight it any longer. Just give up." It's a complete squashing of self. When that happens, I feel about two inches high.

Depression is a bully. A kid who picks on you when you're weak. But if you stand up to him, he'll back off pretty quick. Sometimes he'll put up a fight, but bullies are not strong men, necessarily. They aren't as rough and tumble as they want you to think. If you stand up to it, clinical depression will also back down.

I'm a match for this piece-of-shit depression. I'm not the ultimate match for it. I'm not that arrogant. But I'll stand up to it. I'm gonna lick this. Sports trained me to sit back and say, "Come on, Cliffy. You know what the pitfalls are. But this is the one you really want to win. Let's do this."

Depression is never lying there dead, with no pulse. It might win some isolated rounds. But at the end, I know I will prevail. As long as I'm still alive, I haven't lost the battle against major depression. I'm on the winning side of this war.

Depression is both an enemy and a monster. I really don't view it as the monster I once did. I know I've got my weapons against it. Rather, I view it like the bully in the school yard. If you stand up to it, it will back down almost instantly. And remember: even your biggest enemies can still teach you things.

I feel most alone when I'm worried that I'm going into depression—when my illness starts to rear its ugly head. I know that even the people closest to me are 100 percent powerless to assist me at that moment. There is no human being in the world who can help. That's a terrible feeling. That is when I feel most alone.

When you're on your back with clinical depression, if you've been a sportsman or a super high-achiever in any field, you've got to understand that now you have an opponent who hides his face. The disease itself is trying to take away from you your ability to fight back. It tries to rob you of all of your coping skills in horrible ways. It tells you that your job is not important any more. It tells you that all the things you once enjoyed doing are worthless. Nothing is fun now. It's like this dark cloud. It takes from you the joy, the discipline, the "want-to's" of life.

Wait a second. Stop right there. You've got to sit down and figure out what your abilities have been up to that point. Your auto pilot is busted. Forget about it. Your co-pilot is comatose. You have to manually override the systems that failed you. Find a way to put those manual overrides into play. You're in an emergency situation. All of your hydraulics have gone out, but somehow, some way, you still have to land this frigging plane. About 20 percent of people with clinical depression commit suicide. Don't give in and let yourself become one of them.

This is where it helps me to take that "never say die" attitude I had in tennis and transfer it over to my battle against depression. A few times during the senior tour, I started cramping so badly, they had to carry me off the court to an ambulance. It happened several times, including twice in 1985. I won a senior tournament in Washington, D.C. in 90-degree weather with high humidity. I was 38 years old. I played the final against a Rhodesian, Andrew Pattison. After the match, some newspaper reporters from *The Washington*

I took my "never say die" attitude from tennis and transferred it to my fight with depression. I never gave up and battled through 90-degree temperatures—and leg cramps—to win the senior tennis title in Washington, D.C. in 1985.

Times were interviewing me in the players' tent when I started cramping. I was in agony. Somebody called the park police. They came riding up on horseback. They had some first aid stuff they used to put IVs in my arms to treat me for heat exhaustion.

About a month later, I was playing in Birmingham, Alabama on another stinking hot day. I was starting to cramp during the match. I went up to the umpire and said, "Would you please call me an ambulance?" He thought I was kidding. I had to insist. I wanted it to be waiting for me when the match was over. Sure enough, it showed up and was sitting there by the side of the court. And sure enough, by that point, I really needed it. By the time that match was over, I needed those IVs. That's the quickest way possible to replace your electrolytes.

Antidepressants are like those IVs. Know when to call the ambulance—or in the case of Zoloft, when to call in the prescription. But until it arrives, or while you're still adjusting to the medicine, you have to go right on playing that match.

I know, I know. Believe me, I know what that feels like. You've consumed every ounce of gas in your tank. You're on the last fume. You're under water, scuba diving, and your oxygen tank has expired! But somehow, you have to find what it takes to go on. I achieved many victories while strung out on my last fume.

The first thing you've got to do is believe you really can win it. That you really can seal the deal. A lot of guys on the tour were known as also-rans. I always attributed that primarily to a lack of heart. In their heart of hearts, they didn't believe they were good enough.

I've gone to the mat against clinical depression. I'm not gonna settle for feeling shitty any more. I'm not gonna settle for letting this thing win.

So what about you? What the hell are you gonna do about it? Sit back and let it beat the shit out of you? Remember: as long as you're still swinging, you're dangerous. We're talking about your entire life here. It's a heck of a lot more important than a tennis match! But even out on that tennis court, if I had one nerve left or one muscle fiber twitching, I wasn't ever going to give up.

You're always on the line for more losses. There are no final victories until they plant you in the ground. In the history of golf, the truly professional players always know to watch out after they've shot a record round. You better accommodate your mind to that. Rather than getting cocky, if you make it through an episode, you'd better immediately start thinking another episode will come. Otherwise, you're just asking for trouble. Winston Churchill called it the black dog returning. I have a record of "undefeated" against depression but that is very different from never having another bout. I have learned to prepare myself mentally for more episodes. I do not want to handicap myself through arrogance.

Dogged persistence is a weapon in recovery. People have always judged me to be a driven, persistent person. Depression takes most of that out of you. But if you're that way to begin with, you can still have barely enough left to make it through. It makes me cry just to think about that: how God made certain provisions for me. He left me a reservoir of persistence to survive.

We all, as humans, want it easy. We want our pain relieved in a drive-thru fashion. My intense belief, whether it's with golf or tennis or clinical depression, is that improvement takes discipline. You can have discipline when you're depressed, too. Use that time productively to read, study and learn. Many times in a competitive ball field, you're having to pull out every competitive fiber in your being at a time when you least feel like doing it. You're on the road. You've been through three different time zones and changes of court surface. You're not even getting a good night's sleep. And the third week is the most important event of the three. That's when you've got to somehow muster the discipline, the "want-to's," the steely determination that a coach can't give you. It ain't all autographs and sunglasses. As the saying goes, when the going gets tough, the tough get going. Whenever a champion walks through a room, everybody hopes that magic "something" will rub off on them. A true champion wears an amulet against quitting quick.

I think most people are very competitive. They just don't realize it. They just don't know what they really have inside. My mother is a meek, mild-mannered person. But she didn't want to lose to those women at the club. She felt like she was one of the pros, one of the Richeys. She had a reputation to uphold! And by golly, when it came time for one of us to play, she suddenly turned into a bundle of nerves. I'll never forget, when I was still just a kid, I played the final round of the USTA National Boys' 16s Championship. I played against a guy named Butch Seewagen. Mom was so nervous she couldn't watch. She went over into a sitting room in one of the dorms. She had a straw purse she had been carrying around that week. By the end of the match, without realizing it, she had picked apart half the straw purse!

Richey, Inc. says: no built-in excuses. Some of my opponents would find ways to "bow out" mentally. They didn't want to tangle with me. Ilie Nastase, that year at the CBS Classic, just quit trying. I had gone up to him before that match and said, "Let's just play. I won't complain about any line calls if you won't." That was no fun for him. He liked to pull his *shtick*. I beat him 6-1, 6-0. He didn't even try. He knew that if he did try his antics, I would claw his eyes out and he didn't feel like dealing with that. . . . Boro Jovanovic didn't try against me either. He complained that his racquets were strung too tightly that day. He used every excuse in the book not to have to go out there and play a good competitive match. What I brought to the table helped me against guys who didn't have the *cojones* to put out that day.

If people are honest, those who have bad clinical depression need to take a long, hard look at where they're going wrong—even if it means hearing stuff they don't want to listen to. Most depressed people are doing things that are not helping their situation: unhealthy lifestyles, hate they are harboring in their hearts. These are things that can also lead to illness.

If you end up in clinical depression, don't wallow in self-pity. Instead, maybe you should adjust the way you view yourself. Perhaps your overall bearing to the rest of the world is creating bad feedback. Lack of planning, poor attitudes. You better own it! You better not come up with easy excuses. You've got to be the captain of your ship.

There are no 100-percent-effective antidotes to depression. I haven't found one. I know I will always have another depressive episode.

You're never really in the past tense with depression. You need to be on guard. The minute you think you've licked it, it will come back to bite you in the butt. You have to understand that more than likely, if you've had even one episode, your chances of having another one just rose. Those odds are many, many times greater than for the average guy. If you're 50 years old and have had at least three major bouts, in all probability, you ought to stay on antidepressant medicine for the rest of your life.

I can honestly say that since I've been on Zoloft, I've never had an episode that's lasted longer than three to six weeks. I had one in Denver in 1999 that came and hit me at the beginning of a celebrity golf event. It had subsided by the end of the week. I was functional to the point that I played the tournament (I even played well). I could socialize with people on the golf course. That event later became the John Elway Classic. His foundation bought it and used it as a fundraiser. That year, he invited all the players over to his house for a private party to celebrate his recent retirement from football. I would have been curious to see what kind of house he lived in, but I just couldn't go. There are personal barometers each individual has to use. That should have told me something, right there: I was so down, I couldn't even go to a party thrown by John Elway!

I had a six-week siege in 2002 in Phoenix. I had another one in January or February of 2005. I had a full-month one in March of 2006. That was a pretty bad dip. Even after 10 years of medication, recovery and management skills, still depression can blindside me sometimes. As life happens, you might have something come up on the business end of things. You might get fired or passed over for a big promotion. You might break up with a girlfriend or a spouse. And then, boom! All of a sudden, you're in a five-week depressive episode. You didn't see it coming until it was too late. . . .

Education de-fangs it quite a bit. Just knowing what it is helps. Half the whole problem is not knowing what's happening to you. I've learned to anticipate the depressions, and that makes them less frightening. This isn't necessarily a self-fulfilling prophecy. It just pays to know what the beginning of an onslaught feels like. To pay attention to what's going on.

Lack of patience is a warning sign. I get frustrated quicker. I'm very critical of other people. When I'm going into one of my depressive episodes, I start to scoff. Now, to combat that, I try to flip it around. I thank God for each person. But I still know that one of my "tags" for going into depression is when I feel myself becoming hypercritical toward everyone.

If you can learn to identify your warning signs, they're not as threatening. Now, just because it's thundering and lightning doesn't mean a storm is necessarily going to hit. It doesn't mean you can't use some of your pre-emptive strategies to ward it off. There are definitely ways of getting around certain stresses if you have your little toolbox handy. But even if you do go into depression, you can develop coping skills for that too. I've written in my journal many times:

"This too shall pass."
"It hasn't gotten me yet."
"Eventually, I know that this will go away."

You might ask the question: you're on an antidepressant, so why does this shit still happen? You have to realize, the medicine is only one part of the arsenal. If you only go on an antidepressant and don't try to change anything else, then you aren't doing all you can do to combat it.

There is a syndrome. They call it Prozac Poop-Out. People say, "I've been on Prozac for five years; but now, all of a sudden, it's not working any more." My opinion on that is that the antidepressant is not a fix-all. Your brain starts accommodating to feeling better. You experience, for the first year or two, an initial surge. You start feeling the medicine working. For me, when it started to take effect in 1997, I felt chipper. My mood rose. My sense of humor returned. It almost felt like I had a couple of beers. Suddenly, I was wanting to do things again. But then what happens is, I think your brain actually starts getting used to feeling well. You forget just how bad it was when you weren't on the drug. You pull back, and now the bumps hit you a little harder than normal. When that occurs, don't just assume the medicine's not working any more. Don't forget about the role of cognitive therapy. Don't rely on antidepressant medication alone.

I've had some depressive dips, but not once have I said, "Uh-oh, the Zoloft's not working any more." You're getting into real dangerous territory there. That is—potentially—a real can of worms. Then all of a sudden you're wanting to switch medications. It's the drive-thru or "quick fix" mentality. Your antidepressant can only do so much for you! It would be like a diabetic eating a double cheeseburger and a malt and then when they feel bad, thinking their insulin isn't working. The problem might not be your medicine, dude. Look in the mirror and see if it might be you!

Some day they will invent a drug that can keep you from crashing. I believe that. I would see no reason at all, with the miraculous things that have happened in medicine, why that would not be possible. But it's going to be much easier to come up with a pill that

Me and my daughter Amy in San Angelo, Texas in the summer of 2009.

keeps you from falling than one that allows you to crash normally. What most depressed people don't realize is that ultimately, you're still going to want a normal range of emotion. You don't want a pill that keeps you from crashing altogether. You just want one that provides you a parachute.

That might mean feeling a little down at times. I would say the depressive episodes I have had in the last 10 years would fall pretty close to the normal human range. For a little while there, I was low as a skunk's belly. Unfit for human consumption for three to four weeks. To me, that's not such a bad thing. I go into recovery mode. I might even raise my dose of Zoloft from 200mg to 300mg for a week. Or I might say to myself, "Maybe I'm pushing too hard right now." Some of those episodes, you can use as a barometer—an indicator to tell you that you're doing too much. Your normal down periods are healthy. A-type personalities need a little shaking of the rafters to get them to slow down. Where the hell else are you going to get that nudge?

There's maybe 20 percent of the depressed population for whom medication doesn't do much good. Maybe those are the ones who do end up committing suicide. I can't speak for those people. And there is an appropriate spiritual component of treatment. I will tell God to His face that the antidepressants worked far better for me than I ever dreamed they could. But they are only one part of the solution.

On the other hand, if you don't include antidepressants in the mix, that's irresponsible. If some Christian ministers don't believe in antidepressants, and say it's purely a spiritual problem, that's a bad message. Everything has a spiritual component to it. A diabetic who is 100 pounds overweight also has a spiritual issue. The Christian counselor I saw only mentioned antidepressants once. He only mentioned clinical depression in a minimal way. I think attitudes toward depression within the religious community need to change. We're not living in the Renaissance any more, people. We don't have to rely on exorcism alone. God made scientific research too. Let's use the abilities God gave us to find out even more about the chemical side of this equation—and then, most importantly, to apply what we've learned.

Post-Traumatic Stress Disorder (PTSD) walks right alongside depression. One of the first symptoms that I'm falling into depression is when the PT triggers start setting me off. The PT is more constant than the depression. Day in, day out. But my reactions to those triggers can tell me a lot about whether a depressive episode is coming on.

For example, I might be out there on the golf course and have abnormal fears that I'm starting to lose my game again. That's one of my personal flash points or triggers. It's my same old worst fear of losing skill. Post-Traumatic is not rational. It can happen even if you've played well that day or have been in a good mood. All of a sudden, it's like you're reliving this horror. You're in such emotional pain. You know that no one else in your group understands. This tidal wave starts engulfing you.

Most of the time Post-Traumatic Stress Disorder has been related to greater trauma, like fighting in a war or being slashed by a mugger. Now the experts are starting to include lesser traumas, such as losing one's career. It doesn't necessarily have to be life-threatening. I elect simply not to put myself in certain atmospheres. If you find yourself avoiding certain things at all costs—not wanting to set off those triggers—there's a real possibility you might be suffering from PTSD. For depressed people, it means that another onslaught of depression can trigger the post-traumatic syndrome. I definitely have flashbacks to that major episode in the 1990s when I put black trash bags over the windows. Three long years of major depression. I want to avoid re-living that trauma at all costs.

It doesn't matter how important it is in the great scheme of things. For something to be stressful, it only matters how important it is to you. The world will not collapse if I play a lousy round of golf. But sometimes my sick brain might think it will. The rest of the world has a hard time getting inside any one person's mind. Stress, like beauty, is in the eye of the beholder.

I don't think I have an abnormal fear of going into depression, but I have abnormal fears about certain things that trigger my emotional states. In other words, I'm fearful of triggers. Stressful situations I just tend to avoid.

What's a loss to one person might not be perceived as a loss to another. Try to figure out what your stressors are. Be honest with yourself. Loss is really all in the way you perceive it. I would really hate, at the age of 63, to be divorced a couple times already and be married to a younger wife with whom I have no history. But some guys might enjoy that! An argument with a loved one is not a stressor that I fear will send me into depression. But maybe a guy who used to argue a lot with his mother would react differently. An argument with his wife might be a trigger for him. It doesn't matter what your personal triggers are. None of this stuff is normal! You have to remember that. There's no point trying to rationalize these scary thoughts you get, these abnormal fears. Your brain just goes into a fire storm. You feel paranoid.

Triggers don't have to be catastrophic. They can be anything. It's just a weakness you have. You have a debit in that column. The peace settlement or bargain I've made with it is to know what I can do and what I can't. I prefer to go to a public golf course and preserve my anonymity. I'm OK with that. There are certain things I used to do that I feel like I can no longer handle. I've had to accept that. There are warning signals, signs. Pay attention to your own rhythms. There were certain parts of my life I didn't want to adapt to any more. Some things I never got back to doing.

Always keep in mind that your emotions while in clinical depression are nothing more than just that: emotions. Don't confuse feelings with facts. To me, the existence of God is a comforting fact. That is a belief that I have.

When you're depressed, you need to work doubly or triply hard at thinking right. Constantly try to rearrange the way you're thinking. Manually override your lack of patience with self and others by way of reading good stuff and also thinking good thoughts. A lot of people read inspirational books even when they're feeling good. You need to do double or triple time on that when you're depressed.

In times of crisis, you also need to focus more on things like diet and exercise. I call it reaching into my bag of tricks. Do things to compensate for your injury. It's like having a bad knee. You need to rehabilitate, make better habits in your life. Re-route your "take" on how you try to get things done. Going for a two-mile walk is good exercise. It's healthful. It promotes serotonin flow. The simple act of walking is one of the greatest therapies there is. Here's another trick: make a list of every single thing you have to be thankful for. Sometimes in the morning I'll write down some notes on how I want to react to the day in front of me. Here's a sample:

* *Today is not about you.*
* *See yourself as compassionate and giving.*
* *If you feel like it at all, do something today for somebody else.*

Then after I've made these notes, I'll carry them around in my pocket. I'll keep reminding myself to refer to them throughout the day.

Always remember that depression is a disease. Separate who you are from it. Don't claim the disease as your identity. It would be like coming down with the flu and identifying with that fever. That's not who you are. You will recover. At least on the intellectual level, you can still understand that.

Sometimes I'll say something and then realize, "That's the depression talking." That's my way of trying not to claim it—of putting some space between myself and this disease. Build a wall between it and you. I read that in a book a few years ago: don't claim it. That's not who I want to be. In fact, that's not even who I am any more, most of the time.

You also have to play to win instead of playing to keep from losing. In my battle against depression, I wasn't going to give in. But I had periods where I was scared I might not be able to come back. I knew I was in the fight of my life. I wanted to defeat it, so I studied it. I sized it up. I devised strategies. If I lost, it wasn't going to be for lack of trying with every fiber in my being. I knew I had to make a dedicated effort, to try my ass off. If I had done nothing but get a prescription filled, that would have been playing to keep from losing. But I was willing to pay the price to get better with every means possible. When you're playing to win in tennis, one of the things you do is engage in immaculate preparation. Ivan Lendl used to be the king of that. He probed the brains of experts, even racquet manufacturers, and figured out what would be the best equipment for him. It may not be evident to the average spectator, but most sports champions are highly organized and prepared. I was going to do whatever it took to get out of this, not just tread water. You better not half-ass it, folks. Playing to keep from losing is hoping your way through.

One of my other techniques is to go into what I call the "gray zone." It means consciously choosing not to see the world in black and white. It means settling for less than what I usually do. It might mean shooting 75 on the golf course and having that be OK. Or perhaps playing two or three days a week, not five. The gray zone includes going to a party and only staying 45 minutes. The gray zone is very important for people with clinical depression because it softens their tendency to see the world in terms of stark extremes.

You might have to cut some things out of your life. A high school coach in Phoenix asked me to come talk to his students about what it takes to be a champion. I did it, but sometimes you might have to reschedule certain commitments. Often I jump in and volunteer to do things, like tennis clinics for charity benefits, and then regret it later. Obviously on the day I volunteered to do that, I must have been feeling good. But I might not be feeling well on the day scheduled for that event.

The little things, even activities with your family and friends, can suddenly look like too much to do. I've asked my friends to go on ahead to a nice restaurant and explained to them that I'm going to Luby's across the street because it looks like too big a chore to wait for the server. You realize that maybe you could go buy a new tire, but you know you can't handle getting a haircut too. You feel yourself starting to slip into the pit. So prioritize. You've been there enough times so you can sense it. You might have to go into avoidance mode.

When that happens to you the first time, you don't understand. You get angry. You're upset that you can no longer do the things you once did. You think if you can put enough time between you and the depressive episode, that some day you'll be able to do those things again.

My grieving over all that has come and gone. I've made peace with it. For a period, I was perplexed by this new dynamic. I didn't understand the long-term effects of my disease. There was a residual aftertaste I had not bargained for.

After a while, it becomes a familiar pattern of depression and remission. I have some battle scars. I know I'm not as resilient as I used to be. Many aspects of your life are infringed upon. The very fact that you're trying to avoid certain triggers in turn creates additional stress. The times you're triggered, you feel sick and panicky. It's not always convenient to get the heck out of there. You don't want to make the people around you feel miserable. The traumatized person is doing double duty all the time—managing the triggers and anxiety, while attempting to deal with everyday life. You try to sort of act normal the rest of the day, but it's tough. You're fighting emotional pain. It wears your ass out.

Richey, Inc. says: never quit. If we had one golden rule, it was: no matter how tough it gets, never give in. I watched my sister

Nancy play the final of a tournament in Puerto Rico with a 101-degree fever on a cement court. I ran out on the court after she won. I was so proud of her, I ran out and gave her a hug. I knew how sick she was. But she still went out there and put in one of the gutsiest performances you could ever imagine.

There are no sophisticated indoor tennis courts in San Angelo. In April of 1984, the wind was blowing 40 to 50 miles an hour and we couldn't use our court to practice. So we went and found a little tennis court in between some apartment buildings. (You learn to improvise.) Other times we'd practice at 11 o'clock at night in a public gym. You make do with what's available. It's a "get the job done" mentality. Dad used to tell Nancy: "You may not feel good if you're having your period the week you play a tournament, but you just have to compete against that too." For the true champion, there are no built-in excuses!

The bottom line is: depression can be beaten. Far worse than losing is not staying out on that court. Depression will tell you it's not worth it to keep fighting, but you don't have to listen to that voice. Listen to what I'm telling you instead. Even if you forget everything else, remember these words: NEVER, EVER, EVER GIVE UP.

Epilogue

This father/daughter memoir was written in the fall of 2006 and the spring of 2007. After 41 years, Cliff and Mickie Richey's marriage ended with a divorce on April 17, 2009. Cliff currently resides in San Angelo, Texas and Phoenix, Arizona and devotes much of his time to serving as an advocate for mental health across the country.

Acknowledgments

The authors would like to thank first our family for being supportive of this project. Thanks also to John Falcon, who first suggested that Cliff think about writing a book; Lane Zachary, for getting us started; Randy Walker, our publisher; Dan Rea, for his many talents; Lynn Rutland, for holding Cliff accountable; Jerry Solomon, who gave us confidence that it was a worthy project; Ivan Lendl, who introduced us to Jerry Solomon; Lynn Lasky Clark, CEO of MHA/TX, for mental health expertise; Nancy Richey, for the support only she could give to Cliff; Pro, a great father and coach—he started it all; Betty Richey (a.k.a Nana), for passing on to us her faith; Jackie Shannon, past president of NAMI; Michael Kates—stay strong, Michael; Jimmy Connors, for writing the foreword; Ralph and Tanya Terry, friends and confidants; and John Sutton along with his assistant, Debbie Wall. A special thanks to Craig Kallendorf for remaining amiable through six weeks of cohabitation with his in-laws. Thanks to Mickie Richey, Amy Tremblay, Rick Curry, Celia Carroll, and Eduardo Espina for their insightful comments on the manuscript.

Index

[Page numbers in italics indicate photographs]

AARP, 229
Alexander, John, 124
Ashe, Arthur, 57-59, 64, 65, 91, 93, 94, 96, 119, 136, 143, 177
ATP (Association of Tennis Professionals), 64, 67-69, 160, 218
ATP Champions' Race, 94. *See* also Grand Prix
Australian Open / Championships, 62, 109, 119
Australian Tennis Association, 55
B.F. Goodrich, 100: Jack Purcell, 100
Bancroft Player's Special, 154
Barry, Linda, 70
Barbecue Tour, The, 169, 191
Bartzen, Tut, 15, 132
Belgian Open, 119
Belkin, Mike, 28, 208
Bellville, Texas, 170, 171
Bench, Johnny (baseball Hall of Famer), 235
Berkeley Tennis Club, San Francisco, California, 1, 66
Borg, Björn, 132
Bozarth (school principal), 14

Braden, Vic, 66
Bradshaw, Terry, 164
Brook Hollow Golf Club, Dallas, 61, 70, 138
Buchholz, Cliff, 84, 90
Buenos Aires Lawn Tennis Club, 72
Canadian Open, 84
Cape Cod, 190
Carmichael, Bob "Nail Bags," 131, 146, 155
Carr, Howard (writer), 131
Casals, Rosie, 62, 63, 70
CBS Classic, 160, 253
Century Country Club, Long Island, 13
Checkpoint Charlie, 53
Colony Beach and Tennis Resort, Sarasota, Florida, 100
Connors, Jimmy, 84, 129, 145, 147, 216, 234, 266
Converse, 100
Cooper Clinic, 181, 187, 246
Coral Springs, Florida, 188
Cotton Bowl Invitational, Texas, 28
Cow Palace, San Francisco, 145
Cox, Mark, 223
Curatiba, 79, 80
Dallas Morning News, The, 56
Dallas Tennis Association, The, 47
David (Cliff's childhood friend), 11
Davis Cup, 53-57, 60, 65, 67, 68, 71, 73, 74, 75, 79, 91, 92, 93, 96, 100, 102, 103, 125, 127, 137, 145, 178, 198, 221
Del Rio, West Texas, 169. *See* Barbecue Tour
Dell, Donald, 93, 102, 137, 198
Deford, Frank (reporter), 46
Dent, Phil, 135
DMSO (demethyl sulfoxide), 55, 183
Dowdswell, Colin, 124

Drysdale, Cliff, 212
Dunlop Sporting Goods, 100
Eagleton, Thomas, 229
Eckert, Henry, 14
Ecuador, 57-61, 125
Electra, Texas, 21, 22
Elser Street, Houston, Texas, 13, 40
Elway, John, 254
Emerson, Roy, 174, 198, 221
Evert, Chris, 134
Evert, Jimmy, 134
Federer, Roger, 94
Fitzgibbon, Herbie, 7, 61, 62, 136, 145
Flink, Steve, 139
Foro Italico, Rome, 134
Fort Lauderdale, 86, 194
Fort Wayne, Indiana, 6, 25
Franulovic, Zeljko, 95, 126, 178, 179
Fred Perry, 100
French Open, 42, 63, 68, 87, 92, 94, 119, 121, 142, 178, 180, 187
Froehling, Frank, 132
Gardini, Fausto, 142
Gatlin Brothers, The (musicians), 112
Gatlin, Rudy, 228
Gerrard, Lew, 74, 131
Gimeno, Andrés, 94, 95, 134
Girard, Bonnie (Mickie's mother), 79
Girard, Dr. Louis (Mickie's father), 71, 72, 74, 76, 77, 203
Girard, Lorraine (Mickie's stepmother), 76, 77
Girard, Michelle, 71, 74. *See* Mickie Richey
Girard, Susie (Mickie's sister), 170
Glenelg Beach, Australia, 62
Golf Crest Country Club, 9, 13, 15, 25

Gonzalez, Pancho "Gorgo," 24, 51-53, 113, 131, 142, 198
Graebner, Carol (Clark's wife), 75
Graebner, Clark, 57, 58, 75, 82, 103, 126, 127, 134
Grand Prix, 66, 92, 93, 94-96, 200
Grand Slam, 52, 63, 85, 89, 113, 221, 233
Greatest Tennis Matches of the Twentieth Century, The, 139
Guayaquil, Ecuador, 57
Guayaquil Lawn Tennis Club, Ecuador, 58
Guzmán, Pancho, 58, 59
Gypsy Trail Country Club, Mahopac, New York, 7
Hare, Mary, 135
Harrison Street, West Texas, 13, 19
Hill, King, 169
Highland Park High School, 28
Hoad, Lew, 126
Houston Country Club, 8
Houston Oilers, 169
Hunt, Lamar, 155
Hurlingham Lawn Tennis Club, 52
ILTF (International Lawn Tennis Federation), 93-95
IMG (International Management Group), 220, 221
Italian Championship, 134
ITF (International Tennis Federation), 68
Jack Kramer Pro Tour, 51
Jantzen Sports Wear, 100
Johnson, Walter (Ashe's coach), 143
Jones, Ann, 87, 89
Jones, Tugboat, 28
Jovanovic, Boro, 253
Kalamazoo, Michigan, 36, 37, 228
Kallendorf, Craig, 266
Kallendorf, Hilaire Richey. *See* Richey, Hilaire
King, Alan (comedian), 115

King, Billie Jean (Billie Jean Moffitt), 26, 87, 89, 100

Kissinger, Henry, 103

Kodes, Jan, 162, 180

Kooyong Tennis Club, Melbourne, Australia, 54

Kramer, Jack, 51, 66-68, 95

Lacoste, 100

Lake Nasworthy, San Angelo, Texas, 169

Laver, Rod "Rocket," 51, 52, 64,122, 131, 144, 159, 165, 198, 221, 222, 223

Lee Junior High, 16

Legends Championship, 223

Legends Senior Tour / Legends of Tennis, 96, 221

Legends Trail Golf Club, Scottsdale, Arizona, 98

Lendl, Ivan, 63, 262, 266

Lion's Corner House pub, London, 90

Longwood Cricket Club, 147, 198

Looscan (elementary school), 10

Lupica, Mike (reporter New York *Daily News*), 144, 234

Lutz, Bob, *91*, 93

Madison Square Garden, 64

Maltz, Maxwell (author), 39, 49

Marinaro, Eddie (football player), 3, 231

Mark (Susie's husband), 170

Martin, Dino (Dean Martin's son), 104, 146

Masters' Championship, 95

McAllen, Texas 70

MacCall, George, 53, 55-60, 71, 79,

McCarty, Mike, 16

McCormack, Mark, 220

McEnroe, John, 113, 114, 132, 145, 246

McGovern, George, 229

McManus, Jim, 218

McMillan, Frew, 111, 131

Mental Health
    alcoholic / drinking, 17-19, 32, 62, 90, 107, 155, 158, 163, 170,
       171, 185, 189, 232
      beer, 58, 62, 89, 90, 147, 160, 169-171, 185, 189
      gin, 163, 185
      vodka, 163
      whiskey, 185
    alcoholism, 20, 158, 185
    clinical depression, 4, 12, 29, 33, 35, 79, 113-115, 122, 158,
      174, 180, 190, 192, 194, 195, 201, 204, 205, 211, 229, 231,
      240, 242, 248, 249, 251-254, 258, 260
    cognitive therapy, 208, 210, 256
    counseling, 192, 200, 201, 209, 212, 244
    drunk, 17, 90, 146, 170, 174, 185
    dysfunction, 19, 23, 29, 40, 49, 211, 239, 246
    dysthymia (low-level depression), 84
    neurotic, 19-20, 107, 191
    prescriptions
      Paxil, 206, 207
      Prozac, 230, 256
      Valium, 159, 175
      Zoloft, 114, 206-208, 212, 213, 225, 235, 236, 251, 254, 258
    PTSD (Post-Traumatic Stress Disorder), 124, 125, 259
    schizophrenic, 12, 79
    tobacco, 143, 169, 185, 189, 189
    type-A / A-type , 21, 83, 85, 140, 247, 258
Mental Health/Mental Retardation (MHMR), 230, 235, 243, 244
Merlo, Beppe, 134, 135
Mexico City, 74, 119
Mexico, 55, 74, 75, 111, 125
Midland, West Texas, 18, 79, 169, 198. *See* also Barbecue Tour
Miles Presbyterian Church, 18
Miles, Texas, 17, 18

Milwaukee Town and Tennis Club, 47

Montevideo, Uruguay, 73

Moody Park, Houston, 8

Morrell, Alan (IMG agent), 221

Mr. Ritchie (teacher), 14

NAMI (National Alliance on Mental Illness), 230

Nastase, Ilie "Nasty," 107, 119, 121, 122, 126, 127, 142, 143, 148, 221, 253

 Clown Prince of Tennis, 142

 "pulled a Nastase," 135

National Interscholastic Championship, 28

Navratilova, Martina, 39

New Mexico, 168

Newcombe, John, 79, 221

Newport, Rhode Island, 90

Nixon, Richard (U.S. President), 102-104

No. 1 (ranking), 1, 3, 29, 34, 92, 96, 97, 130, 178, 221

 "Sudden Death," 1, 3, 4, 96, 178

Norris, Bill, 146-147

Olvera, Miguel, 58, 60

Orantes, Manuel, *120*

Pasarell, Charlie, 72

Peugeot Open, 124

Phillips-Moore, Barry, 199

Pilic, Niki, 67, 68

Porto Alegre, 79, 125

Ralston, Dennis, *91*, 137, 140

Rice Owls, 169

Rice University, 13, 25, 41, 71, 169

Richardson, Ham, 29, 37, 47

Richey, Amy (Cliff's daughter), 162, 171, 173, 174, 182, *185*, 257

Richey, Betty "Nana" (Cliff's mother), 266

Richey, Garnie (Cliff's paternal grandmother), 19, 20

Richey, George "Pro" (Cliff's father), 21, 29, 31, 34, 35, 45, 48, 157

Richey, Hilaire (Cliff's daughter), 160, *161*, 167, 171, 172, *173*, 185

Richey, Inc., 23-25, *26*, 29, 33, 46, 48-50, 57, 61, 89, 99, 106, 107, 140, 158, 170, 175, 192, 217, 220, 234, 240, 253, 263

Richey, Michelle "Mickie," 71-77, 78, 79, 80, 90-92, 104-107, 136, 138, 147, 149, 154, 155, 157, 160, 162, 163, 167, 169-172, *173*, *179*, 180, 184, *185*, 186, 190, 192-196, 201, 204, 212, 216, 217, 240, 265, 266

Richey, Nancy (Cliff's sister), 1, 2, 7, 9, 10, 11, 15, 17, 19, 22, 25, 27, 30, 31, 32, 33, 36, 39-43, 44, 45, 49, 53, 62, 63, 75, 87, 88, 89, 91, 151, 157, 180, 195, 264, 266

Richey, Roy "Kewpie" (Cliff's paternal grandfather), 18-22, 61, 158

Richey, Sarah Jane "Hollywood" (Cliff's daughter), 104, *185*, 196, 240, 241

Riessen, Marty, 57, 58, 74

Riley, Jinx, 14

Rio de Janeiro, Brazil, 73, 79

River Oaks Country Club, 76

River Oaks Invitational, 65, 66, 71, 208

River Plate Championships, Buenos Aires, 71

Roche, Tony, 61, 62, 70, 90, 119

Rosewall, Ken, 51, 95, 128, 139, *141*, 200, 221

Sampras, Pete, 94, 113

San Angelo, Texas, 5, 13, 14, 17, 19, 32, 61, 109, 131, 138, 146, 218, 224, 244, 245, 257, 264, 265

Santa Rita (tennis court), 16

Santa Rita Elementary School, San Angelo, 14

Sasiri, Sardinia, 61

Savitt, Dick, 128

Scorpion Gang, The, 14, 242

Shaker Square, Cleveland, 93

Shamrock Hotel, 7-8
Smith, Stan, 1, 2, 3, 42, 82, *91*, 93, 96, 178
Sonora, West Texas, 169. *See* Barbecue Tour
South African Open, Johannesburg, 64, 111, 119, *120*, 122, 124, 128, 219
South American Championship, 125, 154
St. Mark's (prep school), 28
Stolle, Fred, 93, 177, 220, 221
Stone, Allan, 159
Stratton, Vermont, 223
Sugar Bowl Invitational, New Orleans, 29
Terry, Ralph, (New York Yankee pitcher), 104, *243*
Terry, Tanya, 266
Texas High School Championship, 28
Texas Men's Championship, 37, 52
Trinidad, 71-74
Tulsa Invitational, 75, 105, 154, 223
Turville, Ed, 53, *91*
Twofink, Hague (umpire), 143
U.S. Championships at Forest Hills, 27, 36, 62, 77
U.S. Clay Court Championships / season, 44, 47, 178
U.S. Junior Indoor Championships, St. Louis, 19
U.S. Indoor Championships, 63, *78*, 82
U.S. Open, 2, *51*, 63, 64, 68, 77, 92, *95*, 119, 142, 144, 162, 182, 200, 234
USTA National Boys' 16s Championship, 178, 253
USTA National Boys' 18s Championship, 37, 52
USTA, 53, 55, 63, 64, 66, 67, 77, 135, 198
Vilas, Guillermo, 124
Warwick Hotel, 77
Washington Junior High, 16
WCT (World Championship Tennis), 63, 66, 130, 136, 146, 155, 156, 160, 162

Werksman, Roger, 52, 53

West Germany, 67, 93

West Side Tennis Club, 62, 77

Westbury Hotel, London, 68

Wilkinson, Bud (football coach), 103

Williams College, Massachusetts, 28

Williams sisters (Venus and Serena), 42

Wilson Sporting Goods / Wilson, 67, 99, 100, 132, 139, 162, 163, 212

    T-2000, 212

Wimbledon, 44, 47, 51, 52, 61, 63, 67, 69, 80, 84, 87, 94, 119, 125, 136, 137, 139, 141

White House, 102, 103, 104

Wood Harbor Yacht and Racquet Club, Lake Conroe, Houston, 100-102

Woodlands, Houston, 171

World Point Title, 66, 92, 95, 96, 121, 200. *See* Grand Prix

World Tennis, 22, 119

Also From New Chapter Press

The Education of a Tennis Player–By ROD LAVER AND BUD COLLINS

Rod Laver's first-hand account of his historic 1969 Grand Slam sweep of all four major tennis titles is documented in this memoir, written by Laver along with co-author and tennis personality Bud Collins. The book details his childhood, early career and his most important matches. The four-time Wimbledon champion and the only player in tennis history to win two Grand Slams also sprinkles in tips and lessons on how players of all levels can improve their games. Originally published in 1971, *The Education of a Tennis Player* was updated in 2009 on the 40th anniversary of his historic second Grand Slam with new content, including the story of his recovery from a near-fatal stroke in 1998.

The Roger Federer Story, Quest For Perfection–By RENE STAUFFER

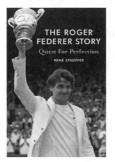

Regarded by many as the greatest tennis player in the history of the sport, this authoritative biography is based on many exclusive interviews with Federer and his family as well as the author's experience covering the international tennis circuit for many years. Completely comprehensive, it provides an informed account of the Swiss tennis star from his early days as a temperamental player on the junior circuit, through his early professional career, to his winning major tennis tournaments, including the U.S. Open and Wimbledon. Readers will appreciate the anecdotes about his early years, revel in the insider's view of the professional tennis circuit, and be inspired by this champion's rise to the top of his game.

The Bud Collins History of Tennis–By BUD COLLINS

Compiled by the most famous tennis journalist and historian in the world, this book is the ultimate compilation of historical tennis information, including year-by-year recaps of every tennis season, biographical sketches of every major tennis personality, as well as stats, records, and championship rolls for all the major events. The author's personal relationships with major tennis stars offer insights into the world of professional tennis found nowhere else.